Discipline and Child Guidance

Karl S. Bernhardt

Director
The Institute of Child Study
University of Toronto

With a Foreword by
W. E. Blatz

McGraw-Hill Book Company

New York
San Francisco
Toronto
London

Discipline and
Child Guidance

Foreword

For nearly forty years, the staff of the Institute of Child Study has been concerned with the concept of discipline: first in the wider implications of the theme and then in the relatively narrow aspect of administration.

No other topic, with the possible exception of the weather, is so frequently discussed as is discipline. In the home, in the classroom, over the bridge table, in the locker room, at the conference table, in the courtroom, in the senate chamber, the questions of human behavior and how to control it are inevitably and invariably aired.

"How do you get him to eat his cereal?" "Juvenile delinquency? Simple! Bring back the strap!" "Frustration is bad." "Love and affection will solve all problems." "Punishment is the only deterrent." Any one of these statements will start an argument that is seldom concluded.

Professor Bernhardt, the author, is now Director of the Institute. He has been associated with its staff since the days of its founding, his main interest having been as head of the Parent Education Division. Throughout the years, under his guidance, the data concerning child development have been sifted and tried empirically in the field.

Throughout the nearly four decades of the Institute's life, many often contradictory techniques have been suggested and employed in other milieus dealing with disciplinary problems of young children. Back and forth, from strictness to leniency, *laissez faire* to rigid regulation, "healthy" neglect to smothering affection, the fads have wavered. But at the Institute, keeping close to the problem by using parents as the natural practitioners and the children as the measure of success, there have evolved a philosophy and a plan that may be described as "understanding first, application second."

One unambiguous note, which has withstood nearly all the tests of time, has sounded throughout: "Violence is contraindicated under all circumstances," which means that corporal punishment is never recommended. What should be put in its place? In this book the author suggests a more effective procedure, which, based on the fundamental principle of self-discipline, works not only for the moment but for the future.

Discussion on the topic of discipline is always interesting. Read this discussion and then start arguing.

W. E. Blatz

Practically all adults become involved in some way in the rearing of the next generation. Of course, the major responsibility falls on the parents of the children, but many other people make their contribution too. Teachers, recreation leaders, Sunday school workers, pediatricians, nurses, social workers, neighbors, and a host of others have a hand in the process. Courses in child psychology, child development, and family life are becoming more numerous and important. This book has been written for all who are interested or involved in work with children. It should be of value not only to parents but to all who advise parents as well as students of child development.

Discipline is the core of child rearing. It is a controversial topic, partly because it is impossible to find conclusive evidence to prove that one method is superior to another. However, much of the accumulating knowledge of child development can be used to formulate principles and to develop a point of view about discipline. This is what has been attempted in this book. A selected group of references has been provided but no specific references are given to prove a point. This is simply because the kind of ideas presented in this book are not proved by any one research; rather, they emerge from a background of many researches. The books and articles listed in the references should be found useful by the serious reader, either student or parent, who wants to explore this intriguing subject further.

To give credit to all who in some way contributed to this effort it would be necessary to mention the scores of individuals who helped to shape the ideas, attitudes, and point of view of the author. This would include his parents, his wife, his son, and the succession of teachers, professors, colleagues, and students who have been a part of his life and experience. And another host of people have contributed through the pages of books and articles the author has read. No attempt will be made to mention any of them by name or to acknowledge the debt the author owes to a large number of people whose ideas he has made his own.

The inclusion of the name of Dr. W. E. Blatz on the title page of this book is an attempt to indicate that it was his interest and encouragement which initiated the project and also that many of his ideas and his basic philosophy of child training are the foundations on which the book was built. However, in fairness to Dr. Blatz, it should be stated that the full responsibility for what is written must be assumed by the author. He only hopes that he has not distorted seriously the approach to child rearing which he has admired as a student and a colleague of Dr. Blatz for many years.

Karl S. Bernhardt

Contents

part i
A Philosophy of Discipline

part ii
Life Situations

part iii

A Developmental View

of Discipline

Introduction

Discipline is an essential characteristic of any society. No family, school, club, or community can run smoothly without rules and regulations and some means of enforcing them. No individual can be a participating member of any group without subjecting himself to control. Control may be external, pressure exerted by the group, or internal, self-discipline or internalized controls. There can be no question of the necessity for discipline, but there is plenty of room for disagreement and difference of opinion about the nature of the discipline, what it is designed to do, and the goals it is to serve. This book is an attempt to elaborate one philosophy of discipline and to illustrate it in a variety of life situations.

This book consists of three parts following this brief introductory statement. These parts may be read in any order. Part 1 presents the main argument—an exposition of the principles of what we consider to be a sound, reasonable scheme of discipline. Part 2 is a collection of "life situations" in which we try to portray these principles in action. Part 3 is a developmental account of discipline as applied in infancy, preschool, school age, and adolescent periods. A considerable body of research literature is the foundation on which this book is built, and reference is made to some typical studies. There are still many areas of child development and child behavior about which research has little to offer. Even when research has accumulated more and more factual information about developmental events and their relations, there will always be the necessity of making individual value judgments in their application to the problems of child rearing.

We hope that you, the reader, will be able to trace the main thread that runs through all sections of this book. It is our belief that parenthood can be a thrilling, deeply satisfying experience. We would go further and state that there is a definite relationship between the degree of satisfaction of the parent and his success as a parent, and if being a parent is a burden with no thrills and satisfactions, then something needs attention and improvement.

There are other beliefs and biases you will discover in these pages. Lest you miss one of these, we shall state it now: parents can solve

1

their own problems; in fact, no one else can solve them for them. Books like this one, parent education courses, consultations with counselors may all help, but in the last analysis it is the parent himself who has to make the decisions, choose the methods, and struggle with the thousand and one puzzles of everyday life with children. The thousands of parents who we know have not only been "good" parents but who have derived a great deal of healthy satisfaction from their hard work provide the basis of our faith in parents.

When men and women become parents, they assume a complex responsibility, whether they realize it or not and whether they welcome it or not. It is the guiding of a young life to maturity, self-discipline, and self-fulfillment. Of course, along the way they will have many helpers: teachers, doctors, clergymen, recreation leaders, and a host of others, but the fact remains that the parents will have the major and central responsibility. Most parents welcome this, even though they may be somewhat frightened by the complexity and seriousness of the task. They know that there will be worries and maybe even heartbreaks, but they know also that there will be fun, thrills, and satisfactions. They know that they will be working with the mysterious forces of Nature: growth, maturation, unfolding potentialities, and life itself. And they know that there can be nothing more important than the task they have undertaken. Serious, conscientious parents may receive much help from teachers, parent education leaders, counselors, and others.

Whenever two or more parents get together, they are likely to discuss children—usually their own. But often the discussion strays off into judgments passed on children of neighbors or relatives. These judgments are sometimes favorable, more often unfavorable. But the point is that parents make judgments. In order to do so they must appear to know what they are judging and the criteria for the judgments.

Passing judgments is one of the greatest of indoor sports, running a close second to giving advice. No subject is overlooked: racehorses, beef cattle, the wheat crop, automobiles, the latest fashion, and so on. In such cases the job is relatively easy because usually only one or two aspects are being judged. For example, can the horse win the race? Is the meat tough or tender? Does the wheat come up to No. 1 Manitoba hard? How many miles does the car run on a gallon of gas? Is the fashion becoming? In each case, there is a clear-cut issue, and an immediate test can be made to support the judgment or refute it. Judging children is not so easy. What is one to judge? What the child is now or what he will become? Can we assume that there is a relationship between what the child is now and the adult to be? Obviously no test can be made right away, and so we must wait for time to pass.

Whenever one is judging a child, comparing him with others, anticipating his future, there is an implied goal in mind. What is the child going to be like when he grows up? And, if it's one's own child, What would I like him to be like? Whether it is vague or clear, there is always a goal in the mind of the parent. Sometimes the goal is in the present. I would like him to sleep longer in the morning. I wish he would eat his pablum. I wish he would come home directly from school. I wish he would do better in his schoolwork. More or less in the background, but still there, is the goal of adulthood, what we would like him to become.

What kind of adult has the parent in mind? There are about as many pictures as there are parents. But most of them are one or another or a combination of the following: (1) Financial success, a brilliant marriage, scientific honors, political power, artistic achievement, athletic prowess, or any other form of success as usually evaluated. (2) Possession of the valued virtues: goodness, benevolence, honesty, and the like, as well as happiness and contentment. (3) Negatively, avoidance of trouble and debt and of being a nuisance and disliked.

These goals are all highly commendable, but the first class are parental goals and may be neither suitable nor acceptable to the children as they grow up. The second class of virtues is difficult to define and also hard to keep in mind, and they have to be practiced by the parents in order to be effective as examples. The third class suffers from all the weaknesses of a negative program. Positive goals are always more effective than negative ones.

Is there a goal that is simple in essence, that may be followed throughout life, that can be recognized at any age, and that fulfills the requirements of civilized man? This question is answered by the following statement which will be made clearer later: the goal is that each person learn to accept the consequences of his own behavior and decisions.

Although we parents are often vague about goals, we are often confident about the method to be employed to reach the goal. If Johnny won't eat his carrots, spank him. If Myrtle leaves her clothes lying around, spank her or pick them up for her, she is still young. If Bill won't do his homework, spank him or let him go to bed, he is so tired. If Jenny won't do the dishes, bribe her or forget it, she will have to do enough dishes when she is married. If Harold breaks a window, take it out of his allowance or ignore it, we were all young once. Thus, "justice" is meted out or mixed with mercy.

The above examples illustrate two of the most common forms of disciplinary methods: (1) force the child to conform or (2) let him grow into it. These two methods are as old as history: dictatorship or *laissez faire*. We'll have more to say about them later.

The ideal plan of discipline is neither one nor the other of these extremes but midway between them, the golden mean. In this middle-of-the-road plan, several aspects will be conspicuous: (1) the sanctity and integrity of the individual, (2) freedom within the limits set by the necessities of social organization, (3) conformity to a set of necessary rules and regulations. So this middle way is a mixture of freedom and responsibility. The individual is respected, and his behavior is restricted only when necessary to ensure the freedom of others. Social organizations including the state are designed to serve individuals, not individuals to serve the state. Violence of any kind has no place in such a society. This is the essence of the democratic way of life.

Obedience is a necessary characteristic of this democratic society. But the obedience required is to a set of moral standards, not to an individual or a set of rules. Obedience is never an end in itself or a virtue, but a necessity. It is never blind obedience or obedience for the sake of obedience, but rather obedience to principles and above all to the ideal of justice.

A child brought up under this plan would become self-controlled, self-reliant, self-disciplined, and self-critical. His self-criticisms would not correspond with guilt feelings associated with offending anyone but would be related clearly to his own shortcomings and thus self-correcting.

The child who comes through this plan of discipline to adulthood should show certain adult characteristics which we value as being related to mental health and self-fulfillment.

1. Physically, he will have learned to adjust his personal appetitive satisfactions to his needs with free enjoyment and gratification. He will accept the responsibility of observing reasonable care of his health, avoiding the dangers of self-indulgence. He will be able to gauge his strengths and limitations. And he will be able to manage his affairs so as to avoid the ill effects of stress and be able to relax at will.

2. Mentally, he will gradually learn his potentialities and limitations and temper his aspirations in accordance with this knowledge. He will slowly build up judgment in terms of his successes and failures, adequately evaluating both. As he accumulates knowledge he will also develop the ability to weigh, discriminate, and choose. He will learn to arrange his decisions so as to reduce anxiety to a minimum. He will learn to feel at home in the world of ideas, opinions, and beliefs, and he will reduce to a minimum the tendency to be prejudiced. He will value accomplishment irrespective of its relationship to the achievement of others. He will learn to distinguish clearly between his work with its responsibilities and his leisure-time activities with their infinite possibilities for variety and enjoyment. He will learn to be open-minded, welcoming new ideas but not necessarily adopting them as good or true. He will be characterized by reason and reasonableness.

3. Emotionally, he will have learned self-control, neither denying nor inhibiting his emotions but channeling them into acceptable and useful behavior. Thus no temper tantrums will interfere with his efficiency. And fears and insecurities will lead to sensible caution and effective learning. He will never be ashamed of being afraid, nor will he allow his fears to keep him from acting in accordance with his standards. His emotions will find their outlet in enthusiasm, sustained effort, appreciation, and admiration without envy or resentment. He will develop a degree of aesthetic appreciation which will enhance his enjoyment of living. In fact, his

enjoyment of living, learning, experimenting, and exploring will be boundless.

4. Spiritually, he will formulate a philosophy of life and find some answers to the purpose of living and this will aid him in achieving a measure of serenity.

Thus briefly, but not exhaustively, we have described the product of the plan of discipline to be developed in this book.

part i

A Philosophy

of Discipline

This first section of the book develops
a scheme of discipline which is characterized as reasonable. It is reasonable
because it is based on reason and a realistic
approach. It takes into consideration
the nature of the child, the kind of
world in which the child is being reared,
and the goals the adult may have in mind.

At first reading, this section may seem
rather theoretical and academic but
when given further thought and study,
the scheme will be seen as practical and
workable. It does not provide a set of
rigid rules to follow; rather it consists of
a number of principles to be applied in
varying circumstances with a full awareness
of the great differences among children
and among adults.

The central ideas developed in this section
can be simply stated. Discipline is
thought of as a plan of training, not
just as correction or punishment. The
positive approach is stressed. Encouragement, support, acceptance, and affection

are necessary foundations of the plan. It can be designated as nonpunitive, since punishment is discarded as a technique. Yet guidance, direction, and control are essential parts of the scheme.

Part 1 will take on added meaning if read for a second time after the other two sections of the book are read.

chapter 1
The Meaning
of Discipline
in Human Life

To many people discipline has a harsh, old-fashioned sound, for to them discipline means punishment, pain, and fear. This is the narrow, negative view of discipline—discipline as essentially correction. But as we shall see later, discipline can be basically positive: training, not correction; guiding, not punishing; arranging conditions for learning, not just inhibiting and restricting.

To some people the "modern" way is the abolition of all regulations and control, at least theoretically and directly. Free expression, permissiveness, and self-demand have been modern slogans signifying a method of child rearing that is essentially an absence of method. But recently many people have become disillusioned, and there is danger of a violent reaction that will throw us back where we were when we discarded the strict and often cruel discipline of a former era.

A brief glance at the history of trends of thought and practice in bringing up children may provide the perspective we need to develop a reasonable scheme of discipline and an adequate background of reasons for it.

Traditional Discipline

What may be called the traditional scheme of discipline seems to be based on the idea that the child is naturally bad and that his badness must be contained. His basic nature is evil and this evil must be dealt with whenever it is in evidence. Thus, punishment is necessary. Punishment has had a long and interesting history. It seems to have started as a kind of revenge. The individual who has violated the rules or taboos of the tribe must be revenged. The method was "an eye for an eye and a tooth for a tooth." Badness in any form, however evaluated, calls for punishment. And punishment is revenge when thought of in this way.

As civilization developed, another idea or reason for punishment appeared. This was the deterrent idea. People could be scared from doing wrong by seeing the wrongdoer punished. Thus punishment and fear became twin instruments of discipline. Public executions, stocks in the marketplace, the child flogged before the rest of the class, the apprehended sinner made an example for others— these were some of the extreme forms of punishment as a deterrent. The idea is still very much with us. It prevents us from abolishing capital punishment. It leads parents and teachers to justify punishment as a method.

The third reason for punishment to appear was punishment as a means of reform. This means punishment as an aid to learning. There is some evidence to support the idea that punishment does help learning but there is likewise plenty of evidence to indicate that punishment can also hinder learning. And there is also evidence that punishment produces resentment and hostility. In the reasonable scheme of discipline we are going to develop, there will be no place for punishment. There is a clear choice between a punitive approach and an educative one, and we have chosen the latter.

We have mentioned fear as being related to punishment in the traditional ideas about discipline. Here also, there seems to be a choice for us between the use of fear and the use of understanding. We have chosen understanding rather than fear as our guiding principle. That is, we have discarded fear as a method of control and substituted training based on reason and understanding.

The traditional discipline has been designated sometimes as authoritarian, that is, the adult commands and the child obeys. Obedience was considered a virtue and thus an end in itself. The most serious kind of misdemeanor was disobedience, especially if accompanied by "talking back," which was interpreted as impudence. The assumption was made that the adult knew what was best for the child who was incapable of any discretion or judgment. The important thing was to be "in control" of the child at all times. A "good" child always did as he was told and "badness" was equated with disobedience.

Another aspect of the traditional approach to discipline which grows directly from the idea of submission of the child to adult control is the use of rewards. As badness was to be punished, so goodness should be rewarded. But one short step from the use of rewards for virtue is the use of rewards to induce goodness. So rewards very easily become bribes. Just as punishment was found to be effective in most cases in producing submission, so rewards proved to be successful in producing the desired behavior. If a bribe is attractive enough the child will do anything in his power to obtain it. Just as a donkey can be moved with a whip or a carrot, so children can be controlled by punishment and bribery. Rewards and punishments are not discarded because they do not achieve immediate results but rather because they do not produce the long-term results in which we are interested.

Still another phase of this same trend in discipline is the use of affection as a directing influence. Because children want to be loved it is possible, in fact easy, to use affection as a means of control. Love can be withheld for bad behavior and bestowed on the child who conforms with adult wishes. This is a powerful method but a dangerous one from the standpoint of personality development. Similarly, approval and disapproval can be used to control the child. Mother loves and approves of good little boys and girls but can neither love nor approve of bad, noisy, dirty, or naughty children. Father is pleased with the polite, submissive, obedient child but annoyed when the reverse is in evidence.

There are, of course, many other aspects of what we have called the traditional scheme of discipline, but perhaps we have mentioned enough of them to see one or two of the central principles involved. One is that the prominent goal is immediate results, the present behavior of the child; success is achieved, then, when the child is well-behaved, does what he is told, and does not "bother" the adult. In every situation in which the adult is dealing with the child there are inevitably two considerations: the present behavior of the child and the effect on his developing personality and character. The traditional approach, while not neglecting this developmental factor, tended to put more emphasis on the immediate results.

Another aspect that is evident is that the control and direction of the child was almost entirely in personal terms. The child's duty was to please his parents (at least this is how it looked from the child's viewpoint). His part was to be submissive to their direction and behave according to their desires and even whims. The weakness in the scheme was its failure to provide adequate training for self-direction, choice, and independent action.

In the traditional plan, punishment frequently meant corporal punishment. Of course corporal punishment is the easiest kind to use with small children. But corporal punishment violates the personal dignity of the child. It is unfair, personal, and frequently emotional. When we see a young child striking out at another child we can be almost sure that he has learned this method of dealing with situations from a parent who slaps, hits, or spanks the child whenever his behavior displeases. There is no place in a reasonable scheme of discipline for the use of any kind of corporal punishment.

Free Expression

Revolts against the traditional discipline have taken several forms in the history of family life. One of these was an almost complete reversal of ideas. In place of the innate badness of the child, goodness was considered to be the basic nature of the child. So Nature should have a free hand in the developing child. Freedom of expression was necessary and desirable. Restrictions, prohibitions, commands were out of place because they would interfere with the "natural" development of the child. The child should be allowed to do as he liked. Of course, this frequently meant that the adult worked to get the child to like what the adult thought he should do. The child's developing personality was considered to be more important than property or the parent's convenience or peace of mind. Thus parents must be "permissive" and homes and classrooms should be child-centered. Authority was to be replaced by love, and control by persuasion, with the result that order gave place to chaos.

Complete free expression for the young child is obviously impossible. His ignorance and impulsiveness would lead him into dangers with which he would be unable to cope. And rather than helping the child move out of the narrow circle of his own self-centered view of things, it confirms him in it. The free expression idea appealed to many parents and they tried to put it into limited practice (at least for a time). But the free expression idea failed to take into account such simple facts as that Nature needs some help to produce a socialized person.

Discipline as a Plan of Training

Many parents have searched for, and a few have found, a position which avoids some of the difficulties in both the traditional and the free expression points of view. This is discipline as a plan of training.

Perhaps "training" is not quite the word we want, because training can call up a picture of putting a trained seal through his paces and throwing him a fish when he does the trick we have set for him. It is not this narrow idea of training that we have in mind. Rather it is a planned program in which we provide the kinds of experiences the child needs in order both to learn how to live and to enjoy living. So we shall think of discipline as arranging conditions for healthy learning and living.

Nor do we want to give the impression that we think of child training and discipline as molding the child into some preconceived pattern, a kind of mechanical conditioning procedure by means of which we can shape the child in any way we want. Rather we think of the process as helping the child to develop his own unique individuality, but in the context of a culture to which he will have to adjust.

It has been said that life is a continuous series of choices. This is certainly true, but the choices seem to have increased greatly in the last few decades. In learning and practicing parenthood, however, we need to distinguish between genuine choices and dilemmas or false choices. A genuine choice is presented when the issue is clear-cut and definite, when the selection of one alternative automatically excludes the other, and when confusion results if one tries to retain both alternatives. Such genuine choices concern, in the main, attitudes and general approaches. Whether we choose deliberately and intelligently, after thought and evaluation, or merely drift into one choice or the other, we have nevertheless done the same thing; we have made a genuine choice.

A dilemma, however, consists of a pair of alternatives, both of which are undesirable. Child training presents several such false choices. These are usually in the nature of extremes or opposites, and the most desirable way is usually somewhere between the two. The only way to deal with such dilemmas is to refuse to be caught on the equally undesirable horns.

A third kind of problem demands a decision as to the relative importance or priority to be assigned rather than a choice between clear-cut alternatives. Here, instead of accepting one alternative and discarding the other, it may be possible and even desirable to retain both but give one rather than the other more emphasis and importance.

Some Parental Dilemmas or False Choices

Areas of human thought which are deficient in factual information are often characterized by pendulumlike swings from one extreme to the other. In such circumstances we are presented with false choices or dilemmas, alternatives which are equally undesirable and unacceptable. This is especially true of the field of child training where some of the swings have been rather extreme, posing unnecessary dilemmas in which many parents have been caught.

Parents are sometimes faced with dilemmas because they demand simple rules and formulas. They ask, "What is the right thing to do?" or "What formula applies here?" When we try to reduce the complex business of bringing up children to a few simple rules, we are inviting dilemmas. To try to apply a rule of thumb to varying situations and different individuals and family circumstances is to invite trouble.

There is one old dilemma that keeps recurring in each generation. This is expressed in the two words "freedom" and "discipline." When the two words are put in opposition—freedom or discipline —we have a false choice or dilemma. This same dilemma is expressed in a number of ways, for example, free expression or control, self-demand or regular routine. But there is no real choice here. Both freedom and discipline are necessary. Rather than being opposed, they actually complement each other. Discipline implies responsibility, order, and regulation, and it is only when these qualities are present that freedom is possible. We make freedom possible for the child when we help him to learn to be responsible and self-disciplined.

Another false choice is well illustrated by the remarks of a mother who had been listening to a talk on discipline. After hearing reasons why corporal punishment should be discarded as a method of keeping children in order, she finally burst out, "But you can't reason with them all the time!" She was caught in the dilemma of punishment or reason. Evidently she saw only these two possibilities. Of course she was right, one cannot reason with children all the time. Reasoning often deteriorates into arguments or a battle of words. But this is a dilemma we do not have to accept; punishing and reasoning are not true alternatives. Narrowing down the possibilities to either spanking the child or talking him into a line of behavior shows a serious lack of thought and imagination. There are many other possibilities.

Another old dilemma, which used to cause considerable soul searching and which is still fairly common, was expressed as a choice between a home (or school) that is child-centered and one that is adult-centered. This dilemma was posed at a time when people were beginning to doubt the wisdom of the old idea that children "should be seen and not heard." Previously the home had been clearly mother's or father's. The convenience, comfort, and whims of adults determined what was done and not done. "Life with Father" marked the transition. Still later came the so-called child-centered home which was often a child-dominated home, in which everything revolved around the children. Children were not to be frustrated and in some cases were allowed to run wild so that their budding personalities might not be stifled. We have learned that this is another of these false choices; the home does not have to be adult- or child-centered but can be run for the benefit of all. Today we are trying to build homes in which all members, young and old, are considered important—democratic homes which are neither adult dictatorships nor child anarchies.

Not long ago a newspaper article claimed that parents are faced with the choice of returning to the "tried and true" method of spanking, or seeing a continued increase in juvenile delinquency. Present-day advocates of corporal punishment (and they seem to be increasing in number) pose this false choice: spank the child or watch him become a delinquent. But this is an obviously false choice; there are other possibilities. To be effective, discipline does not have to involve pain, fear, or torture. In fact we are finding out that, to be effective in the long run, discipline must be based on methods which help the child to understand and accept the necessary controls of civilized living rather than merely learn to do what he is told through fear of punishment by adults.

The most recent dilemma presented to parents is in some ways the most puzzling. Perhaps it is so new that we have not gained sufficient perspective to see what it means. It can be stated thus, "Are you an authoritarian or a permissive parent?" When we first look at this question it seems to present a genuine choice: one must be either authoritarian or permissive. But this is because the question has forced us to think in terms of extremes, and these extremes are clear enough. The authoritarian parent is in effect saying to the child, "You do what I say, and don't ask why; I'm the boss, I know best." At the other extreme, the permissive parent seems to be saying to the child, "You do as you like." We pose this dilemma for ourselves when we think in extremes, and perhaps all extremes produce false choices.

But no parent has to accept such a dilemma or make such a choice. There is a place for authority and a place for permissiveness, just as there is a place for both discipline and freedom. A good parent is neither a dictator nor a wishy-washy adult who can never say "You must" or "You must not." A child feels more secure in a home where there is a measure of decision and a clear statement of the boundaries. Parents should be able to make rules that are necessary, reasonable, and understandable, and to enforce them consistently and impersonally. At the same time there can also be a large measure of permissiveness—freedom of choice within the child's ability to choose wisely.

The twentieth century has been called the century of the child. During its first half, the old authoritarian approach was fast going out of fashion and the "love them and let them learn" method was being given a trial; today a return to authoritarian ways is being advocated. But there is no need to adopt either extreme. The way out is to deny the soundness of the apparent choice and to find another method, one that is better than either the "command-obey" or the "let them do as they like" method. This way is to guide the behavior of the child by the use of logical, impersonal, relevant, and consistent consequences. This idea will be developed in more detail later. For about three decades now we have been suggesting to parents that they need not choose between the "Do as I say" and the "Do as you like" approaches. We have said that it is possible to build up a child's understanding of what is involved in happy, effective living. The key to such an approach is in making sure that the child experiences the kinds of results from his own behavior which help him to learn to choose for himself. While the child is learning, parents win his trust by being not stern but consistent, not merely permissive but just, and by unhesitatingly making decisions for the child until he is able to make them for himself.

There are many other dilemmas in the field of child training. There is only one solution for all of them: refuse to be caught on their horns. "Do you beat your wife or send her to bed without her dinner?" This is a silly question; dilemmas are frequently silly.

Apparent Choices: A Matter of Relative Emphasis

We are sometimes asked which is better, direct or indirect control, as though we had to choose between them. Direct control is influencing the child's behavior directly through commands, directions, suggestions, and requests. Indirect control is influencing the child through the arrangement of his environment. Obviously both methods are necessary, but the better we arrange the environment the less we will need to use direct control. Both fences and commands can keep the child from the danger of street traffic. In meeting the "TV problem" for example, if we arrange an environment that has many interesting possibilities of which television is only one, and in which discrimination, planning, and choice are demonstrated, we will not remove the necessity for direct control but we will make the direct control more effective.

Another apparent choice is between love and discipline. It has been said that the important thing is to surround the child with abundant love and set him a good example; if we do this, all will be well and we can dispense with discipline. This sounds as if no discipline were necessary so long as love is present; but this is another of those traps for unsuspecting parents. If love is chosen and discipline discarded, then almost inevitably love will begin to be used as a means of discipline. Then parents will say or imply that mother cannot love bad little boys and father will be annoyed (fail to love you) if you behave that way. If, on the other hand, discipline is chosen and love discarded or submerged, then discipline will become less effective because it is functioning in a deficient context. Discipline as a plan of training must be carried on in a context of love, warmth, and acceptance. There is no choice between love and discipline; they are complementary and both are necessary.

Still another apparent choice confronting parents concerns goals: Do they want a good child or eventually a mature, self-disciplined adult? But can we not try to have the best of both worlds here? We may be tempted to stress immediate results, to try to have a well-behaved child today and let the future take care of itself, yet undoubtedly it is also important to think of the kind of person the child is becoming. We can try to do both things at the same time; while we are using the necessary controls to take care of the immediate situations we can also be thinking of what the child is learning and becoming. We can use controls in such a way that he will eventually learn to manage without them.

Genuine Choices

There are some real choices which parents make either deliberately or unwittingly. There is the choice, for instance, between what we shall call punitive and educational approaches. This is a difficult choice because the centuries-old punitive approach has been built right into our personal attitudes and values, yet at the same time punishment is unpleasant and even barbaric. When a child lies, steals, disobeys, or acts inappropriately, we tend to turn immediately to the technique of punishment. The child must suffer for his badness. Of course he must be punished, and we rarely stop to ask ourselves why. And even though we may not think of spanking, we do think of some kind of punishment. It may be sending him off to his room, curtailing his privileges, or restricting his freedom. All these techniques, however, may be used either as a punishment or as an educative device, and which it is will depend on how we think about them. The punitive way makes the child feel guilty and realize that he has been bad and that we think he is naughty or sinful. The educational approach conveys to him as clearly as possible that we are trying to help him learn how to fit in and be adequate. "We do not think you are bad but rather that you have a lot to learn yet, and it is our job to help you learn it." The educational approach leaves out name-calling, blaming, and any such elements as disgrace or disapproval. Here we are doing a very difficult thing; we are trying to separate the child and his behavior. We still love him and are "for him" but we do not approve or condone his undesirable behavior. We are helping him to see that every situation demands something of him and that he must live up to these "situational" demands.

Another example of a genuine choice which is not easy for a parent to make, but which he must make, is whether he is to train his child to adjust to the world as it is or to the world as he would like it to be. Take, for example, the perennial question of fighting. If we believe that fighting is never a good way to settle disputes and differences of opinion, even though it is still a prominent technique in our imperfect world, then should we not decide to train our children to get along without it? Many parents make the opposite choice, arguing that because the child will be faced with fighting, he should be trained to "stick up for himself." The parent has a real choice here and with similar situations, and he should be aware that he is making such a choice and why. Reasons such as, "The world is like that" and "We must help the child to conform with things as they are" are not good reasons. The world will become a better world only when there are enough people who are not satisfied with things as they are. The most powerful technique of reform is education, especially the informal but important education of the child in the home.

Such are some of the many traps, dilemmas, unreasonable extremes, and puzzles for unwary parents. Being a parent takes a lot of thought, study, and planning. It would be nice to be able to supply a set of simple rules and some tried and true techniques, but we do not have them, nor does anyone else. We offer instead goals, principles, general ideas, and attitudes—and the very comforting thought that parents are allowed quite a few mistakes.

The fabric of personality that is the product of our efforts is woven of the many seemingly small incidents which pile up day by day and year by year. The values the parent treasures, his general approach to life, his attitudes towards people and ideas, and the principles in which he believes and which he holds most precious will determine not merely what he does with his children but also, more important, *how* he does what he does. In the long run our choices will depend on our values. It should not be too much to ask that parents take stock of what they value most. This stocktaking will be the test of their parenthood.

chapter 2
Basic Considerations
for a Reasonable
Scheme of Discipline

To develop a plan of discipline it is necessary to take into account a number of considerations: (1) the nature of the child, (2) the kind of world in which the child is living, (3) the results we hope to achieve, and (4) the best techniques available. We shall look at these in turn before we attempt to outline a scheme of discipline and see how it works in practical situations.

The Nature of the Child

It is well to consider the material with which we have to work. Our views of human nature in general do influence the kind of discipline we plan and how it is applied. For instance, there is the often-repeated contention that you can't change human nature. This has been taken to mean that the character or personality of the child is predetermined and nothing much can be done about it.

Is the Child Naturally Good or Bad? Some people have considered the child naturally bad and have built their plan of discipline on that assumption. With this as their starting point they have found punishment and fear both necessary and central to their plans. Punishment they thought necessary to combat the child's bad nature and to keep the badness in check. In some cases they have literally tried to "whip the devil" out of the child. Others have built their philosophy of discipline on the assumption that the child is naturally good. With this natural goodness as a base, they thought the child should have complete free expression, and that left alone the child would demonstrate in his behavior his basic, innate goodness.

However, the more we learn about child development the more we see how impossible it is to think of the child as either innately good or bad. These terms have no meaning when applied to the newborn child. He is neither good nor bad, he is just a bundle of possibilities. He can become good or bad depending on what happens to him, the kind of treatment he receives, and the kind of experiences he has. He will probably become a mixture of both goodness and badness as his accumulating experiences shape his personality and character.

This, then, is our first consideration and we are proposing that we build our scheme of discipline without being influenced by the original-sin idea or the "little angel sent from Heaven" concept. Rather we shall try to free ourselves from such preconceptions and proceed on the assumption that the child has no innate moral predispositions, he is neither good nor bad to start with.

Heredity.   Another aspect of the nature of the child that must be considered is the part played by heredity in the development of the child. Without going into too much detail about the process of biological heredity, we can make some general statements which should aid us in our attempt to build our plan of training.

It is not possible to separate the influences of heredity and environment completely and adequately. They work together and every aspect of the child's development and nature is affected in some ways by both sets of factors. However, heredity has more to do with physical structure than do environmental influences. Heredity provides the structures which mediate activity. Thus, appearance, body build, muscles, nerves, glands, sense organs, and physiological systems are determined mainly by hereditary factors carried in the genes of the germ cells. But even physical structure and systems are influenced to a certain extent by the influences from without, including the materials for growth which the environment provides. Because basic capacity is dependent upon the structure of the central nervous system it would seem that it is largely determined by hereditary factors. The child's level of intelligence will depend on the nature of the cell structure and will be affected to only a limited extent by environmental influence.

No one has, as yet, discovered a way to transform a child with limited capacity to a person of average or above average intelligence. When we move from physical structure and basic capacity to special abilities, personality characteristics, emotional stability, and character, the influence of heredity becomes less noticeable. Here we are fairly safe in assuming that we are dealing with the results of experience or what is generally called environmental influence and not with something that is set and unchangeable.

This, then, is our second consideration in building our scheme of discipline. Remembering that heredity will set limits of structure and capacity, we can assume that the personality and character of the child will depend more on what happens to the child, the kind of treatment he receives, and the experiences he has, than upon anything that is a result of biological heredity. We must beware of using heredity as an excuse or as a reason for "letting Nature take its course."

The Child's Equipment for Behavior. There are two statements that can be made about children which are true even though on the surface they seem to be contradictory. They are: all children are alike, and all children are different. They are all alike in that they have the same basic structure, needs, and potentialities. But each child is unique, different from every other child in the details of the structures, the strength and mode of expression of his needs, and the way he develops his potentialities.

Every child is endowed with sense organs, nerves, brain, muscles, and glands, the structures essential for activity. And although all children have the same general structures, there are important differences in the details. For instance, all children have eyes, but some children are color-blind, shortsighted, or even blind. All have muscles but there are important differences in size and functioning. So in terms of basic equipment we can see this general principle of similarity and difference. All children are human but each is unique. So in thinking of a plan of training we shall keep in mind that we can count on some basic human characteristics but shall expect to find important differences between children which we must take into consideration.

The most important feature of the child's equipment for behavior is his ability to learn and profit from experience. The child is a learner by nature. Every experience he has leaves some effect. Everything he does, sees, hears, smells, and tastes makes some kind of impression and is retained for possible later recall and use. It is true that he forgets too, but this forgetting may be merely a temporary inability to recall. We can be sure that all experience leaves some trace, some experiences having a profound effect and others fitting into the stream of numberless items that impinge on and affect an impressionable individual. This can be summed up in the statement that every experience that the individual has leaves him a slightly different person. This is another of the considerations in our planning: the fact that we are dealing with a learning, remembering individual.

This fact of the almost limitless possibilities for learning is at the same time our most optimistic asset and our greatest danger. For the child can learn undesirable as well as desirable patterns of thinking, feeling, and acting. It means, also, that the child will learn much more than we teach him or mean him to learn. On the other hand, what has been learned can be changed, and so we have the basis for reeducation as well as education, retraining as well as training. But it should be said that learning is always easier to arrange than relearning. This is the central clue to a good scheme of discipline; the child is flexible, modifiable, a learner, so our job is to arrange the conditions for the right kind of learning.

Another aspect of the child's nature is feeling: not just occasional feelings of pleasantness and unpleasantness but continuous and fluctuating feelings. Every experience the child has contains a feeling component, not just something added to it but an integral part of the experience itself, so everything he does and everything that happens to him is either pleasant or unpleasant, sometimes very pleasant, sometimes moderately pleasant, and sometimes only very slightly pleasant, or it may be some degree of unpleasantness. Not only do these feelings lend interest and variety to experience and activity but they also serve to direct activity as well. Objects, situations, and activities that are experienced as pleasant are approached, prolonged, and repeated if possible. Similarly, experiences that are unpleasant are avoided, withdrawn from, shunned, or resisted. That is, feelings of pleasantness are accompanied by an attitude of approach and feelings of unpleasantness by an attitude of withdrawal.

We sometimes take pride in thinking of ourselves as rational beings and we are, to a certain extent. However, it is wise to recognize the large part that feelings play in human experience and activity. This is especially true of young children. It would seem that the experience of the very young infant is mainly feeling and as we shall see later it is very important that the infant's experience be predominantly pleasant. As the child grows older, reason and understanding play an increasing part but he never completely leaves behind the influence of feelings on his behavior.

This universal human characteristic of evaluating things, situations, and activities in terms of feelings needs to be taken into account in any training or educational program. For instance, the child can acquire likes and dislikes for food (or anything else) that become powerful directing forces in what he does and how he thinks about things. What we call interests is another example of the functioning of feelings. When we say we are interested in something, what we mean is that we have built a pleasant feeling evaluation of it and that we tend to approach it.

So, we have another feature of human nature that must be taken into account as we build our plan of discipline. This does not mean that the road must be completely smoothed for the child, that he must never experience anything unpleasant, must never be frustrated or required to do what he does not like. But it does mean that we must be aware of the large part that feelings play in human life.

Another aspect of the child's equipment for behavior is the emotions. All children are emotional, that is, capable of being disturbed. Any emergency, either real or imagined, is a potential stimulus for emotional disturbance. Emotions can be valuable sources of energy and stimuli for learning and activity. They can also be disruptive and unhealthy when they do not lead to adaptive behavior. Threats to safety, well-being, or even reputation may result in the kind of disturbance which we call fear. Hindrances to activity, difficulties and obstacles to free satisfaction of needs and wants can produce the kind of disturbance we call anger. Fears and angers of low intensity can be the spur to effort and learning. However, more intense or prolonged disturbances which do not lead to activity designed to take care of the cause of the disturbance can be unhealthy and disruptive. Emotional education can be directed to training in how to deal with emergencies and need not, indeed should not, be merely training in repression.

Still another aspect of the child's equipment for behavior consists of needs and wants. Needs are recurring conditions that require periodic satisfaction. Thus all children have the same fundamental needs for food, liquid, sleep, elimination of waste products, sex expression, and changing experience. These needs direct behavior and dictate much learning. A large part of the time and effort of the preschool child is given to learning how to satisfy these needs in socially acceptable ways. Most of the training of the child in the first five years of his life is concerned with some aspect or other of need satisfaction. And most of the difficulties and problems that parents report are related to this training. On the foundation of these universal needs each child builds his own unique pattern of wants. Thus he has need for food but learns to want certain kinds of food. He has a need of a changing pattern of experience, and he builds his play wants and activities.

The training procedures in need satisfaction are a part of the larger scheme of discipline. Our concern will be to find ways of directing this training, in such a way as to help the child learn how both to manage his need satisfaction and to build a healthy personality structure.

Every child is endowed by nature with equipment that provides the potentialities for almost any kind of activity. He has needs and develops wants, which must find some kind of satisfaction. His experience is colored by feelings which affect his behavior. He is disturbable and can be stimulated to effort or thrown into confusion. He can remember, and he can also anticipate and imagine. He is, above all, a learner and can profit from experience. He is flexible and changeable. This is the material for child training. Almost any kind of development is possible. He will become the kind of person he does partly because of the kind of organism nature has provided, but more because of the kinds of things that happen to him along the way. A scheme of discipline is planned to see that the right things happen to him.

The Nature of the Child's World

To plan a scheme of discipline it is necessary to take into account some aspects of the child's environment. He is born into an organized society with laws, rules and regulations, customs, taboos, and mores. Part of the business of growing up is to learn how to fit into this complex organization and get what he wants in acceptable ways or to learn to want what is acceptable.

The most important part of the child's environment is people. He will find some of his deepest satisfactions in his relations with other people. But he will find also that some of his greatest annoyances and frustrations come from the same source. Social considerations are inherent in every aspect of child rearing. The process which is sometimes called socialization is the core of child training and dictates much of what is done. It poses many questions and problems for parents. How much conformity to social custom should be demanded and how soon? Toilet training, eating habits, washing, dressing, learning to read and write, language habits, manners, and moral standards are some of the obvious examples of situations in which society makes demands, sets standards, and restricts the individual's freedom.

Living with other people means that individual freedom must be curtailed. Freedom, in the sense of doing what one wants, is never possible. Membership in any group, family, school, club, team, or community imposes demands and restrictions on the individual. To belong, one must give up some of his individual freedom. Growing up requires that the individual accept and fulfill these social responsibilities. It requires also that the child learn that every situation has activity that is appropriate to it, and that social adjustment is behaving in a way that is appropriate to the social situation. Discipline is the help and guidance the child receives in learning these lessons.

The child's environment is not static or unchangeable, nor is it by any means perfect. Training, therefore, need not be designed to produce blind obedience or unthinking conformity. This problem of conformity has always been central in schemes of discipline.

One solution has been to stress obedience; the child conforms to adult direction. One difficulty about this has been that the adult is not always present to give the directions. Another is that it does not provide adequate training for self-direction later. Because some rules and regulations are essential, training should be planned to help the child understand the meaning and necessity of these laws. And during the growing-up period it should provide plenty of opportunity for participation in making rules and changing customs.

Sometimes it is suggested that the child should be trained to adjust to the world as it is. For instance, it has been said that because we live in a highly competitive society it is necessary to train the child to be a good competitor. But there is another solution, that is, to train the child not just to fit into the world as it is but to provide the kind of training that will enable the child to help change the features of the society which he feels are undesirable.

The fact of social change is something that must be taken into account in all child training and education. Certainly the world of our childhood was very different from the present-day situation. And there is no reason to believe that the world of our children's adulthood will not have changed considerably from the present. This means that the best kind of training for a changing world is not so much training in specific rules and set habits of thought and action, but rather an emphasis on understanding and general principles.

A difficult decision, which nevertheless has to be made, is as to how much conformity is desirable. This implies that there is no virtue in conformity per se. Blind conformity, or conforming for the sake of conforming, is not the goal. Rather a blend of conformity and nonconformity seems to be the answer. This suggests that there is a core of necessary rules and standards that should be accepted and followed, but that there are areas in which individual taste and preference are desirable. Perhaps we can sum this up by saying that a scheme of discipline should enable the child to develop an understanding of the need for conformity to a solid core of morals on which his society is founded, but at the same time it should allow him to develop a wide margin of nonconformity or individuality of taste and preference.

There is an implication in what we have been saying that should be made explicit. It is that conformity should be intelligent, that is, based on understanding of the reason for the rule or standard of behavior. This makes training in conformity more than just seeing that the child meets requirements. It requires that the child be helped to understand and appreciate the meaning of the rules themselves. It may be enough for the very young child to know that "this is what is done" and "this is not done" but later on as he grows older, he will need to know why.

The child's world will not provide easy and immediate means of satisfying all his needs and wants. There will be difficulties, obstacles, delays, and problems. Part of his growing up will consist of learning how to accept and deal with such frustrations. Some of the self-demand or permissive ideas would suggest that all delays, difficulties, and frustrations should be removed and the child provided with immediate and easy satisfaction of all his wants. This position is as extreme as an earlier one which advocated that we arrange hard, difficult tasks for children in order to strengthen their characters. This "formal discipline" idea has gone out of fashion just as the extreme "free expression" and permissiveness idea will be discarded.

In building a reasonable scheme of discipline, therefore, we must take into account the nature of the world into which the child has been born and in which he will be living. Our job is to help him learn to meet and deal with his difficulties, to accept the challenge of frustration by learning what to do about it. Of course, it is only sensible that the child be protected from more frustration than he can tolerate while he is learning how to deal with it.

The child's world will provide opportunities for activity, learning, and satisfaction. It will also provide hindrances, restrictions, and some regulation. His world will make demands on him as well as presenting him with problems and difficulties. Training should be designed to help the child learn to know his world, to accept the world as it is while not necessarily approving of all of it, to find ways of achieving satisfaction in activity and also to participate in the reshaping of his environment. In short, he should be helped to learn to be the master rather than the slave of his environment.

The Goals of Discipline

Having looked at the nature of the child and the kind of world into which he was born, we must now consider what our training is supposed to produce. A clear picture of the goals will help to determine some of the details of a plan of discipline. All parents have goals of some kind. If you ask a group of parents to tell you what they are striving for with their children, you will get an interesting variety of answers. They will say they want a happy child, a good child, a successful child, a well-behaved child, and only occasionally will they mention the more remote goal of a mature, happy, mentally healthy adult.

All parents, whether or not they express their thoughts, have ideas about the kind of person they want their child to become. These ideas are important because they dictate the kind of training they will provide. For instance, if they want submissive, obedient individuals who spring to obey whenever they speak, then their discipline will be planned to produce that kind of behavior. If, on the other hand, they want thoughtful, self-disciplined persons capable of running their own lives, then their methods will be different.

If the parent thinks mainly of the immediate situation, then the techniques used and the emphasis will be on what will work in taking care of the present behavior. That is one reason why rewards and punishments have had such a central place in most plans of discipline. When we think of how to get the child to do something the most available answer is to make the activity as attractive as possible to the child. And it works, for the child will do almost anything if the reward is attractive enough. However, when we think not just of what the child does, but of what the child himself is becoming, the reward method is at least doubtful. Similarly, punishment will be effective in keeping children from undesirable behavior but there can be other effects that may be serious when viewed in a larger perspective.

Of course, immediate results are important and cannot be neglected, but there can be no doubt that the long-range results are

more important. When the methods used in getting "good" behavior today leave scars of resentment and smoldering hostility, we
are paying a big price for immediate results. When we bribe a child
by the offer of a reward to work hard at his lessons, we may get
results evident on his report card but at the same time we may
be helping to develop a "reward habit" of expecting tangible returns for all effort, which will become a part of his personality
for life.

Every parent must decide on his own values and the goals he
adopts. What we are suggesting is that the parent should be aware
of the importance of the longer view. We mean by this that what
the child is becoming is more important than what he is doing at
the moment. The two are related because what he does today
helps to determine what he will do tomorrow. Our point is that
it is possible to sacrifice the child's development to present order
and the immediate result. But when we do, we lose out in the
end. Children who have learned to hate school, parents who have
lost contact with their adolescents, persons who resent anyone
in authority, and a great variety of unhappy, maladjusted, or confused people are all products of this emphasis on the immediate
results rather than the developmental approach.

We are suggesting that goals which take into account the end
product of child training are to be preferred over goals which are
more narrow. Our job is to produce adults, people who can run
their own lives satisfactorily, who can make their own decisions and
accept the consequences of these decisions, and who are truly self-
disciplined. We hope to see our children grow into interesting,
effective people who will be good friends, good husbands or wives,
and good neighbors and citizens.

Techniques and Attitudes

It would make things much simpler if we could offer a list of
simple rules of child training and some clear-cut techniques to be
applied. But it would be something less than helpful to do so; it
could be misleading. Because no two children are alike and no
two situations are ever identical, simple rules are not possible.

When a parent asks "What is the right thing to do when...?" the only honest answer possible is the unsatisfying one, "It all depends...." It depends on so many things: the age of the child, the context of the behavior, the relationship of the adult and the child, what the adult is trying to achieve, what has gone before, and a host of similar features. This sounds as though child rearing were a matter of trial and error, guess work and chance. But this is not true, for there are some guiding principles, goals, and values.

The essence of child training is time. Personality development is a slow, gradual process. More mistakes are made by parents because they are impatient with this slow growth than for any other reason. Development cannot be hurried. One fact stands out clearly in all the accumulating knowledge of child development and this is the great differences that exist between children in the rate of their development. Just because one child or even the majority of children learn to walk or talk at a certain age is no reason why we should expect all children to conform with this timetable. The parent who tries to hurry a child's development usually hinders the process. Many young children, for instance, are dawdlers mainly because their parents tried to hurry them when they were unable to hurry. One of the young child's defenses against being pushed is to dawdle. An adult may be able to wash a two-year-old's face and hands in half a minute but most two-year-olds take about ten times longer to do the job for themselves. Just because the neighbor's child was able to learn to read before he was five years old does not mean that all other children are ready for the same learning at that age.

There are two very prominent parental tendencies. One is to try to hurry development and the other is to be unaware of the child's readiness for the next phase of development. Perhaps the hurrying is more noticeable in the everyday routines of eating, washing, dressing, and the like and in the acquisition of skills such as walking, talking, reading, and writing. The tendency to lag behind the child's development is more apparent in such things as the time to let the child have an allowance, own a bicycle, drive a car, start dating, and similar activities. What seems to be necessary is abundance of patience to allow the child to develop and learn at his own rate, and at the same time a sensitivity to the readiness of the child for new activities, experiences, and developmental opportunities.

As we have said, all personality development takes time and during this time the infant, child, or youth needs guidance and support as he learns to manage his own affairs and accept the consequences of his own decisions and behavior. There are two major parental functions. One is the establishment of a relationship of trust and affection with the child, and the other is the planning and carrying out the details of a scheme of discipline while the child is slowly building his own inner controls. These functions, affection and discipline, are dependent upon each other, for adequate discipline is only possible in an atmosphere of mutual trust, respect, and affection, and affection is wasted if there is not a background of order and reasonable regulation.

Normally the relationship of the parent and the child is a progressively changing one. At first, the child is completely dependent on the parent, but as he learns and accumulates experience and skills, he gradually moves out from complete dependence to a degree of independence. When he starts learning to do things for himself he has started his journey toward independence, but while he is growing up there will always be a degree of dependence. So the parent-child relationship is a mixture of dependency and independence on the part of the child. The parental contribution to this ever-changing relationship is a mixture of protection, care, guidance, respect for the child, and abiding affection. As the child learns, there will be diminishing protection, care, and guidance with no decrease in affection, trust, and respect. At first, the parent acts as an agent accepting the consequences for the child's behavior, but gradually the child becomes more responsible and is accepting more and more the consequences of his behavior and decisions.

Recent research has indicated how essential for healthy development is a base of consistent, warm, ever-present care and protection by the parent. This enables the infant to feel completely secure in his dependence on the parent. The child must develop this trust and dependence on his parent if he is to acquire the necessary self-reliance as well as trust in others that is essential for growth toward independence and self-discipline. This basic trust is the necessary foundation from which he can move out to explore his world and attempt to form relationships with other people. Without this trust and dependence he will have difficulty and may never be able to achieve friendly, satisfying relations with others.

A great deal has been written and said about parental love, especially mother love. It is assumed by some that mothers instinctively love their offspring. But there is no reason to believe that there is any such instinct. In fact, there is much evidence to the contrary. However, in our culture it is the accepted thing for mothers, and fathers too, to love their children and most parents do. Such love, if not misused, can be a valuable part of the parent-child relationship, almost an essential part. It is when the parent uses love as an excuse or reason to be inconsistent, to smother or hinder the child's development, or to keep the child too dependent too long that love becomes a menace rather than a help. But love which includes respect for the child's individuality and right to be a person is healthy, desirable, and helpful. The warmth of human love is the atmosphere in which children thrive. It aids the feeling of trust and provides the kind of haven the child requires because of his insecurity growing out of his ignorance and lack of skill. However, if the love is used as a method of directing the child, it not only cheapens the affection but confuses the child. It is never fair to the child to say to him or even imply that mother will not love him any more if he behaves in that way. Love should be taken for granted. It should be something like the air we breathe, always there, necessary but free and unearned. Most parents expect to love their children and should not be ashamed to do so, but if they are wise they will never "use" love as a method of discipline.

It is difficult to overemphasize the importance of the intangible but real atmosphere that finds its expression in the relationship of the parent and the child. It is this atmosphere that determines the effectiveness of what the parent tries to do with the various techniques and details that make up a scheme of discipline. It isn't so much *what* the parent does that is important as *how*, and the context of attitudes, feelings, and meanings in which it operates. One simple example of this is the use of the technique of isolation. The child can be excluded from the family group as a way of helping him to learn that what he was doing was inappropriate, and he can be welcomed back when he is ready to behave more fittingly. Or he can be sent away in disgrace, feeling that he is not wanted. Or isolation can be a punishment with all the overtones of blame, hard feelings, and broken relationships. It may be the same technique but completely different in meaning, feeling, and results.

Another example of the way attitudes and feelings function in the parent-child relationship is seen in the mistake frequently made by parents in expecting gratitude from their children. The only legitimate gratitude that the parent can expect is the wordless gratitude of the child who grows, learns, and gradually becomes an independent, interesting person. The parent receives many returns for his hard work. He has the thrill of watching this miracle of development take place and of realizing that he has had something to do with it. That is reward enough for the mature parent. Of course, he sometimes gets extra dividends when the child does say, "Thanks." But to expect gratitude is to express an attitude which we hope our children will not acquire, that of thinking first of what they get in the way of returns rather than what they can contribute.

These are the considerations we shall try to keep in mind as we outline a reasonable scheme of discipline: what the child is like, what his world, present and future, is like, what we want to achieve, and the atmosphere in which we work.

chapter 3
A Reasonable
Scheme of Discipline

We build this reasonable scheme of discipline with two pictures in mind. One is the picture of the newborn infant, helpless, immature, and ignorant. The other is that of an adult, mature, capable, and functioning effectively in a complex world. These two pictures span a period of about twenty years. In these years the helpless infant becomes the active toddler, the preschool child, the school age child, the adolescent, and the young adult. The growth potentials inherent in the constitution of the infant combined with the multitude of experiences that come to him determine what kind of person he will become. We can do little about the constitutional factors, but it is our responsibility as adults to see that the experiences he has are conducive to healthy growth and development. This is discipline: arranging conditions for learning.

As has been said, "Love is not enough." Besides providing the child with a secure, dependent relationship, the parent has to have a plan of control, regulation, and training. It has been suggested that the child can be allowed to direct his own activities and growing up; that Nature is wise and if left alone will take care of development. This "free expression" or "leave the child alone to grow" technique came largely as a reaction to a too rigid and unintelligent kind of control and regulation. But it is quite unrealistic, as any parent or teacher knows. The combination of ignorance, lack of skill, and impulses can lead the child into activities that are dangerous and undesirable. Even more serious is the fact that the child under such a regime would fail to learn some of the most important lessons in living. There must be some kind of control and regulation. The only problem is what kind of control. It is on this point that there has been much controversy.

The nature of the plan of discipline adopted or drifted into by

a parent will depend on the kind of values, memories of childhood, and goals that are prominent in his own experience. The
actual techniques he uses will be colored by his attitudes, prejudices,
and scale of values. In a very real sense what one *is* is more important that what one *does* as a parent. This is because the parent's
behavior will be interpreted by the child and the meaning he gives
will depend on the kind of person the parent is. This does not
mean that techniques and methods are not important. They are.
A well thought-out plan can save a great deal of anxiety and also
cut down on the number of mistakes the parent is liable to make.
All parents make mistakes but their frequency will depend on the
adequacy of the plan that is made and carried out. No plan, or
haphazard kind of hit-or-miss plan, will lead to inconsistencies,
and as we shall see, consistency is the core principle of an adequate
scheme of discipline.

Progressive Change in Discipline

Discipline changes as the child grows and learns. It changes both
in amount and kind, and the change needs to be both gradual
and continuous. There are two kinds of control, external control
and self-regulation. From birth until maturity both kinds of control are present but vary in amount, the relative amounts of each
depending on the learning of the child. At birth the child's activity
as it relates to his environment, especially other people, is controlled or directed entirely from without, usually by his parents.
At maturity the control is now completely self-control, since the
adult no longer needs to be directed, policed, or supervised. At
least this is the ideal, although there are many so-called adults
who are incapable of managing adequately for themselves and who
still require policemen and others to keep them in order. It is our
contention that if there were adequate discipline during the first
twenty years of life the individual would be self-disciplined; he
would even drive the same whether he is being watched by a police-
man or not.

In between the landmarks of birth and maturity there is a gradual
but continuous shift of control and responsibility from parent to

the child. Each month sees new areas of activity in which the child can take the responsibility and manage for himself. The shift parallels the child's learning. When he acquires enough skill he feeds and dresses himself, looks after his toilet needs, manages his possessions, his time, his work, and his play. There is much for him to learn, and in the learning process he will make many mistakes. The process cannot be hurried but it can be continuous. We are usually allowed about eighteen or twenty years to guide the child from complete dependency to independence, from external control to self-discipline.

No child will conform to such a simple smooth picture of the transition. There will be many irregularities, some regressions and even spurts in development. In actual life, some months will show no progress or even some shift in reverse, and other months may show a great leap forward. The important thing is that there be overall progress from external control toward self-discipline.

Kinds of Control

There are three kinds of control: direct, indirect, and self-control. By direct control we mean deliberate attempts to influence the behavior of the child so as to ensure a degree of conformity with the necessary, sensible rules of living. Indirect control is the use of the child's environment to bring about desirable forms of behavior. Self-control is where the directing influences are within the individual himself. Every situation has some of all three types of control but in each situation one or another kind of control predominates. The self-control should slowly but surely take over until at maturity it is the main element. In the meantime, as self-control builds up, the parent must exert external control, either direct or indirect.

Indirect Control. The more adequately we can arrange the environment of the child the less need there is for direct control. In fact, when the child's environment is well-planned direct control is very little in evidence. Visitors to a well-run nursery school are often surprised at how infrequently the adults need to interfere with the children. Parents frequently ask what to do with the child who is bored, destructive, or showing any one of a score of patterns of behavior that are puzzling and nearly always annoying to parents. The most helpful answer that can be given is to do something about the child's environment, rather than anything directly with the child. Thus, providing interesting opportunities for activity, variety in play materials, ideas for activities, and the like, directs or redirects the child. This is one kind of indirect control. Most of us are so sure of the value of teaching that it is sometimes hard for us to realize that many of the important aspects of living are acquired by the child without tuition as he deals with everyday life situations. Manners, morals and attitudes develop more from the adoption of patterns of behavior than from any verbal repetition of rules or precepts.

Just because this kind of control is not direct or obvious does not mean that it need not be planned. It requires much thought and effort to provide an environment for the child which will yield the kinds of experiences that will foster healthy development. We shall look briefly at some examples of such planning, make clear what we mean, and then leave the reader to fill in other details in keeping with his own set of values and circumstances.

Even though the physical environment is not so important as the social environment, it is not without value as indirect control. The provision of a place to play, a variety of suitable play materials, and a place to keep these materials can be of great value, not only in preventing difficulties but also in laying foundations for interests with boundless possibilities for development. With older children, most of us are aware that the children who get into trouble are those who live in an environment which provides virtually nothing of a stimulating, interesting nature.

A visitor to our nursery school was heard to say as he was leaving, "I didn't see any bad behavior." (Maybe he had expected to find that nursery school children were problems!) He went on to say, "They were all busy doing things." And then he put the two observations together and concluded, "I guess they were too busy to be bad."

The fact that "the devil finds work for idle hands" is only part of the reason for paying attention to the child's physical environment. The more important consideration is the positive stimulus to development that results. Consider, for instance, the enormous stimulus to intellectual development the child receives from having access to interesting literature in which he discovers new worlds to explore.

It is not necessary to describe all the facets of this principle of provision of materials for educative experience. It applies to all areas of the child's experience and at all ages, not just in play activities but also in routines and work activities. Once the principle is accepted as important by the adult, he will find many suggestions from observing the child's interests and enthusiasms, from the experience of other people, and from the wealth of literature available.

The other aspect of indirect control is the social environment: the people in the child's world and the interpersonal relationships in which he participates. It would be impossible to overemphasize the importance of this for a plan of discipline. Without doubt the most powerful single factor in shaping the personality of the child is his relationship with people and especially his own family.

The young child can build a feeling of confidence and trust in people, if he is handled consistently with warmth and affection. He can build up a feeling of belonging when the atmosphere in which he lives is one of acceptance and respect. On the other hand, inconsistency, confusion, and conflict produce a setting in which it is practically impossible for the child to develop in a healthy way. Methods of direct control are important, of course, but their meaning to the child and their effectiveness depend on the context in which they are used. This is one reason why child study cannot provide a set of clear-cut, straightforward rules and techniques and guarantee that if they are followed the result will be a happy, well-adjusted person. The same technique used in different settings, with different adult-child relationships and varying "atmosphere," produce very different results. This is why some people talk about "born teachers" and imply that good teachers are not produced by training. What they are really saying is that it isn't so much the techniques that are used but the attitudes and atmosphere that provide the meaning and significance of the technique for the child that spell success in education. The same principles hold in the home with parents.

Someday we may be able to analyze in detail what is involved in atmosphere, interpersonal relationships, and attitudes. At present, however, we can be sure that these factors are involved in effective child training even though we cannot reduce them to precise, objective measurement or appraisal.

Two words which are commonly used to express an aspect of indirect control are imitation and example. Imitation is not by any means automatic. Children tend to copy those for whom they have respect and admiration. They tend to be highly suggestible toward those for whom they have affection. Suggestibility is accepting uncritically ways of thinking and behaving. If mother or father behaves that way, that must be the way to behave. But nearly every child has periods when he seems to be rebelling against his own suggestibility. It is as though he wants to assert his own individuality or growing independence and so he appears to be "negative." With most children this phase passes; the child loses his tendency to be negative although he may not be as suggestible as he was previously. But with some children it is not so much a phase of development as an indication that the child's relationship with his parent is not what it should be. These children are expressing their lack of trust in the adult or possibly even antagonism toward the adult, or in some cases, all adults. However, the usual picture is one of the child absorbing and expressing the patterns of behavior he sees in the people with whom he lives. Thus his manners, moral standards, values, and attitudes usually reflect those of the rest of the family. For instance, it is not very difficult to find, even in preschool children, attitudes of intolerance when such attitudes are prominent in their parents.

The atmosphere of the home is created by the parents. This atmosphere has many parts. The goals and ambitions of the parents help to determine the nature of what they value. There are, of course, as many shades of value as there are people. It is possible to place a high value on almost anything: neatness, kindness, consideration for others, material success, social approval, justice, happiness, honesty, social status, money, friendship, appearance, and so on almost indefinitely. The point is that the child will almost certainly absorb some of the values prevalent in his home.

Another part of this picture is what we shall call an attitude of expecting. We get from children about what we expect. When we expect a battle we usually have one. When we expect the child to conform he usually does. The attitude itself has a great deal to do with the result. For instance, contrast two attitudes in the introduction of new food in the child's diet. The one is uncertainty, expecting difficulty. "I hope you'll like it" or "Won't you just try it, it's good for you" or "You may not like this, but I hope you will." The other is an attitude of confident expectation, placing the food in front of the child with every expectation that he will eat it. The attitude helps to determine what will happen.

Attitudes are conveyed by such intangibles as tone of voice, posture, and facial expression. Observing adults in dealing with young children provides many examples of what we mean. Here is a beginning student in the nursery school who approaches a child timidly and says in a hesitant manner, "Would you like to come and wash now?" and is met with a blunt "No." An experienced teacher in the same situation would approach the child with a confident attitude, take the child by the hand and say, "It's time to wash now," and be halfway to the washroom before the child realized what was happening.

The so-called emotional aspects of home atmosphere are also important. The child thrives in an atmosphere of acceptance, affection, consideration, and friendliness. The lesson many parents have learned is that it is possible to be both good friends and effective parents. In fact, when there is a feeling of trust, understanding, and friendliness, supervision and direction of the child are easier and more successful. The fear that such an approach will undermine the authority of the parent is unfounded. One does not have to be cold and stern to enforce requirements; what is needed most is consistency. What has been called a good home atmosphere is a compound of a healthy adjustment between the parents, sincerity, a real liking for the child, willingness to consider the child's feelings and point of view, a sense of perspective, and a sense of humor.

Indirect control is stage setting. It is providing the environment and background conducive to desirable behavior. It is building a climate in which mutual trust and affection make happy, satisfying relationships possible. The more adequate this indirect control is, the less need there will be for direct control. But direct control will still be required because no amount of stage setting or atmosphere will do the whole job.

Direct Control. Direct control is not in good repute, at least with some parents. They seem to be afraid to make demands of their children or restrict their behavior in any way. They try to talk the child into doing something. They have adopted as their main technique "reasoning" with the child. But reasoning often becomes arguing and the parent does not always win the argument. Perhaps this is because they have heard so much about emotionally disturbed children who are said to be the products of too much frustration. Perhaps they have heard of the importance of what we have been calling indirect control and have thought that no direct control is ever desirable. Perhaps they think that the "experts" advise against any direct control of the child. Or perhaps they are reacting against the extremes of cruelty and regimentation of an earlier time. Some direct control is not only respectable and desirable, but essential in any reasonable scheme of discipline. There are two important aspects of direct regulation of the child to be considered: the context or setting in which the control occurs, and the why and how of the control itself.

We have already had something to say about the first of these when we discussed indirect control, so a brief summary is all that we need here. Commands, suggestions, requests, and prohibitions which are given in an atmosphere in which justice, understanding, and affection prevail have a very different effect on the child than when these are absent. When the child feels secure and wanted, he can and does accept direction and restriction. But when the child does not have a feeling of belonging he may not be so ready to accept direction. In fact, when adults have difficulty in enforcing regulations with children, it is wise to see if the general atmosphere and what we have called indirect control have been well managed or not. When there is a good relationship between the adult and the child, direct control is usually fairly easy; in some cases the child is almost too ready to conform.

Planned Requirements

Life consists of two kinds of activities: those things which we must do whether we want to or not, and those which we can do or not just as we like. The first of these we shall call requirements. They may be positive or negative, the "musts" and "must nots" of civilized life. Even though the parent must plan the requirements they are not (or should not be) parental whims, merely what the parent would like the child to do. They are requirements because of other considerations. They are necessary for some other reason than personal desire. They are required for the safety and well-being of the child, for his progress toward self-discipline, or for the smooth functioning of the group—family, classroom, or community.

Requirements are planned and periodically revised by the parents. In his early years the child is incapable of taking part in this planning. However, as he learns and accumulates experience he is brought into the planning and helps to formulate the rules he is expected to live by. Finally, as he reaches maturity the requirements will be his own, the rules will be internalized, and he will be self-disciplined.

Every parent has to decide what is to be required of the child, what are the boundaries he must not violate, what are the necessary, reasonable demands that should be made of the child. Obviously no two parents will have the same requirements, but if the parent is too different from the rest of the community he will have difficulty making the demands seem reasonable.

The requirements are planned on the basis of a knowledge of what the child is capable of doing. Thus the requirements change as the child grows. So we have a picture of a dynamic, ever-changing pattern of planned requirements. At first all responsibility rests with the adult, he makes the decisions and accepts the consequences of them. Then as the child acquires the necessary skills and understanding the parent makes the rules and sets the boundaries, and the child has to live up to the things that are required of him. Still later, with further learning and greater understanding, the child takes part in formulating the rules and accepts the responsibility for fulfilling them. Finally, the control moves into the area of self-regulation and the individual behaves appropriately without any necessity for checkup or supervision. Of course, not all areas follow this sequence at the same rate; some aspects of everyday living move into this area of individual responsibility early while others do so years later.

In the stage between the time when the parent has to take full responsibility and manage completely for the child and the time when the child manages completely for himself, is the period when the adult plans, imposes, and enforces requirements. It is in this stage that the following principles apply.

The requirements are kept to a minimum, only those which are necessary are included. One of the easiest things to do is to have a number of rules and requirements, many of which are merely nuisances and some of which can never be enforced. For example, there is no use requiring a child to sleep, because it is impossible to enforce such a rule. You can require a child to go to bed at bedtime because if necessary you can put him there, but to require sleep can only be enforced with a baseball bat or drugs. So the only requirements that are planned are those which are within the child's capacity, enforceable and necessary. By necessary, we mean important for the child's safety, health, and development, and the convenience and peace of mind of the rest of the group.

Requirements with young children are usually in the nature of limits, boundaries, or general rules within which the child has some freedom. They are made to appear to the child as reasonable as possible. So the parent must ask about each regular requirement: is it necessary, is it reasonable, is it within the child's capacity, and can I enforce it?

Requirements that fit these standards are really situational rather than personal. They are not merely whims of the parent. They are required by the situation, not by mother or father, even though mother or father will have to administer them. It becomes clear to the child that it isn't just that mother wants him to go to bed but rather that sleep is a necessity and a regular bedtime a reasonable, sensible way of managing it. It isn't just that father wants the child to have clean hands at the meal table. It is simply what is done in the best of families. The idea we help the child to see as soon as possible is that there are some things that are a part of the business of living, some things that are done and others that are not done, some activities that are sensible and others that are undesirable. There is a behavior that is appropriate and fitting in every situation, so that one has the most fun and gets the most out of life when he behaves in this way. Conformity then becomes not merely doing what you are told to do, but doing what the total situation requires of you. Often so-called bad, naughty, or un- desirable behavior is behavior that is out of place in that setting. It may be quite all right to run, jump, climb, and shout on the playground but such behavior is inappropriate in the living room.

When requirements are personal the usual formula is, do this because I say so, or do this or I will be annoyed. When require- ments are situational and impersonal all that is needed is a simple statement of what is required and some indication of why. This can be summed up by saying that the core principle is consistency.

By consistency we mean that the same requirement is made every time in the same situation. This is saying in effect to the child that the situation requires this way of acting. In this way it is pos- sible for the child to learn and accept the daily demands of civilized living. Of course he will not learn it overnight, but each month should add to his store of knowledge of how to behave. Consistency banishes personal resentments because consistency says more clearly than anything else that this is not just a personal parental whim but a simple necessity of life itself.

Consistency divorces the requirement from a person for it means that whoever is supervising the situation requires the same thing. It should also reduce the amount of "reasoning" with the child. Reasoning with the child usually means that the adult is trying to talk the child into doing something or behaving in a certain way, and it invites argument. Some children make a kind of game out of this and keep arguing until the adult loses patience and "lays down the law." When there is a routine requirement there should be no argument. There can be and indeed needs to be dis- cussion about requirements with the child but not at the time the requirement is being enforced. At this time the adult carries through and sees that the child conforms. However, the whole issue can be discussed at another time when both parent and child are sure to

be less emotional about it. Resistance by the child to reasonable requirements can mean many things. It can mean that the child has
not yet seen the necessity and reasonableness of the requirement.
Or it can mean that there have been exceptions, lack of consistency,
so that the child has learned he can avoid the requirement and thus
will strive to do so. Or his resistance may be a part of a larger pattern of resentment and hostility built up by unjust, unreasonable,
or inconsistent treatment. Sometimes the resistance simply means
that too many demands are being made on the child and that an
adjustment in the plan is necessary.

As adults we realize that no two situations or circumstances are
ever exactly alike and therefore the demands from these situations
vary. However, in order to help the child learn, we try to make
the same demand or requirement of the child in what is basically
the same situation. Thus bedtime for the young child comes at
approximately the same time each day even though the circumstances of bedtime may vary from day to day. The same requirement of eating the first course before he gets his dessert is made
at each meal even though the foods may be different and the child's
hunger vary as well.

There can be no standard answer to the question, What should
the requirements be for a two-year-old? The details of the requirements will vary from home to home. And not all two-year-olds are
ready for the same requirements. One home may have a requirement that hands must be washed before coming to the meal table,
while in another home it may not be thought necessary. In one
home putting play materials away neatly and promptly after use
may be considered a reasonable, necessary demand, while in another
home it may be left for mother to do. So each adult will have to
decide for himself what is important, what should be required, and
what not bothered with.

Enforcing Requirements with Consequences

There is no use having rules or imposing requirements on the
child unless we have some way of enforcing them. The method
we are suggesting is summed up in the phrase: the arrangement

of consequences. We take our cue from examples of simple learning we can see in the child. He learns that water is wet, that fire is hot, that floors are hard and thousands of similar items of knowledge from the constancy and consistency of the relationships experienced. After all, water is *always* wet, otherwise it wouldn't be water. So we accept the principle that if a consequence always follows a behavior the child will learn to connect the two. All behavior has consequences. But there are some consequences that are too remote for the child to see the connection and so he has to take our word for it. This he is usually ready to do if he has found us to be trustworthy and reliable. Thus, when we tell him that certain things are dangerous or harmful he accepts this as true. But if he has found that our warnings are not true he learns to disregard them. After we have said to him dozens of times, "Don't run or you will fall and hurt yourself," and he runs and does not fall or falls and does not get hurt, then he begins to doubt our statements about possible consequences. In social situations the consequences are rarely sure and immediate, so to help learning we have to introduce the artificial, arranged consequences.

Life is a series of choices. Some of these are deliberate and thought out, some are habitual and thus the result of a series of previous choices. Child training is a program to aid the child in making choices and then making some of his choices so much a part of himself that he does not have to think about them very much. Intelligent choice depends on the adequacy of the individual's anticipation of consequences. That is, when a person makes an intelligent choice he knows what the consequences of the alternatives are and selects the line of behavior which will end in the desired results. We think of discipline as a plan of training and the enforcing of requirements as helping the child to learn how to behave adequately through a knowledge of the consequences of various ways of behaving. Some consequences are pleasant and will thus lead to the repetition of the activity. Others are unpleasant and will be conducive to the elimination of that behavior. Some will happen naturally and automatically while others will need to be arranged.

Consequences of Desirable Behavior.   When the child's behavior is appropriate, that is, when it conforms with the requirements of the situation, the natural consequences are feelings of satisfaction and enjoyment. The child feels "at home" in that situation and has thrills of achievement and the tonic of success. But these natural consequences can be easily obscured if we complicate the situation with rewards, approval, or other artificial consequences. Effort which results in achievement carries its own reward and needs no added incentive. Sometimes the child needs encouragement because achievement is delayed or progress is slow. And sometimes we need to emphasize the desirable behavior by expressions of approval and applause. However, such approval should be used intelligently because we do not want him to learn to do things merely to get this approval. Nor do we want to make it difficult for him to experience the more valuable consequence of his activity, the feeling of success and achievement. When the child's efforts do not seem to produce immediate results, approval can serve to bridge the gap between effort and results. This is especially necessary with the timid child or the one who is easily discouraged or inclined to give up easily.

Rewards are an easy kind of artificial consequence to use but not necessarily desirable. They can so easily become a kind of barter: you do this for me and I'll give you something in return. This becomes a form of bribery. If you will be good all week I'll give you a dollar on Saturday. If you will eat your dinner quickly I'll buy you an ice-cream cone. If you work hard and beat the other children in your studies I'll buy you a wristwatch or a bicycle. The person who gets the highest grades gets a scholarship. The winner gets the gold cup. The list is endless: prizes, honor rolls, awards, ribbons, gold stars, and rewards of all varieties. These are all artificial consequences used to bring about desired results. One difficulty in their use is that they tend to produce the "reward habit," that is, thinking of activities only in terms of what tangible return it will bring. When we meet this "What's there in it for me" attitude in child or adult we can be pretty sure that the reward technique has had a large place in their bringing up.

Rewards often obscure the issue. When the child is rewarded for living up to the necessary requirements of everyday life, it is difficult for him to realize that they are requirements after all. The child who is rewarded for working hard at learning may become so interested in the reward as to lose the fun and thrills of learning. One of the common ideas behind the reward technique is that if we can get the child to do something often enough the habit will be formed. So by the artificial stimulus of a reward we get the child to do something over and over again. But the child does not just learn by doing, rather he learns *what he practices.* So if he is practicing working for a reward that is what he learns and not to be tidy, or punctual, or whatever goal was in the mind of the adult.

Rewards are often coupled with competition, especially in the schools. Here the emphasis is on winning and the important thing is to get ahead of others. Most school competitions are unfair because the competitors vary so much in intellectual equipment that the winner may not be the child who worked the hardest but the child who had the longest head start in terms of IQ. Such competitions teach the child that winning is more important than the activity itself. Learning can be interesting, challenging, and self-rewarding if these extraneous incentives of winning and getting prizes are left out of the situation. It has been demonstrated that a school or a home can function efficiently without rewards, competition, or prizes.

Consequences for Inappropriate Behavior. The natural consequences of inappropriate behavior are feelings of failure. These feelings can be valuable incentives to learning if they are not complicated with blame and disgrace. Failure is a part of learning. A feeling of inadequacy can be a starting point and a stimulus to effort. However, when it is considered to be something to be ashamed of, it leads to emotional disturbance rather than improvement. It is when one feels inadequate because of not knowing enough or not being able to do something well enough, and at the same time feels that he *can* learn, that a feeling of inadequacy is healthy. But when adults make children feel small and inadequate, and intimate that making mistakes or not being able to do something well is a disgrace, then what we have is not a healthy feeling of inadequacy but a crippling condition that some people call an inferiority complex.

The natural consequences of inadequate behavior are not always sufficient and adults must find some artificial or arbitrary consequences to apply. Such artificial consequences can be anything that the adult can devise and administer. There are a number of guiding principles to help the adult decide on what is an effective consequence for inadequate or undesirable activity.

The first principle is that of relevancy. The more relevant, that is, related, logical, and connected with the behavior itself, the better it will function. Taking an amount off the child's allowance for failure to return home in time for a meal is not relevant unless, of course, the allowance is considered to be pay for punctuality. Having to eat a cold meal alone is related. Spanking the child for failure to learn his spelling words has no logical connection with his behavior unless we want to tell the child that such failures on his part are annoying to us and the spanking then is our expression of annoyance. In most cases it is possible to find a relevant consequence for the child's behavior and thus help him to learn both that the activity is undesirable and also why.

Another principle is immediacy. The more closely related in time a consequence is, the more effective it will be in helping the child to learn. What we are trying to do is to have the child learn that certain consequences follow a certain kind of behavior. When the result follows the event after a delay it is difficult for the child to see the connection. This is one reason why consequences are not put off until father comes home but are applied immediately.

Besides being logical or relevant and immediate, consequences should be consistent. The same consequence always follows the same behavior. Just as requirements need to be consistent, so consequences for nonconformity should also be consistent. That is, consistency from time to time with the same adult, and consistency from adult to adult. Mother, father, grandparents, and anyone else supervising the child should all use the same requirements and the same consequences if the child fails to live up to them. In this way, the requirement is attached to the situation and the consequence is related to the behavior; it is not merely an expression of one adult's desires. Consistency does not mean that there will be no change, no progress in privilege and freedom, that a child will always be treated as he is at present. Rather, he should know that when he learns to make good use of the amount of freedom he has he will get more and that increased responsibility will bring increased freedom. However, the principle remains the same, that abuse of privilege brings loss of privilege for a time; that failure to abide by the necessary boundaries of his present freedom means a temporary loss of that freedom; and that this happens inevitably and consistently.

As we have said, almost anything may be used as a consequence for undesirable behavior. But this does not mean that all are equally desirable or effective. Some of the more common techniques in use are evaluated in the following paragraphs.

One of the most common of these is corporal punishment. There are still many people who believe that such a technique is indispensable. The administering of pain (either bodily or mentally) seems to appeal to some people as a sure and quick way to bring about learning. Punishment as a method has had a long and sordid history and still continues to play a large role in dealing with undesirable behavior in both adults and children. But merely because it is centuries old does not make it good or bad, acceptable or unacceptable. It must be evaluated on its own merits. When viewed in a narrow way and considering only immediate results, it seems to have had considerable success. But looked at from a wider perspective, that of personality and character development, one can doubt if punishment is ever justified with children.

To inflict pain deliberately on a young child cannot be justified on any grounds. It is an easy method, always available and requiring little intelligence or thought in use. It appears to accomplish what is wanted because it does keep the child in order. However, when we think of what it does to the relationship between child and adult, when we think of the resentments and antagonisms it can produce, when we think of the fears and timidity it creates, and when we realize the emotional scars it can leave behind, we are ready to consider the possibilities of other ways of helping the child learn how to behave.

There are many forms of punishment; in fact any consequence for undesirable behavior can be punishment if the attitude of the adult is one of blaming the child, thinking of him as bad and sinful and deserving of pain. But when we think of the child as a learner, immature and ignorant at present but capable of learning, punishment does not fit into the picture. Arbitrary consequences for undesirable behavior do not have to be punishment.

Another form that arbitrary consequences for undesirable behavior takes is verbal expression of disapproval. This is probably the most frequently used technique. Thousands of words are used daily by the average parent in dealing with the child, and many of these words are words of disapproval. And many of them are wasted as the child is almost forced to develop defenses against this flow of words. His easiest defense is to learn not to hear or at least heed the disapproval. Lecturing the child, bawling him out, ridicule, sarcasm, belittling, name-calling, and many more make up the content of this common method. Besides the fact that this technique is relatively ineffective, it should be discarded as much as possible because it is so highly personal, giving the child the impression that the main reason for good behavior is that the parent wants it. And it tends to be inconsistent, depending, as it does, so much on how the parent feels at the time.

Depriving the child of possessions, freedom, privilege, or opportunities for particular forms of activity can be the consequence of undesirable behavior. There are some occasions where this is undesirable. When, for instance, the child misuses possessions, he can be helped to learn through his mistake by losing the possessions for a time. When the young child uses his crayons to mark on a wall, the crayons can be taken from him and he can be deprived of their use for a time. The child who shows that he cannot manage the amount of freedom he has at present may have to lose some of that freedom so that he can be helped to realize that responsibility goes along with freedom. Of course the important thing is how the technique is applied. It can very easily deteriorate into a punishment with all the overtones of blame, hard feelings, and resentment. When, however, it is used as an educative procedure it can be relevant, logical, impersonal, and helpful.

Social isolation is another consequence of undesirable behavior. It is a legitimate technique when the behavior is related to the group and is undesirable because it is disruptive or is violating some social rule. Thus the child who is disturbing other children can be removed from the group to help him learn that being a member of a group requires that he behave in such a way that he does not interfere with the enjoyment of the others. When he fails to abide by the simple but necessary rules of the situation he can be removed from the situation to help him to know that membership in groups means that he cannot do as he likes but must take the other members into consideration. Again, isolation can be used as a punishment, and sometimes a very cruel punishment, if the isolation is in a dark closet or locked in a room by himself for a long period. Whether it is a helpful educative procedure or a punishment will depend mainly on the attitude of the adult. If the parent means it as a punishment it will have that meaning to the child, but if it is used as an educational device the child will realize that the parent is being helpful and not mean.

One adult attitude that colors all that is done for and with the child is the degree of respect the adult has for the child as an individual. Listening to parents and teachers talk about children and observing some of them dealing with children, one can see all degrees of respect for the individual personality, all the way from a complete absence of respect to an intelligent acceptance of the right of the child to be a unique individual. Another attitude that helps is that of thinking of the child as a developing, changing, learning human being. This enables the parent to accept the child as a child and not a miniature adult. This attitude is the basis of a realistic understanding of the stage of development that the child has reached at present. It keeps us from expecting either too much or too little from the child. It enables us to keep in step with the child's development and thus progressively modify our program of discipline as we gradually hand over to him more and more areas to manage for himself. And above all, it enables us to manage the requirements and their consequences without recourse to punitive methods.

Related to this is an attitude of faith and confidence in the child. Even though he may not know much today or be able to do much for himself, we believe in him and his ability to learn and improve. He feels that we are on his side, that we are cheering for him, and that we have confidence in him. This attitude of expecting the best is a strong influence in stimulating him to give his best. But even more important than this, it will help him to build self-confidence and reliance. It is a fortunate child who has parents who love him, respect him as an individual, think of him as a learning, developing person, and have faith in him. Fortunate, because he has the kind of social climate that will aid his progress toward maturity and becoming a functioning adult who will fulfill some of his potentialities. Fortunate, also, because adults with these attitudes will arrange reasonable, sensible requirements and will enforce them consistently and fairly.

Children need discipline; so do adults. But children must have discipline from without as they are acquiring the inner discipline that is the mark of a true adult. The discipline that is best for this purpose is a planned program of reasonable demands consistently enforced, which help the child to understand and accept the core of sensible standards of civilized living and at the same time keep the individuality of his own taste and preferences.

chapter 4
Relax and Enjoy
Your Children

If you have read all that has gone before, perhaps you are wonder-ing if bringing up children has to be that complex. Actually it *is* complex in the sense that every day brings new situations and problems. But parenthood need not be a continuous strain or worry. There's a lot of hard work about it and it does take some hard thinking and planning as well. This does not mean that we have to worry and fret about it. In fact, it is much better done if there is not too much strain and worry.

It is easy to say, "relax and enjoy your children," but it is not always easy to do. Here are a few suggestions that might help. Children are extremely flexible and so a few mistakes need not be too serious. All parents and teachers make mistakes, and children are not ruined for life by the occasional mistake. There are no perfect parents, just as there are no perfect children. Both parents and children are human, and to err is human. The main thing is that the general day-by-day picture is sound; if it is, then the oc-casional mistake makes little difference. And by the way, children appreciate it when parents admit that they have said or done some-thing they should not have. It gives the child a fellow feeling with the parent to know that even parents are human and can err like children.

Another help to relax and enjoy our children is a well-developed sense of perspective so that we realize what is important and what is trivial and can be safely ignored. Of course there are some things that are important and must receive our attention but there are many features of the child's activity that are of much less im-portance and can be overlooked. It is comforting to remember that immaturity is a stage on the way to maturity and that the behavior we call childish, although a characteristic of childhood, is not permanent. Children grow out of a lot of things besides their clothes. "It is just a passing phase" does actually apply to much of the behavior of the child.

Relax and enjoy your children is not just a catch phrase; it is a basic condition of effective parenthood. If things are not going well it is a good idea to take off the pressure, let up, not try so hard, and take it easy for a while. This sometimes works in golf and it is even more effective in being a parent. Parents who have come through the mill say that most of the things they worried about never happened anyway. The parent who is tense and worried cannot be a good parent; for one reason, the strain is catching and soon the children are irritable and fretful too. Sometimes a few hours away from the children is a help. The mother who is so tied to her job and her children that she cannot bear to leave them in the care of a competent baby-sitter for an afternoon, evening, or weekend is probably not a very good mother. She could be a better parent after being away from them for a while. It is good for both parent and child to get away from each other occasionally. That is one of the reasons why a nursery school is so valuable. It takes the young children out from under mother's feet for a few hours and allows her to catch her breath, and also carry on other activities and interests which make her a more interesting and relaxed person. So, relax and enjoy your children for the sake of the children as well as yourself.

So much has been written in newspapers, magazines, pamphlets, and books about child rearing that many parents today are confused and even afraid that they may not be doing the right thing. This fear is unnecessary. There is no right way to bring up children. The right way for any parent is the way that is most comfortable for him, as long as he has thought about what he is doing, knows what he is trying to achieve, and is not just taking the easiest way out. Children are not brought up by the book; they are raised by people called parents. Of course, parents can get a great deal of help from books and lectures, but only if they are used intelligently and critically and not as blind guides. Being a good parent requires a lot of love, abundant patience, considerable study and planning, and a large supply of common sense. But being a parent can pay big dividends.

Relax and enjoy your children. You will not find any more drama on any stage than you can see in your own home and your own children's behavior. You will not find anything more interesting if you travel the world over than the changing picture of your own developing children. Do not let the seriousness of the job of parenthood rob you of the enjoyment that should go with parenthood. Perhaps some parents could take a lesson from those grandparents who find that when they are not too concerned about the serious responsibility of managing children they can enjoy being with them. Of course, parents cannot shrug off their responsibility, but perhaps if they did not take themselves too seriously they would be able to find more enjoyment and satisfaction in the job. Without minimizing in any way the serious things we tried to say in the preceding chapters, we now say, relax and enjoy your children; they will not be children for very long.

References on Discipline

Auerback, A. B.: *The Why and How of Discipline,* Child Study Association of America, New York.

Bacmeister, R. W.: *All in the Family,* Appleton-Century-Crofts, New York, 1951.

Bakwin, H., and Bakwin, R. M.: "Discipline in Children," *Journal of Pediatrics,* 1951, **39,** 623–634.

Baruch, D. W.: *How to Discipline Your Children,* Public Affairs Pamphlet No. 154, New York.

Bauer, W. W.: *Stop Annoying Your Children,* Bobbs-Merrill, Indianapolis, 1947.

Benedict, A., and Franklin, A.: *Your Best Friends Are Your Children,* Appleton-Century-Crofts, New York, 1952.

Bernhardt, K. S.: "A Philosophy of Discipline," *Bulletin of the Institute of Child Study,* Toronto, 1959, No. 80.

————: "Building Security in a Changing World," *Bulletin of the Institute of Child Study,* Toronto, 1959, No. 79.

————: "Freedom and Discipline as a Means toward Self-discipline," *Bulletin of the Institute of Child Study,* Toronto, 1960, No. 86.

————: "A Positive, Non-punitive Scheme of Discipline," *Bulletin of the Institute of Child Study,* Toronto, 1962, No. 94.

Blatz, W. E.: *Understanding the Young Child,* Clarke, Irwin, Toronto, and Morrow, New York, 1944.

Burgess, H. S.: *Discipline: What Is It?* Child Study Association of America, New York, 1948.

Cutts, N. E., and Mosely, N.: *Better Home Discipline,* Appleton-Century-Crofts, New York, 1952.

Dolger, L., and Ginandes, J.: "Children's Attitudes towards Discipline as Related to Socio-economic Status," *Journal of Experimental Education,* 1946, 15, 161–165.

DuBois, F. S.: "The Security of Discipline," *Mental Hygiene,* 1952, 36, 353–372.

Estes, W. K.: "An Experimental Study of Punishment," *Psychological Monographs,* 1944, 57, No. 263.

Havighurst, R. J.: "The Function of Successful Discipline," *Understanding the Child,* 1952, 21, 35–38.

Krug, O., and Beck, H. L.: *A Guide to Better Discipline,* Science Research Associates, Chicago, 1954.

Langdon, G., and Stout, I. W.: *Bringing Up Children,* John Day, New York, 1960.

Lippitt, R.: "An Experimental Study of the Effect of Democratic and Authoritarian Atmospheres," *University of Iowa Studies in Child Welfare,* 1940, 16, 43–195.

Meyers, C. E.: "The Effect of Conflicting Authority on the Child," *University of Iowa Studies in Child Welfare,* 1944, 20, 31–98.

Miller, D. R., and Swanson, G. E.: *Inner Conflict and Defense,* Holt, New York, 1960.

Mowrer, O. H.: "Discipline and Mental Health," *Harvard Educational Review,* 1947, 17, 284–296.

Muuss, R. E.: *First-aid for Classroom Discipline Problems,* Holt, New York, 1962.

———: "Mental Health Implications of a Preventive Psychiatry Programme in the Light of Research Findings," *Marriage & Family Living,* 1960, 22, 150–156.

Radke, M. S.: *The Relation of Parental Authority to Children's Behavior and Attitudes,* University of Minnesota Press, Minneapolis, 1946.

Sheviakov, G. V., and Redl, F.: *Discipline for Today's Children and Youth,* Association for Supervision and Curriculum Development, National Education Assn., Washington, 1956.

Spock, B. M.: *Dr. Spock Talks with Mothers,* Houghton Mifflin, New York, 1961.

Stendler, C. B.: "Climates for Self-Discipline," *Childhood Education*, 1951, 27, 209–211.

Whyte, D. K.: *Teaching Your Child Right from Wrong*, Bobbs-Merrill, Indianapolis, 1961.

Wittenberg, R. M.: *Adolescence and Discipline*, Association Press, New York, 1959.

Wolf, K. M.: *The Controversial Problems of Discipline*, Child Study Association of America, New York, 1953.

part ii

Life Situations

In this section a sample of life situations
is presented in the hope that by discussing
these practical everyday situations
we shall be able to see how the theoretical
principles outlined in Part 1 work out.

These sketches of family life reflect no
hard and fast rules but rather a point
of view which is a compound of common
sense, knowledge of child development,
and a fairly clear set of ideas of what
aids progress toward personal fulfillment.
This is not meant to be a set of easy
lessons on how to bring up children but
rather a source of insights and understanding. We do not believe that anyone
has all the answers about child rearing,
and we are sure that we do not. Nor
do we believe that any set of techniques
will ever cover the problem adequately, for
we know that what is important is not
the technique but the way in which it is
used. Two parents may employ the same
technique with very different results,
just as two teachers may employ the same
teaching methods and get almost completely opposite results. Adults working
with children need more than a set of rules
or a ready-made formula, for the adult's
attitudes, feelings, goals, and values will

have more to do with the results than any
formula or set way of behaving.

There is no particular order or logic in
the areas covered. About the only reason
for including or not including a situation
was whether we had anything to say
about it. If we felt we had anything that
might be helpful to say about an area,
it was included, but if not it was left out.
In these sketches of life situations an
occasional suggestion of "what to do" is
offered, but these situations are not so
much rules to follow as something to think
about and possibly try out. We have tried
to keep these sketches as simple and
concrete as possible in the hope that they
will have relevance in the day-by-day
family life of those who read them.

Over seventy-five thousand meals! That is the number you will eat if you live to be threescore years and ten. And if you average a half hour a meal (I hope it will be more), you will spend over four years of your life at the meal table. And if you enjoy your meals, or at least most of them, you will want to make sure your children do too.

True, we have to eat to live but surely meals should contribute more to life than just the provision of fuel for the body. Eating can be enjoyable. What makes it so? Certainly the satisfaction of the need for food. But that isn't all. The kind of food and how it is prepared has a lot to do with it, and so do the surroundings, and, of course, the company. Think of those very special meals you have had, the candlelight, the spotless linen, the shining silver, the charming companions, and the flow of wit. Perhaps you remember the food or some part of it, but certainly the highlights you remember are not just food. There is more to mealtime than eating, even though that is what meals are for.

Nature (or heredity) has provided the newborn infant with the mechanisms to get food easily. He has dependable sucking and swallowing reflexes and he feels hungry (or at least he shows all the signs of discomfort). So when anything touches his lips he starts right in to suck. A little later he will have to learn a whole new set of activities associated with eating, but even at this very early stage parents have decisions to make. Whether the infant should be fed "on demand" or "on schedule" is one of these.

This problem is one of those controversies or differences of opinion, about which some people get quite concerned. It need not be either of these choices—of extremes. There is something to be said for taking the infant's hunger into account just as there is much in favor of regularity. It is when we think only in terms of extremes that we take sides. If we think of a schedule as something that is timed to split-second precision, and of the principle of regularity as meaning that we must not vary a minute one way or another, then we shy away from the schedule idea. Or when we think of the "demand" idea as meaning that the infant is fed whenever he shows distress by crying, we discard this approach. But no one (or at least very few people) would think of a schedule that did not take into account the infant's own hunger rhythm. A schedule that was planned without reference to the child's needs would be silly, just as discarding the schedule idea and "letting Nature decide" would be equally undesirable.

Perhaps this is the place to say something about frustration and the fairly widespread idea that frustrations are always bad for children. Some of our clinical friends have pointed out that some maladjustments and unhappiness stem from situations in which frustration has been prominent. It seems easy to conclude from this that *all* frustrations are bad for children. Nothing could be further from the truth. If we think of frustration as hindrance or delay in satisfaction of wants, we must realize that such experiences are not only inevitable but desirable. Without them there would be very little learning. It is only when we put forth effort to overcome such frustrations that we acquire new patterns of activity. Also, it is one part of growing up to learn to delay satisfactions. It is one sign of maturity to be able to want something today and start working toward getting it days, months, or even years later. But we are wandering a long way from eating. What we are trying to say here is that frustrations in the life of the child are inevitable; they are also healthy and desirable as long as they are not too serious or too frequent.

So it isn't a clear-cut choice between "demand" and "schedule" feeding. It is rather a matter of working out a schedule which is custom-made to the child's needs, and gradually working toward the time when the child will learn to fit in with the plan of eating that is a part of the culture into which he was born. This usually means that eating is reserved in the main for *mealtimes* and these times are a matter of group (family) convenience.

Even in these early months eating can be enjoyable. This means that the infant is fed (or gets his food) in a comfortable, relaxed atmosphere—that he is fed often enough so that he is not made too uncomfortable by delays, but not so often that hunger does not have a chance to make the activity pleasant.

Weaning seems to be difficult for some parents to manage. This is the process of substituting new eating activities and new kinds of food for the early liquid diet. The key to weaning is to make it gradual. It should not be hurried. Only one new feature at a time should be introduced. Too much of the new and unfamiliar will produce withdrawal, refusal, and resistance.

Food dislikes often originate from the way new foods are introduced. It is very common for young children to refuse a new food because it is unfamiliar. It may be different in taste, temperature, smell, consistency, or just appearance. If there is an emotional storm at this time or if the food is forced on the child, this refusal may be fixated and a full-blown food dislike occurs. No child or adult is going to like all foods equally, nor would we want him to do so. It is natural that there should be preferences. However, the goal parents have in mind is to get the child to accept all or most foods even though some will be preferred.

You can lead a child to food but you can't make him eat. But hunger is a strong force and a hungry child will usually eat if he is left alone. Many food dislikes and eating difficulties occur when there is pressure on the child. We know so much about calories, vitamins, and nutrition today that many parents are concerned about getting their children to eat a well-balanced, adequate diet. But their concern leads to difficulty, because they are tempted to try to force the child to eat, coax him, bribe him, or talk him into it, sometimes even try to trick him into eating: "Now one bite for Grandma, a bite for Fido, and a bite for Charlie."

The eating situation is a good example of the indirect method of control. The food is attractive, the setting is conducive to acceptance with no distractions, and the attitude of the supervising adult is one of calm expectation. The stage is set for eating and it's up to the child. No one seems to care. If he doesn't eat then the meal is over and there's no more food until the next meal. But no emotion, no recrimination, no punishment here.

Some simple common sense suggestions have been found very helpful with preschool children. If the child has his own small table and eats there rather than at the family meal table it makes things easier. For one thing, his food will probably not be the same as the rest of the family and he will have no temptation to beg for adult food items. There will be less distraction. And he will not have the chance to put on a show to gain attention and start a fuss. He needs all his concentration for the still difficult job of eating with a spoon and other utensils. He is not yet ready for the combination of eating and conversation; that comes later. His low level of skill of manipulation makes the adults uncomfortable. He will spill food and make a mess of his place until he has learned how to manage better. It is better that this happen at his own little table rather than with the rest of the family, who could hardly keep from showing their disapproval. How long should this last? Until he is "ready" for the family meal table, that is, when his skill in eating is sufficient and his food is approximately the same. His introduction can be gradual—starting with special occasions—once a week, then once a day. It can be something of an incentive. "When you can eat well enough, we'd like to have you with us."

And now the child has been promoted to the family meal table. Let us look at the meal situation with school age children. Here are two pictures. First, we'll visit the Blacks—father and mother and three children. At the start of the meal it is a race between father and mother, and this time father wins and starts on his tale of woe—what is wrong with his boss, his job, the streetcar company that lets the cars get so jammed and doesn't have enough cars, the government and its shortcomings. When he pauses for breath mother gets her chance and she is away in a cloud of words about the stores and the neighbors and the women's committee at the church and then she gets to the children. Through all this they have been sitting in gloomy silence but now their apprehension replaces their gloom. Mother tells about Charlie's failure to do his chores, Mary's low mark in arithmetic, and little Fred's tracking mud into the house. With every incident father glowers at the culprit and administers his usual lecture, sprinkled with threats and penalties. It is not a very happy picture. When Charlie starts to tell about some of his activities his grammar is corrected and he is told to eat his carrots. Mary's story about her girl friend meets a similar fate as father breaks in with, "Is that that terrible Brown girl you are talking about? Haven't I told you before that you are not to have anything to do with her? Why, her father is a disgrace to the neighborhood." The meal finally ends and everyone is relieved; they are glad it is over.

Now we'll go across the street to the Whites who are at their dinner. As we enter we hear laughter; father has told one of his jokes. Then Charlie tells about the basketball game at school and the rest of the family are interested. Mother has her worries but she doesn't bring them to the table with her. Father asks Fred about his hobbies and friends. All members are enjoying each other's company. The attractive food is relished by all. Mary did remark about the carrots, "Why do we always have carrots?" But the rest of the family good-naturedly remind her that they haven't had carrots for a week, so Mary nibbles at her least-liked vegetable and surprises even herself by eating all her serving as the conversation ball is tossed back and forth. And so the Whites finish their meal. They have had a good time together—mealtime is fun.

Of course the Blacks and the Whites are fiction and the contrast is extreme, but there's no doubt at which meal table you would prefer to be. You see, atmosphere, that intangible, is important. It makes all the difference. The tragedy is that both Mrs. and Mrs. Black are charming people when they are not at their own dinner table. They have just got into the bad habit of using the mealtime at home to air their grievances and "discipline" their children. Unfortunately the Blacks haven't learned to enjoy their own children either, and they are really nice children too.

Manners are somewhat of a worry to some parents—especially at mealtime. Children should learn to be mannerly, they insist. So they keep at them, every meal. "Say please." "You forgot to say, Thank you." "Sit up in your chair." "Don't wiggle." "You reached in front of your mother," and so on, in an almost continuous stream of corrections and admonitions. Is this necessary? Do we have to keep at children all the time this way? Some people think so. But we have observed that children pick up this polish of outward manners just as quickly without the nagging, sometimes more quickly. And even more important, they catch the idea of consideration and courtesy of which manners are the outward expression, more easily without the persistent insistence on the outward forms.

Manners, like many other features of human activity, are caught more than taught. Children inevitably reflect the patterns common in their homes. But, this doesn't happen all at once. It is a slow gradual process. In later childhood and adolescence most children become interested in manners and etiquette and ask about various customs and folkways. This provides parents with the opportunity to extend the children's understanding of social customs and traditions and to provide them with a basis for the acceptance or rejection of customs. Many customs are a matter of taste and preference and not essential to effective social relations. Other customs are based on true consideration for the feelings and comfort of other people. Of course what we are interested in seeing happen in our children is not just blind and mechanical conformity but thoughtful adoption of ways of behaving which are based on social sensitivity.

To get back to family meals, we have been implying that mealtime is the core of family life. It is the time when the family is together as a group. It can be a time when they enjoy each other's company. They can find a common satisfaction in eating, but more, they can enhance the enjoyment of eating with the pleasure of companionship. Many children have interesting, charming people for parents but do not discover this because the parents are so concerned about their teaching, supervising, correcting functions that their charm is hidden from their own children. We could suggest that a very good rule to follow is: mealtime should never be used to settle problems of control. There are other more appropriate times for discussion of serious issues. Mealtime should be a time for happy discussion. This means that direct control should be at a minimum. This requires considerable self-control on the part of the parents, who are tempted to stress the child's behavior usually in a "Don't do this" way. Don't slouch, don't wiggle, don't fiddle, don't grab, don't bolt down food, and so on. Slouching, wiggling, fiddling are childish forms of behavior. That is, they belong to childhood and only maturity will eliminate them. Certainly nagging helps very little and it does make the meal an unpleasant event for all. I suppose one of the most difficult things for some parents to accept is that children cannot act like adults until they become adult.

There is only one form of direct disciplinary action which is appropriate and that is isolation; the child has to eat by himself. This is really demotion to the earlier phase of eating by himself because he isn't ready to eat at the family table. This rather drastic procedure should only be used when the child's behavior is such that the meal is spoiled for the rest of the family. When used it should be done without rancor and recrimination and not as a punishment. Rather it is a device to help the child learn that there is a minimum standard of appropriate behavior which he must live up to if he wants to be with the group. Of course, it will have little meaning or effect unless the mealtime is such that he wants to be there.

Meals, their preparation, serving, and clearing up afterward require a lot of hard work. All members of the family can share this work. In a later section we'll talk about chores, but just a word now about work in relation to meals. There is a real fascination in cooking and serving food, and more than one member of the family can be interested in it, and not just the girls in the family either. In some families each member develops his own culinary specialty. And in some families certain meals are the responsibility of individual members. It does not matter particularly how it is done as long as all have a chance to participate in more than the eating. Even father can be a specialist in scrambled eggs or waffles. And the twelve-year-old son can have his favorite hot dogs for Saturday supper, being responsible for buying the wieners and buns and also preparing them. If he is not interested in the tossed salad to go along with his beloved dogs, maybe he can enlist the cooperation of his sister to be the salad chef for that meal. It may be a useful stimulus to self-discipline for father to have to nibble at the preferred food of his young son just as the son has to put up with the preferences of his father at many meals.

The real point is that the spirit of family eating is communal: cooperative effort, group participation, and common enjoyment. There is an old Eastern custom that if you have eaten together you cannot be enemies. Perhaps this is true in the family too. At least it is true when the whole meal is shared and enjoyed. Mealtime is one of the best indications of family atmosphere, and this vague atmosphere or climate is the foundation of home discipline.

But what about the irritating happenings? What should be done about lateness for meals, dawdling, lack of skill, messy eating, food dislikes and refusals, lack of manners, and a host of other "problems"? These are the questions many parents ask. But these questions can only be satisfactorily answered in the context of the general picture of mealtime which we have tried to sketch in the preceding paragraphs. Some of these problems turn out to be behavior which corrects itself with time. Others are created by the general mealtime procedure and atmosphere. Some problems, such as being late for meals, can be handled in a logical manner, letting the inevitable consequences function. For instance, the member of the family who is late has to be content with what is left, which may be cold or just lukewarm. He will have missed the fun and interesting conversation and companionship. These are the consequences of lateness, whether the lateness was the result of mere thoughtlessness or some more legitimate reason. There will be few problems if mealtime is a happy, shared family gathering; those present will have a simple self-correcting solution in which the child suffers the consequences of his own failure to live up to the necessary sensible requirements of appropriate behavior. All is done in the spirit of friendly companionship.

References

"Eating," *Bulletin of the Institute of Child Study,* Toronto, 1953, No. 57.

Kirkpatrick, M.: *Feeding the Pre-school Child,* Copp Clark, Toronto, 1963.

Spock, B., and Lowenberg, M.: *Feeding Your Baby and Young Child,* Little, Brown, Boston, 1955.

Wishik, S. M.: *Feeding Your Child,* Doubleday, Garden City, N.Y., 1955.

chapter 6
Relaxation, Rest, Sleep, and Bedtime

Another important part of every day is sleep and rest. Life is a succession of activity and rest, sleep and waking, effort and relaxation. And life cannot go on without the relief from effort that is rest and sleep.

The Nature of Sleep

We do not know much about sleep, though there are many theories, such as that sleep is a retreat from reality. But we do know that sleep is a need; we cannot get along without it. And we know that adequate sleep both in amount and depth is basic to health, even though what is adequate for one person may not be for another. And we also know that sleep requirements change with age. The newborn infant sleeps most of the time while the "average" adult spends about one-third of his time asleep.

Relaxation

Rest and relaxation, while not the same as sleep, serve some of the same purposes. And relaxation is a prelude or necessary condition for sleep. The adult who is unable to "let down," to inhibit effort and relax periodically, is robbed of one of his greatest potential assets. The strains and tensions of the complex society in which he is living must have the relief and restoring that comes from rest and relaxation if he is to continue functioning in a healthy way. Without adequate rest and relaxation he is susceptible to irritation and emotional disturbances that would never happen if his defenses had been restored. Stress is the inevitable concomitant of effort and channeled activity. But stress need not have the damaging results demonstrated on research animals. It depends on how the person handles stress situations, and this in turn depends on the restoring, refreshing results of rest, relaxation, and sleep. What we are trying to say is that sleep, rest, and relaxation are extremely important for the health and efficiency of the individual.

What has all this to do with discipline and child training? Just this, that the basis for healthy habits of sleep, rest, and relaxation is laid down in childhood. Because life is so much a unity, a continuum, what happens in childhood does make a difference in all later stages. True, habit patterns are subject to change at any age but it is always easier to learn than to relearn or change what has been learned.

Learning to Sleep

The infant sleeps most of the time, goes to sleep easily, and wakes up easily. Any discomfort or intense stimulus will wake him up. But otherwise he sleeps; at least this is true in the first few weeks. Soon, however, his waking periods are longer as he develops a stronger need for activity. His growing muscles seem to call for activity. And also, the world is slowly becoming more meaningful to him. There are now things to stay awake to see and hear. The child's world continues to increase in meaning and interest so that by the time he is two years old he seems to have to learn to go to sleep even though a few short months ago he was doing it without any difficulty. But now to go to sleep he has the very difficult task of inhibiting activity. This is hard enough for an adult but infinitely more difficult for the young child. Sleep occurs naturally and easily when all response to stimuli ceases, when even thought is reduced. This is an important fact to keep in mind. Sleep is easy when you are bored. I suppose this is why some students go to sleep in lectures. It isn't difficult for the child to go to bed and sleep when there is nothing interesting to do and nothing interesting happening. Another facet of the same idea is that emotional disturbances hinder sleep. If possible, the child's emotional books should be balanced for the day before bedtime, so that there are no nagging fears of guilt hindering his relaxation.

The Details of Sleep and Bedtime

With the infant there is little we need say. The main things are to see that he is comfortable, that his day is ordered and fairly regular, and that he is undisturbed in his sleeping times. He gets a feeling of security from the comfort and pleasure of needs satisfied, and also from the regularity of the care provided. He soon comes to depend on being fed, washed, changed, played with, and put to bed. It's a good world for the infant when he is comfortable and can depend on regular care. That is, "loving" care does seem to make a difference. We do not know why exactly, but we can guess that loving care includes pleasurable fondling, more gentle handling in the bath or while being changed, and the comfort and warmth of being held.

As the child gets older the periods of activity lengthen and sleep gradually decreases in length. The decrease, at first, is in the amount of daytime sleep. During the first year the baby will have both a morning and an afternoon nap. Then early in the second year the morning sleep may drop out and the afternoon nap continue. This afternoon nap usually continues until about five years when it drops out for most children. Even though the child may not sleep every afternoon, a rest period is very valuable and should be continued until school attendance interferes. We are of the opinion that an afternoon rest period would be valuable at all ages.

The management of the afternoon sleep or rest period can be very simple. Regularity is one principle. When exceptions are made the child will look for reasons for other exceptions, so resistance, coaxing, and pleading take place. Naptime has been classified by the child as one of those activities that depends on whim and choice, and it takes on a kind of personal meaning. He is resting because mother wants him to. It has lost the meaning of one of those things that always happens and thus is to be accepted like darkness (or later, taxes).

What we are calling indirect control (or stage setting) is also important here: a time for sleep (immediately after lunch), a place for sleep, darkened and quiet, an unhurried unemotional adult attitude which says very surely, "This is rest time," and no competing distractions and usually there are no difficulties.

We cannot enforce that the child sleep, but we can enforce rest. If the child does not sleep we are satisfied that he remains quietly on his cot. The afternoon rest or sleep period should not be so extended as to interfere with night sleep. He should be up and out to play by three o'clock.

Bedtime

Bedtime is often "battle time" in some homes. This is another of those sensitive indicators of the effectiveness of discipline. Scenes at bedtime usually mean that things are not well planned or handled, or that the general atmosphere of the home is not as healthy as it should be, or that some feature of the child's experience is making him feel insecure. Perhaps the discipline is too personal, which really means inconsistent. The child has learned that bedtime depends on parental whims. When mother is "out of sorts" bedtime comes early—she wants to get rid of the children. When mother is in a happy mood, coaxing will get an extra half hour of play. Or perhaps the child's resistance to bedtime is a part of his battle for independence and an indication that he needs more chances to choose and do things for himself and less detailed direction. Perhaps his battle is a sign of some childish (he *is* still a child) fear of the dark or being abandoned. Or maybe the indirect control idea hasn't been used enough so that he is asked to leave a very exciting, interesting activity while it is still in progress. Sometimes the child's resistance to bed is due to overfatigue. He is so tired that he is cranky, irritable, and resistant even to that which he needs most.

Some simple procedures have been shown to help. First and

foremost is the acceptance of the regular bedtime idea and that this is not subject to discussion or change every night. Of course there can be discussion about bedtime, especially with the older child (over ten), but not *at* bedtime. Bedtime is bedtime; the clock decides. Another helpful procedure is a warning, "In ten minutes, or when the big hand gets to the top, it will be bedtime." This gives the child a chance to finish up what he is doing. And, of course, if we can arrange that the time just before bed is filled with a relatively quiet activity, it serves as a kind of prelude to sleep. A hilarious romp with father is hardly conducive to the let down in activity needed for sleep. Exciting, stimulating experiences hinder sleep. The just-before-bedtime stories on television programs have to be checked with care to assure that they are not too exciting and that they end in time.

Some Questions and Answers

How much sleep should the child have? Average amounts of sleep advocated for each age are not very satisfactory. It is so much an individual matter. The main thing is to be alert to signs of fatigue, irritability, and fussiness, because these and related conditions are often indications of insufficient sleep. During the growing period sufficient sleep is a must.

Parents ask many questions about sleep and bedtime which are difficult (and possibly undesirable) to answer in a straightforward, dogmatic way. For instance—Should the young child be rocked or sung to sleep? Should the child be allowed to take a doll or favorite play object to bed with him? Should he have a nightlight? Should the child be scolded or spanked if he refuses to stay in bed? What should we do when the child takes more than an hour to get to sleep? These and many more specific "problems" arise in parental discussions.

To give direct answers to questions of this kind would imply that there is a set of rules to follow, and if we follow all the rules all will be well. But it doesn't work out that way. This is true of all life situations, because no two situations or the people in them are ever exactly the same. The same activity can mean different things. For instance, a child wanting a Teddy bear in bed may mean that he feels insecure and needs the presence of this familiar, loved object to reassure him, or that he is afraid it will be lost or used by another child, or that he wants to tickle his nose with Teddy's hair, or that he can get an argument by asking and thus more attention and a delay in being left alone. Every parent can, and indeed must, answer these questions for himself. The answer will come when the parent considers what is involved, what the child wants and is learning, and what he wants him to learn. And these problems never occur in isolation. They are always part of a bigger situation which has to be taken into account.

Some Suggestions about Sleep

Even though we are unable to answer such questions directly and give a rule of thumb to follow, we can offer some suggestions which we hope will help parents solve their own problems. One has to do with discussion and argument. Some children dearly love an argument and persist in it as long as they have breath, or an antagonist. These arguments are frequently staged at bed-time. We hear children on the playground carrying on a "You will," "I won't" series almost indefinitely, and sometimes the same thing happens in the home at bedtime. "I won't go to bed"—"You must go to bed"—"I won't," and so on until voices rise and mother and child are shouting at each other followed by tears, hard feelings, and a battle which the parent has to win, but frequently loses. But this need never happen. It takes two to have an argument. When the seven-year-old invites an argument by saying "I won't," take him by the hand and lead him to the bedroom and do not worry that he says "I won't" at every step he takes. It is too bad to disappoint him by not entering the verbal combat but it is better that way. It isn't easy for parents to be good-natured, patient, and unemotional all the time, but it is worth the effort.

Emotional storms cannot always be avoided because parents are people too. But the more they can avoid being drawn into battle, the better. Children frequently do and say things to get a "rise" out of their parents. A sense of humor helps immensely. It helps to be able to "laugh some things off" and not allow them to become a serious issue, with parent and child squared off for battle. True, issues *have* to be resolved and sometimes children have got to get some of their resentments off their chests. And sometimes, too, they just have to "save face" and we can let them do so.

As the child gets older, bedtime is adjusted and the child has more to do with setting when bedtime is to be. It helps to talk the matter out (but not *at* bedtime) and come to an agreement about it. This should be reviewed periodically (maybe once a year). When we get to adolescence, it will be pretty much a matter of understanding, sympathetic advice rather than laying down the law.

Now a word about relaxation. As we said before, relaxation is a valuable asset. To be able to take a few moments in one's busy day, "clear the board" of all worries and serious effort, and just "let down" and relax pays big dividends. This takes practice to do. The yoga system shows how possible it is. But we don't have to be yogis to benefit from relaxation. And children can be helped to develop the ability.

It is an interesting sight, to see the little children in a well-run nursery school relax under the stimulus of soft music, a partly darkened room, and quiet voices. It is used there both to help the children learn to relax and rest, and to bridge the gap between play and mealtime. But any child (or adult) can learn to let down from activity to rest and relaxation, and our children can be helped to do so. It is mainly a matter of setting the stage and providing conditions conducive to it.

References

Chant, N.: "Sleeping Habits," *Parent Education Bulletin,* University of Toronto, Toronto, 1942, No. 18.

Renshaw, S., Miller, V. L., and Marquis, D. P.: *Children's Sleep,* Macmillan, New York, 1933.

Reynolds, M. M., and Mallag, H.: "Sleep of Young Children," *Journal of Genetic Psychology,* 1933, **43,** 322–351.

chapter 7
Cleanliness,
Toilet Habits,
Dressing, and Clothes

Our culture puts a high premium on cleanliness and appearance. Some of our strongest taboos are concerned with elimination habits. Public nakedness is more than immodest, it is immoral. Elimination is a private activity and mention of it is bad taste. The child has a lot to learn—not just the voluntary control of bladder and bowel but all the complex social customs related to it. And the matter of clothes is also very complicated, for clothes serve a number of functions: protection from the weather, hiding the body, enhancing the body, social competition, membership in special groups, and prestige. Clothes are affected by taste, fashion, fads, desire for variety, ego enhancement, utility, beauty, and many more factors.

Infancy

In early infancy, parents make all the decisions and take all the responsibility for cleanliness, dressing, and selection of what is worn. Even here, social custom, fashion, and competition play their parts. The cleanliness of the infant and what he wears is accepted as an indication of parental care and family position. The infant's comfort and serenity sometimes take secondary place especially when he is on display. Swaddling, restricting clothes are still traditional even though there are signs of more sensible infants' wear becoming more common.

At first, the infant has no voluntary control of his eliminative functions. Time and place have no meaning for the infant and the body excretes its waste materials with no relation to social taboos. Sometime he will have to acquire voluntary control and learn to fit in with the accepted customs of the group. But this learning cannot be hurried; nerves and muscles must develop, experience must pile up so that he can recognize pressures and their meanings and voluntarily control muscles.

Of course it is a nuisance, but thousands of diapers will have to be changed before he can manage for himself. Most mothers and even fathers accept this as part of their job. When irritation is shown and the infant blamed for his infant behavior, unpleasant feelings color the situation and store up trouble for later. And if the parent tries to hurry the learning before the infant is capable of it, tensions and strains can develop which influence the whole developmental picture.

Infancy is a time for comfort, as feelings are so much of the child's experience. He is busy building up meaning and this meaning is mostly feeling. Directions of development are set in infancy which tend to go on the way they start. Avoiding, disliking, withdrawing, shrinking, and feeling insecure can result from small but unpleasant experiences and continue for years. So toilet habits, cleanliness, clothes and such matters should not be unpleasant or a matter of strain.

It may sound peculiar to hear that the routine toilet, washing, and dressing activities should be enjoyed. But why not? After all, these are daily activities that take up some of every day and so why not find satisfaction and enjoyment in them? Certainly enjoyment is better than the reverse—dislike and shrinking. So we keep this in mind with the young infant—and we see that his bath, the changing of clothes, and all the other attentions for cleanliness are as pleasant as possible.

Building Habits of Elimination

Training in habits of elimination is really just arranging things so that learning will take place. One of the most important features is the attitude of the adult. It is a lot easier to write down that this attitude should be relaxed, unemotional, and unhurried than it is for the busy parent to attain such an attitude. But experience shows that when anxiety, hurry, and impatience are in the picture, the child's learning is not very adequate. Actually the child will "train" himself if he's given half a chance. But he will not do so before he is able to recognize and remember sensations of pressure and to maintain muscle tension. We have to wait until he is ready. This occurs at different ages for different children so it is not possible to say that when the child is so many months old he is ready to learn. But when the stools have formed, we can try him out, placing him on a comfortable toilet seat or chamber after a meal, and doing so regularly. The parent should not make too much fuss about it or be too disappointed if there is no success for a while. And it should not be made an ordeal. The child should be left alone to experience the sensations and not distracted by coaxing or urging. And he should not be left there too long either. Scolding or punishment for failure is definitely undesirable.

Later he will learn the more difficult control of the bladder. Setting up a planned routine of times to take him to the toilet is the main part of the arranging for his learning. He can be helped to associate a word with the activity so that, as his command of language increases, he can ask to go to the toilet. It is simpler if some word is used regularly rather than some slang word or euphemism. When the child has acquired daytime control, then he can be helped to learn night control. This may require taking him up and putting him on the toilet once in the late evening, for a time.

The preschool child has usually made considerable progress in toilet habits. He has learned to have his bowel movements in the toilet, usually after breakfast. He has learned to control the bladder between the planned routine times and is no longer in diapers. Periods between toilet routines are lengthened and he is beginning to anticipate his needs and ask to go to the toilet. He may even manage a dry bed with the help of the evening trip to the toilet and early morning attention. But he will have accidents, and he will have days when things go wrong and he will seem to have forgotten all he has learned. There are times when parents have to work hard not to show annoyance or scold, blame or punish.

"Training" the child takes time, patience, planning, and regularity. It cannot be hurried and it is not helped by fuss and emotion. Some adults have strong attitudes of shame and disgust associated with toilet habits. Of course, it is not a subject for drawing room conversation but it *is* a part of normal healthy living; certainly the child can have healthy feelings of satisfaction and desirable feelings of achievement when he is mastering or has mastered the habit. The child can have some understanding of the process, its relationship to eating, digestion, and the use of food for energy.

There are social conventions which the child needs to learn to accept. These conventions have to do with the time and place of elimination and discussion. The child can learn these without developing a feeling of shame, disgust, or impropriety about the act itself.

Washing

The preschool child can learn to wash his hands after he has gone to the toilet and make it a usual routine. There are other times when washing seems sensible, such as before meals. Preschool children can learn to wash themselves if things are arranged so that it is possible. Bathroom fittings are made for adults—size, height, and tap handles—but can be adapted for the use of young children with a sturdy step or block and sometimes a change in the hardware. With his own washcloth, towel, toothbrush, and comb all within reach, a little unobtrusive supervision and limited help, he is soon able to do it all for himself and proud of it too. Of course, it will take him longer than if you did it for him and he will not do as good a job, but he is learning and he is growing up in the process. Preschool children are characteristically interested in everything, and washing and cleanliness are not exceptions. They can get a feeling of independence and advancement from doing things for themselves. The standards of performance must not be too high, for their skill is still not too great.

Dressing

Dressing and undressing are daily activities that take quite a bit of time. The preschool child can begin early to learn to do much of this for himself. The kind of clothing provided has a great deal to do with how soon he can manage for himself. He will need help with the more complicated items of clothing for some time, but he can do a great deal for himself if the adult can be patient enough to allow him to do so. Low hooks and cupboards where he can put away and get out his clothing also help. By the end of the preschool period the child can manage practically everything in the dressing and undressing situation. Up to this time the decisions about what is worn will be made by the parents. But starting in the early school age period the child will begin to do some of the choosing.

The School Age Period

The school age period will be a time when difficulties about cleanliness and clothes will occur. The child who a few years before was interested in washing and proud of his achievements in personal care may become something of a backslider. He may become careless and neglectful, wash only when the adult checks up on him, and rather than being proud of neatness and cleanliness may seem to be proud of the reverse. This may be one of those "phases" of development that pass with time. But it may be a period which causes a lot of irritation and annoyance to mother and a temptation to nag, scold, and snipe at the child. One or two things help— one is being content with a minimum level of cleanliness; and another is some simple, impersonal way of enforcing this minimum without a constant verbal barrage. This means some regular routine before meals and in the morning that can be enforced without fuss.

The school age child should have some part in the selection of the clothes he wears. Where possible he can help pick them out when they are purchased and can have some choice as to what he wears.

Some parents have been amazed at the battle a school age child can wage when they have bought him an item of clothing which he refuses to wear. It may be warm, comfortable, and good looking, but if it is too different from what other children are wearing his resistance may be extreme. He does not dare be too different for he fears the ridicule of the other children. The older school age child is a faddist—he must, if at all possible, be in the swim.

What about cosmetics? It is natural for the girl to want to be "grown-up" and to follow the pattern of her older sister or mother. Of course, what she sometimes fails to realize is that she is far more attractive without artificial make-up—that her natural school girl complexion is far ahead of what comes in jars and boxes. Also, when she makes a start on make-up, she is liable to overdo it. So she needs sympathetic help. Forbidding, sarcasm, and the like are of no avail. Positive help and instruction may be quite acceptable.

Grooming in all its aspects becomes important to the preadolescent girl and later to the boy. Good taste does not just happen; it is acquired. What should be remembered is that there is no absolute standard—taste can and should differ and mother and daughter need not prefer exactly the same color combinations, hairdo, or length of skirt. Practice in choosing is essential to learning, so the school age girl is given an opportunity to help select her clothes and to be involved in the planning, which may entail discussion in which mother does not try to "win her points" but rather tries to talk over the various considerations: financial, appearance, suitability and so on.

With each stage of development there is increased maturity of independence, choice, decision and responsibility in cleanliness and dress. In the adolescent period, most of the responsibility has been shifted to the child and the parents' role is now one of advice, discussion, and support.

The adult who is the product of this guidance is one who has acquired healthy habits of cleanliness, healthy attitudes toward conventions, and taste and modesty. Clothes are not too important to him; they serve their purpose as clothing and are not used for prestige or display.

chapter 8
Self-chosen Activities—
Play, Leisure Time,
and Family Fun

Freedom is a current slogan. We fight for it. We talk about it. We believe that "man must be free." Freedom with no restrictions or compulsions is an impossibility in any society. We cannot do as we like. But freedom within sensible limits or boundaries is an important aspect of living. One place where such freedom is essential is in the self-motivated activities of play and leisure-time activities.

It used to be thought that play was a kind of necessary evil of childhood and that as the child grew older he left it behind with other childish activities. But that idea has long since disappeared as the work week has steadily decreased and as we have learned the great importance of leisure time and how it is used for the total adjustment and health of the individual. Our ancestors found it necessary to work from dawn to dusk and even at that, "Mother's work was never done." But today forty-hour work weeks for wage earners and even housewives are common. We have time for self-chosen activities, and for freedom in activities in our leisure time. And we have the responsibility of seeing that our children learn how to play, to entertain themselves, to find a variety of interesting, satisfying activities that will persist throughout life and help to keep them happy and healthy.

Play in Infancy

The infant shows a pattern of rest and activity, with rest predominating at first but more and more wakeful periods of activity as he gets older. His activity first shows very little meaning or interest—it is just activity, but it does seem to satisfy his need for change. There is satisfaction in just being active. Developing muscles seem to require exercise and this activity is pleasant. And what is more important, he is learning through activity. He is acquiring control and coordination—he is learning how to master his muscles and make them work for him. So the infant should have a time each day when he is unrestricted by clothing and when he can kick, wiggle, and try out his musculature. And he can have things to handle, manipulate, and explore.

As the days go by, his periods of wakefulness increase, and his activity becomes more controlled and directed. He is still exploring his immediate world, feeling, tasting, following moving objects with his eyes, and storing up experiences that slowly and gradually achieve meaning. He doesn't need many play materials but he does need some. What he has should contribute to his sensory explorations—cutaneous, visual, and auditory. His muscular activity continues and takes on patterns—patterns related to posture, sitting up, holding his head up; to locomotion, creeping, rolling, later walking; and to prehension and handling, manipulating, grasping, holding, dropping, banging. A safe spot on the floor where he can wiggle, roll, and later creep, a time for this each day, and the simple play materials he requires can be provided so that he gets the opportunities for self-chosen activities that are suitable to his level of development.

Preschool Play

The preschool period is a period of dramatic happenings in development. The child has learned to walk and is learning to talk. He sleeps less in the daytime. He is beginning to learn how to manage some things for himself and he has an enormous appetite for activity. He spends about six hours a day in play—in "free" activities, things that he does for fun and enjoyment, and not because of any outside compulsion. But this does not mean that this activity has no value. Quite the contrary, for through play the child learns a great deal—motor coordination, skills, ability to entertain himself, social attitudes and skills, and the foundations for his cultural development. Through play, also, he finds relief from the tensions of his required activities, and the satisfaction of freedom in doing what he wants to do.

The adult's function is to provide time for play, places for play, materials for play activity, companions some of the time, ideas, and unobtrusive supervision.

Time for play means blocks of time in which the child is relatively uninterrupted, time that he can feel is his own; time for outdoor play, for indoor play, for social play, and solitary play. It is very helpful to the child to have a fairly ordered, regular daily plan and for him to learn that there is a time for eating, for sleeping, for toilet routines, for active play, for quiet activities, for companionship, and for self-entertainment. When things are sorted out in this way, there is less likelihood of difficulties; play does not interfere so much with the serious business of the routines.

A play place both indoors and outdoors is another essential. One very common parental complaint is that their preschool child is always underfoot, that his play materials are scattered all over the house, and that furniture and walls are all marked up. All of this is unnecessary. When the child has a place to play that is suitable for his various activities and when he has a place to keep his materials, such as low shelves and baskets or boxes, it is relatively simple to keep both the child and the materials within sensible bounds. It is not necessary to make the child feel that he is restricted or cooped up in his play place. Rather he should get the feeling that here is his very own place with his own materials and the freedom to carry on his own activities in his own way.

Outdoor play is obviously important. But outdoor play for preschool children is only possible if there is a place which is relatively safe and in which there are materials suitable for interesting activities. To dump the child outdoors and say "play" is not enough. He should have an enclosed space, with freedom within these boundaries. And he should have things to do: locomotor toys, climbing, swinging, sliding apparatus, and construction materials. Some of the best materials are the least expensive—a sand pile, water, packing boxes and homemade building blocks, old pots and pans, and dishes are just a few of the things that can easily be supplied.

Playing outdoors need not be reserved for days of perfect weather. Suitable clothing can be provided for cold and drizzly days and even muddy times.

It is possible in most districts for families to cooperate in arranging for outdoor play, working together to provide the play facilities and taking turns supervising the little play group.

Volumes have been written about play materials, and many pamphlets are available with suggestions. Some of these are listed in the references at the end of this chapter. One of the main things is variety. The attention span of young children is short and they need different materials to keep them busy and interested. Many materials which are available in the ordinary household will provide many happy hours of activity. Wrapping paper, cardboard boxes, tin cans from which the top has been removed by the wall-bracket can opener, spools, and dozens of other discarded objects make interesting materials. Plenty of building blocks and nests of cans or boxes, pegboards, crayons, poster paints, plasticine, and all kinds of housekeeping materials are perennial favorites. Toys made to interest adults are frequently of little value for young children. A visit to a nursery school, examination of suggested play materials listed in pamphlets, and conversation with other parents are all sources of ideas. Special materials to be brought out when things get difficult can be very useful. Rainy-day materials, special visitors' toy boxes, and special reserve materials can provide a little extra interest when needed.

Some of the play activity from about age two should be social. That is, about this time the child is ready for companionship in some of his playtime. Social play has its own special values. It can stimulate cooperation, taking turns, consideration for others, ability to lead or direct, and ability to be led to take a subordinate position. It isn't always easy to provide for companionship in the preschool period, but it is important. The nursery school fills this very important function. When nursery school is not possible, other means must be found to provide opportunities for social play.

Preschool children need ideas for play. In a nursery school the ideas come naturally from seeing other children, what they do, and how they use the materials provided. But when the child is pretty much on his own, in the home, it is necessary for the parent to show the child some of the things that can be done with the materials: how to use scissors, paste, plasticine, crayons, paints, blocks, and so on. The little preschool boy who threw his new building blocks around the room had never seen blocks used to build towers and houses; he had to be shown what blocks are for. But when he got the idea, he had many happy hours of building and never threw them around again. The child who used his new crayons to mark up the walls and furniture had never been shown how he could make pictures on paper and color drawings. Yes, young children need ideas and models to imitate.

Finally, preschool children need supervision. This is especially true of social play where rules have to be made and enforced. It is necessary to avoid too much danger, enforce the boundaries, and redirect when materials are being misused and when boredom appears. But supervision should be very much in the background so that the child can feel that he is free to carry out his ideas.

Play in the School Age Period

In the early years of the school age period playtime diminishes as school takes up a large part of the day. The seriousness of school-work makes the freedom of playtime even more important. True, school should not be a strain or too serious, but there is an important difference between the assigned tasks of school and the freely chosen activities of play. Watch children getting out of school at 3:30. Often you see a kind of activity explosion, a release of inhibited boisterousness. Even though the modern classroom is not overly restrictive, there is this release which clearly says "I'm now on my own and I can do what I like for a while." This is a valuable feeling and should not be dimmed by the scheduling of too many required activities. I remember one little girl whose overambitious mother had arranged something for nearly every waking moment, music lessons, ballet, practice periods, home chores, and other planned activities that left practically no free time. All the activities were good but what was not so good was the lack of time for doing what she wanted to herself. She became a rather unhappy, whiny little girl who wasn't having much fun. So in the school age period there must be free time also.

Variety and balance are key words, but variety and balance viewed over a period of time, not necessarily in one day or week. Variety in activity is important because the foundation is being laid for the whole cultural life of the individual. Specialization in interests will occur but it is best that it does not happen too soon. Balance means both active and relatively inactive interests, both spectator and participator pursuits, both solitary and social activities, and both appreciation (listening and watching) and creative behavior.

What is the function of the parent? Mainly, provision rather than direction. Indirect stimulation rather than direct suggestion. A very simple way to keep a child from developing an interest is to nag at him—"Why don't you do this?" or "Why do you spend all your time with that trash?"

Interest begets interest. The child who lives in a family where everyone has interesting things to do and obviously enjoys them is stimulated to do similar things himself. But the child's talents will not be the same as the adult's. Some of them will be childish interests (after all he *is* a child). Some of them will seem senseless to the adult and others will be a nuisance and hard to live with. But they are all part of a pattern that has meaning for the child. One mother had to learn to accept frogs and snakes when her young son developed an intense interest in such animals. Of course, she had to draw the line and keep the reptiles out of the living room and kitchen.

Children's interests frequently move in fits and starts and parents have to be prepared for the sudden enthusiasms and the just as fast dropping of the activity. It is disconcerting, of course, when expensive materials or equipment have been purchased to find them forgotten and gathering dust after a few weeks. But even this can be taken care of with a little thought and planning. Interests are given a tryout before too great an investment is made and expensive equipment is only purchased after discussion with the child and some understanding on his part as to what is involved. It is also well to remember that activities which are dropped are frequently returned to if we do not make too much fuss about it. It is a mistake to get rid of the equipment because of temporary loss of interest. It may not be so much loss of interest as a supplanting of interest by something else, and the child may return to the earlier interest.

Reading usually becomes a prominent interest somewhere in the school age period. It cannot be hurried but it can be stimulated by seeing that appropriate books are available. The child may go through a period of concentration on comic books or literature which you may think of as trash. Be careful that you do not make good literature distasteful to the child by your contrasts and comments. "Why do you read that trash, why don't you read good literature?" Some children have been kept from an interest in good books for years by such comments. Good literature should not be made forbidding by being classified with medicine and spinach as something "good for you."

Parents can be so inconsistent. The same parent who wished her child would learn to read for himself is found later deploring the fact that "he always has his nose in a book." And the parent who deplores comics for children may read pulp magazines herself.

Taste and preference in literature can only develop from experiencing a wide variety of material. A preselected diet is not the answer, nor is a rigid censorship, nor is the imposing of our tastes and preferences on the child. He needs to explore a wide domain of printed matter to develop his own preferences and standards of taste. But he will not do this in any one year. He is more likely to concentrate on an author or a kind of literature until he has exhausted it for the time being. So the boy may go through scores of space-ship books or airplane stories and the girl may complete the whole series of the modern version of the Elsie stories. The main thing is to keep the way open—have other reading materials handy, make occasional gifts, talk about what you find interesting, and get him to talk about what he is reading.

Music is another area in which people can find enjoyment. It is rather easy to spoil music for children. If lessons are imposed on the child and the teacher is an unfortunate choice, music can become a burden and a task to be done rather than a leisure-time activity. We believe that music should be play, a self-chosen activity. So if the child is provided with an environment where music is appreciated he may develop an interest and want to learn, and then lessons become something he wants rather than a required activity. Discussion can deal with the details, such as amount of practice and when. Music should be the child's own choice and responsibility and not the same as arithmetic, which is a required task. One of the reasons why parents put on the pressure and make music lessons a required part of the child's life is their false idea that if he doesn't learn now he never will. This is not necessarily true. He can learn any time, even after he has become adult.

Handicrafts is still another area of leisure-time activities which has many values. Everyone can learn to make something and there can be a great deal of satisfaction from creativity. The variety is infinite. There are many kinds of materials which can be used to create beautiful or useful objects. Every child should have a chance to use at least the ordinary tools and materials. Some children become quite expert in even very complicated areas such as radio or television. To take an old alarm clock apart and see how it works, to dismantle an outboard motor or a motorcycle is not beyond the interest or ability of some school age children. And it isn't too much to expect that every boy and girl should learn how to change a fuse or wire a lamp. There is an enormous area of interest in the mechanical, the construction, and the handicraft field. Even sewing, knitting, and crocheting can be included.

Collecting has almost limitless possibilities and most school age children become interested in collecting something. It may be stamps, coins, pictures of movie stars, nature specimens, or just bottle tops, but all have a fascination. It does not matter that the collection is stored away and forgotten; it is the fun of the activity itself more than the product that is important.

Games and sports have a big place in children's leisure activities. At first it is the game itself; later the team or group becomes important to the child; and belonging to the team may be even more important than the game itself.

What the school age child does—his hours, companions, boundaries and related features—are of concern to his parents. However, this does not mean that the parents have to direct, legislate, and lay down the law as to what is done and when and with whom, but it does mean that they are interested and have a hand in planning and decisions. This often means setting limits, safeguarding health, and requiring a reasonable degree of punctuality for meals. The main point is to see that the opportunities for enjoyable, satisfying activities are provided and that the restrictions and requirements are reasonable.

Leisure Activities in Adolescence

The use of leisure time changes with age. The young adolescent shows a different pattern with social activities, organized clubs, and team sports predominating. Many of the school age activities drop out altogether—dolls are put away, model airplanes gather dust, collections are forgotten, music lessons are dropped; sitting for hours listening to the hit parade, just doing nothing, interminable telephone conversations, and just being together in groups take over. It is as though the adolescent had discarded anything and everything that belonged to his childhood but has not yet developed more mature activities to take their place. Leisure-time activities seem to have lost their zest and meaning. Ask an adolescent what he does in his spare time and he'll either deny that he has any spare time or tell you he just "fools around." It is a puzzling time for parents. The whole pattern of worthwhile leisure-time activities seems to have disintegrated. Adolescent scorn is poured on all the things which a few short months ago engrossed his interest.

But adolescent pictures vary greatly. Some young people throw themselves into an activity, sport, or club and everything else is shut out. Others seem to have no absorbing interest and look as though they were marking time. Still others become so emotionally involved in dating that nothing else seems to matter.

There is little the parent can do during this period except be as understanding and sympathetic as possible and be ready to provide advice and help when called upon. The main thing is to keep the lines of communication open so that the adolescent can feel he has a place to talk things over. Moral support, faith, trust, and confidence are what he needs most from his parents.

This puzzling period of early adolescence may not last very long. It is followed by a semiadult picture of interests and self-chosen activities. The concerns of the young man or woman are still with the big problems of vocational choice, heterosexual adjustment, emancipation from parents, and the development of a philosophy of life, and his leisure time is usually related to these major adjustments. He is trying to "find himself" and some of his leisure time will be spent in trying himself out. Organized social groups will play a large part, membership will be important, and leisure time will almost certainly include to a large extent his current date.

Emerging finally from this long and varied journey from infancy will be an adult, interesting because he is interested, enjoying life because he has a number of things he finds thrilling. He is entertaining because he doesn't have to be entertained. He has skills and knowledge which enable him to contribute to groups. He is never bored with life because life is enjoyable and because he has too many inner resources to call on.

Family Fun

Try this little experiment. Think back to your own childhood and jot down those experiences you remember with the greatest feeling of pleasure. Then look at the list carefully and ask yourself why the particular memories are so pleasant. You will probably find, like most people, that what you have remembered are those times when the family was playing together, having fun as a group. There will be holidays, parties, picnics, festivals and perhaps such times as special Sunday breakfasts, family games, songfests, and such. Or perhaps you look back to special family occasions such as moving into a new house or a new family car, or some special project that meant the whole family worked together for something. The glow of pleasure which has persisted down through the years shows how much such experiences meant to you and how valuable they were in providing a happy relationship between family members and in building a feeling of a happy family group.

It is with this in mind that we include this section on family fun. Many people today have suggested that the family is a declining institution and wish for the "good old days" when the family used to gather around the piano on Sunday evenings to sing hymns.

We cannot bring back any good old days even if we wanted to but the same principle of working, playing and having fun together can find expression in this automobile, television age, even though the details may differ.

Each member of the modern family has his own interests, friends, and activities, and these will differ from the rest of the family. This is as it should be. But this does not mean that family activities have to be completely shut out. It does mean, however, that there has to be planning and also the seizing of opportunities when they arise. It means using those times when the family is all together as times for mutual enjoyment.

One of the first essentials is to develop a feeling of family—"we are all friends together." The atmosphere of a home depends largely on the parents, on how they think of their job as parents, whether they enjoy their roles as well as enjoying the children themselves. When being a parent is mainly a duty and a burden it is almost impossible to have a happy home. What some people do not seem to realize is that it is possible to take the job seriously and work at it conscientiously and still enjoy it. Also, enjoyment doesn't mean being lenient or neglecting discipline. Reasonable discipline does not require a cold, stern attitude or the creation of fear. It is possible for parents to be warm, understanding, sympathetic, friendly, and still enforce necessary standards of behavior. Nor does the discipline have to be based on a personal relationship, the "do it for me" or "I can't love you if you don't" idea.

If you ask parents who have achieved a happy friendly home atmosphere how they did it, they will probably be surprised at the question. "Why, I don't know, we didn't do anything in particular, we just happen to like each other and enjoy living together. We just have fun, that's all." Perhaps this is the main secret of a happy home: the attitude of expecting to enjoy it, taking it for granted that home is for living and living should be satisfying.

There was a time when homes were adult-centered; that is, when things were done and planned for the parents and especially the "head" of the household. Then we went through a period when homes were supposed to be child-centered. The old idea of "being seen and not heard," was discarded in favor of the reverse—everything had to be done for the convenience, comfort, and well-being of the children and adults did not count. And some homes became child-dominated homes where the parents' interests, comfort, and convenience had to take second place to the child's demands. I'm not sure which is worse—a parent or a child tyranny, but I am sure that any tyranny is bad. The current idea, which is being worked out fairly satisfactorily in many homes today, is what can be called a group-centered home. In this the idea is the good of all rather than that of any one individual. Of course the child's comfort and convenience are important but so is that of the parents. The result is a kind of compromise in which the whole family is considered and the individual members all give up some of their personal freedom for the good of all. Cooperation or mutual working together is the pattern.

Discipline takes on a new meaning in such a setting. It is not then the imposing of one person's desires on another, nor the coercion of activity to a preconceived pattern. It is rather the development of sensible rules or ways of doing things so that a group of people can live together in harmony. This theme will be developed in more detail in a later section. Here we are dealing with the less formal side of the picture, family fun.

There is no one pattern of family enjoyment. Every family discovers and works out its own unique pattern, but some suggestions can be offered that may help.

Family fun is based on situations in which all have a stake, all take part, and all contribute. The mere fact that all members of the family are there isn't enough. Sometimes all this means is an opportunity for bickering, hard feelings, and resentments. The twelve-year-old complaining about family outings, "Oh, it's no fun, we always go to the same old place and do the same old things and even have the same salmon sandwiches," provides one clue: variety. The ten-year-old who whines, "We always have to do things *your* way," reveals another principle: cooperative planning. And a little thought and observation show other features that are important. Two little girls crying and screaming and making a whole coach full of people uncomfortable on a long train journey illustrate another point: there must be things to do which are suitable and interesting to the age level of the persons involved.

Let's look at some of these a bit more—the "same old place," the "same old things to do." Some adults like ruts and some children enjoy the familiar, too. But it is still true that variety is the spice of life and family outings are enhanced by new scenes and different activities. Every occasion can be an adventure. Just because the family had fun together going somewhere doesn't mean that the same fun can be recaptured by a repeat performance.

It helps to take turns deciding what should be done. Take birthday parties as an example. These can become as routine and as dull as sandwich lunches. But when it is Mary's birthday shouldn't she decide what form it should take? Maybe she will chose the same old program but at least she did the deciding for her own party. Or the family vacation, if the family takes its vacation together. This could be a matter for family discussion with the wishes of all taken into account. If the family did what father wanted last year, perhaps it's mother's turn this year to decide. And next year the family might do what some of the children would like to do.

There can be a fairly regular family fun time. Maybe it's Sunday morning breakfast with the members of the family taking turns with surprises of new dishes and even new locations for eating them—one morning in the parents' bedroom, another around the living-room fireplace, another at the kitchen table. Or maybe it's Sunday evening supper, or Saturday noon, or some other time that's suitable for all. Or perhaps Saturday evening can be a family evening with each taking his turn deciding what the group will do together—an evening of games, music, the movies, exploring, or anything as long as all have fun together.

There are very special occasions such as Christmas when the family let down their hair and have fun together. The main thing is the fellowship and companionship, not how it is achieved.

The home is more than a boardinghouse providing meals and shelter, a base for work and play outside. The home is the secure emotional haven, the foundation of living, the center of its members' world. It is a place where sympathy, understanding, and affection form the source of strength for living. It is a place where you can be comfortable. It is a place for fun. I have heard parents deplore the fact that their children seem to want to be anywhere else but at home. "Why does my fifteen-year-old son want to hang around the corner or the poolroom every evening? Why doesn't he stay at home once in a while?" asks one mother. The answer is so obvious she missed it. There was nothing in the home worth staying for. None of the things he was interested in could be done in that home. None of his companions was welcome. There was no fun in the home. His parents could be pleasant companions to their own friends, but they changed into nagging, sniping, complaining persons when they talked to their own son.

A good home is a place where all members feel at home. It is a place where work and play, satisfactions and problems, pleasures and worries are shared. It is a place where each individual's wishes and ambitions are considered. It is a place for serious discussion, a place for mutual decisions, a place for living—a place for fun.

References

Arnold, A.: *How to Play with Your Child,* Ballantine, New York, 1955.

Bernhardt, K. S.: "Leisure Time Activities for the School Age Child," *Bulletin of the Institute of Child Study,* Toronto, 1957, No. 49.

"Music," *Bulletin of the Institute of Child Study,* Toronto, 1956, No. 68.

Fletcher, M., and Denison, M.: *The New Highroad of Song for Nursery Schools and Kindergartens,* W. J. Gage, Scarborough, Ont., 1961.

Frank, J.: *Your Child's Reading Today,* Doubleday, Garden City, N.Y., 1954.

Grossman, J. S. and LeShan, E. J.: *How Children Play,* Science Research Associates, Chicago, 1954.

Hartley, R. E., Frank, L. K., and Goldenson, R. M.: *Understanding Children's Play,* Columbia, New York, 1952.

—— and Goldenson, R. M.: *The Complete Book of Children's Play,* Crowell, New York, 1957.

Johnson, J.: *Home Play for the Preschool Child,* Harper, New York, 1957.

Kepler, H.: *The Child and His Play,* Funk and Wagnalls, New York, 1952.

McKenzie, D., and Raymond, J. M.: *Parties for Preschoolers,* University of Toronto Press, Toronto, 1958.

Millichamp, D. A.: "Another Look at Play," *Bulletin of the Institute of Child Study,* Toronto, 1953, No. 59.

chapter 9

Companionship,

Friends,

and Siblings

The most important as well as the most interesting part of the child's world is people. Growing up in this world of people requires that he learn to shape his behavior in such a way that he can enjoy and profit from his association with other people. When the child is born he is nonsocial. That is, he has no social skills and no knowledge of other people. He has it all to learn. Not only does he have to become socialized in the sense of learning how to live with people, but everything he does later will have a social significance. In the kind of world in which he lives he can be mentally healthy and adequate only if he is socially effective.

Infancy

The little infant, in between periods of sleep, satisfies his needs for food, liquid, and elimination and in doing so has to have the help of someone else. So because every time he is fed and made comfortable there is another person present, he learns to associate satisfaction with the person or persons. He has begun his gradually widening discovery that other people are important to him. He learns very early also that what he does has an effect on other people; he discovers that when he cries he gets attention; and he thus learns to cry for attention. He has started his social development.

If the infant's needs are satisfied adequately and his life is generally serene and comfortable, he has the foundation for trust in other people. That is one reason why a regular and adequate routine is important during infancy. But regularity is not enough, for it has been shown that infants thrive better when they get not just care, but loving care. Some time in the first few months the infant begins to recognize persons and to distinguish between the familiar and the unfamiliar, and to prefer the former. He is now making social responses, that is, his behavior is affected by other people. His social relations during about the first two years are mainly with adults and especially his own parents. He is usually not ready for other social contacts before his second birthday. He is not ready, partly because of his limited skills and his very slight knowledge. If two infants are placed together in a playpen, they will be observed to treat each other as though they were other objects. But at about age two, the child is ready for the beginning of social play with other children.

Preschool Period

Preschool children need the companionship of other children for a number of reasons. They need a pattern to imitate, practice in the give and take of play, opportunities to start taking part in cooperative activities, and the experience of being a member of a group. A nursery school, junior kindergarten, or neighborhood play group provides the setting for this important beginning in companionship with contemporaries. Naturally the child's first social contacts are inept. He may treat other children as though they were inanimate objects. His approach, at first, may be to shove, hit, or bite. Or he may not approach the other children at all, being content to be near them, watching what they do, then later doing the same things but at a distance. Gradually he becomes drawn into the group, and the long process of learning how to get along with other people has started.

Getting along smoothly and peacefully with other children is an art that is learned slowly. It does not just happen; it has to be cultivated. Children need a lot of help in this learning, because it is so complicated. Their natural way of settling disputes and difficulties will be to strike out at each other. It is only when we help them see that taking turns, sharing, and compromise are better methods that they make progress from savagery to civilized living. And there will be many times when they will revert to fighting and struggling. Some parents seem to welcome fighting, especially if their child wins, because they say it shows courage and "sticking up for his rights." But if we believe there are better ways of settling differences of opinion, then we will help our children find and use these better methods too.

Friendships and preferences develop in this early period but they may change quickly. The child is not yet ready for more permanent friendships. That is still in the future.

The School Age Period

In the school age period, being a member of the play group and being accepted into the school gang are very important to the child. Sociometric studies indicate that nearly every school classroom has its "outsiders," the children who are left out, who do not belong. These are the children who have to try to find a substitute for their denied satisfactions. Sometimes they do this by being aggressive and resorting to bullying and other undesirable patterns. Sometimes it takes the form of withdrawal and seeking solitary activities. These children need help. There is no satisfactory substitute for companionship and belonging to the group. Perhaps the best way to help the child to be accepted by his contemporaries is to make sure he has the skills and knowledge valued by the group and that he is able to contribute to group activities.

During the elementary school period boys and girls tend to separate into their own sex groups. This separation need not be complete; in fact, it is better if it is not. They can be together for many of their activities, and when this is so, they learn to appreciate and understand each other and this makes adolescent adjustment easier.

It is helpful when the child associates with a variety of other children so that he learns to appreciate the fact of individual differences. Children, if uninfluenced by adults, usually cross the artificial boundaries of class, race, and religion, and it is desirable that they should. The artificial standards of social class, wealth, racial background, and religious affiliation are very inadequate standards for judging personal worth. Adults frequently impose these standards on the children and many children adopt the intolerances of their parents. The socially mature person is free of these artificial and unjust methods of appraising people so steps need to be taken to help children to avoid this common error.

In the period just prior to adolescence the gang or self-organized play group is important to the child. After adolescence the picture changes to a mixed group and pairing off starts. Dating days are in the offing. This grows naturally out of the play groups and earlier companionships. Now, belonging to the group is secondary to having a boy (or girl) friend. Although the young people are not thinking much about life partners, their parents usually are. The boy or girl is thinking only of having a partner for the party or being accepted by someone of the opposite sex, and marriage is far from his thoughts. Parents usually see the friendships as preludes to marriage and many of the misunderstandings between parents and adolescents are based on this difference in approach.

Friendships, companions, membership in social groups are obviously central to the happy and efficient adjustment of the person to life. Companionship is so satisfying to the individual because it includes interest in people, a sense of belonging, sex, and competition. There are so many satisfactions that are impossible alone. People are interesting because they are unpredictable, and because their activity is so varied. A sense of belonging includes a feeling of self-importance, social approval, and being liked. Sex is much more than a biological urge. In human living there are many experiences which provide satisfaction. Just being with a member of the opposite sex, being recognized and accepted, participating in social events, are all a part of this aspect of living. Competition is fun when the result is not as important as the competition itself. Competition is what adds zest and thrills to games and sports. However, when the emphasis is put on winning, then the only fun is to win and to lose is something of a tragedy.

Companionship can be thought of in many ways. For instance, it is possible to think of it in terms of what we get out of it, or it is possible to think of it in terms of what we can contribute. It is clear that companionship is always healthier when we adopt the second view. "You must not play with these boys because they do not use good language" or "because they do not come from good homes" is an expression of the "what can I get out of it" attitude. Parents can so easily pass on their attitudes to their children and produce this "what can I get" approach in their children. This is one reason why children should be free to choose their own companions.

Parents sometimes worry because their children have too few friends or too many. They worry about the kinds of friends they have. They worry because they think their children spend too much time with other children or not enough time. What parents should be most concerned about is whether they have provided enough chances for their children to acquire skills which will make them interesting, desired companions who have something to contribute. When that is taken care of they can safely leave these other aspects to the children themselves.

Children should feel free to bring their companions into their own home and to feel that they will be welcomed. This does not mean, of course, that the whole household has to be disturbed by them, nor that the child can have his friends to a meal without warning.

Companionship of contemporaries is a shifting pattern of dominance and submission. Dominance or leadership rests on bright ideas for the present situation. Submission or followership depends on the recognition of the bright ideas and their acceptance along with their author as the leader. So healthy companionship is a shifting pattern in the sense that the dominance is not permanent or forced, and the submission is willing and intelligent. When dominance is based on secondary features such as size, strength, family position, wealth, or ownership of materials, it is an undesirable social pattern.

Sibling Relations

Why do the children quarrel with each other all the time? Why do brothers and sisters have such difficulty in getting along with each other? Can't siblings be friends? These and similar questions are frequently asked by parents. Is sibling rivalry inevitable? Is it unhealthy? What should be done about it?

There are many reasons for sibling rivalry, quarreling and bickering. For one thing they know each other so well! They do not feel that they have to put on a front. They can be themselves. Then, of course, their lives are so intertwined that they get in each other's way. What one does may interfere with the activities of the other. And, also, there usually is much that they have to share: playthings, rooms, the television set, even clothes. Perhaps the most important feature is that they have the same parents. Some children find it difficult to share their parents with brothers or sisters.

Sibling rivalry is not inevitable, or at least need not be serious or bitter. Siblings can be friends, and many are. But parents need to be on the alert for signs of jealousy, feelings of resentment and injustice, as these may indicate the beginnings of unhealthy relations between children.

When a child, either rightly or wrongly, feels that a parent prefers a brother or sister to him, he will almost certainly become a jealous child. Jealousy distorts thought and colors feelings, often with unfortunate results. It finds expression in many ways but all are related to the basic meaning of jealousy—a fear of the loss of security of some social relationship. But jealousy is not just fear, it usually also includes some anger. So the jealous child may vent his anger on the source of the threat, his brother or sister. Or he may brood and build unhealthy feelings of resentment and hostility. There is not one pattern but many.

Peter was a bright boy of fourteen. His schoolwork had deteriorated seriously, so much so that he was in danger of failing. This was not at all like Peter, who had always done well in school, and who still showed signs of interest and effort; yet his academic record was way below what could be expected of him. Why? The answer was eventually found, not in anything to do with school but in the fact that Peter had an older sister. He seemed to admire her, for she was an accomplished young lady, popular, successful, and well-liked. Yet Peter reluctantly admitted that he and his sister quarreled nearly every day. The occasions of the squabbles could be almost anything: doing dishes, the use of a portable radio, a simple comment about something, the use of the bathroom, friends;

in fact practically any simple everyday happening or situation could be the start of a quarrel. And according to Peter, his sister always won. Or at least Peter thought that he always lost and what's more, he was sure that his parents were always on her side and against him. Nearly every evening Peter retired to his own room to do his homework, but instead he brooded, licked his emotional wounds, and was sure it wasn't fair. And he carried his brooding to school next day. Peter was failing, not because of low ability, lack of interest, or any of the usual reasons, but because he was not able to handle the family situation where he felt he came off second best in everything that involved his sister.

Peter's parents were quite unaware of the serious effects of Peter's encounters with his sister, unaware that Peter was becoming disturbed by jealousy that was gradually dominating his whole approach to life and making it impossible for him to concentrate on his schoolwork. They thought they had been teaching Peter to be courteous to women but had succeeded in making Peter think that they favored his sister and had virtually rejected him. Of course, after some hours of discussion, Peter was able to see that he was mistaken and that his feelings of insecurity and jealousy were unnecessary, but only after he had wasted a year of school.

Perhaps the most important thing we can learn from Peter and his difficulties is that the unhappiness and his school failure could have been prevented. A little insight on the part of his parents into what was happening and they could have taken the necessary steps to see that the natural disputes and differences of opinion between the two children did not have the serious consequences that have been described.

It is very easy for parents to make another kind of mistake: expecting brothers and sisters to be almost constant companions. For instance, two brothers, Charlie and Ed, with two years' difference in age, were expected to play together almost to the exclusion of other children. When they were preschool children, young Ed tried to do what his older brother did. Of course, he was always less capable, and always a nuisance to his older brother. In his immature way he would try to get even; if he couldn't build things as well as Charlie, at least he could knock things down. If he couldn't create things as his brother did he could destroy them. Naturally Charlie found this annoying and so nearly every playtime ended in a fight and tears. Their mother blamed Charlie; after all he was older. So Charlie learned to resent his young brother and having to have him spoil his play. And Ed learned to feel insecure because no matter how hard he tried he could not catch up to his big brother. Charlie and Ed could have gotten along together if they had not been faced with a day after day adjustment. If possible, they should have had other playmates some of the time.

Another related difficulty comes when the older sibling is not given the added privileges that go with his greater age but must conform with the requirements necessary for his younger brother or sister. This arises when the parents, in an attempt to be fair, try to treat both alike even though there is the age difference. Thus in their attempt to be just they are really unjust, robbing the older child of his just dues. Children in the family cannot be treated alike because differences in age and maturity must be taken into account. For instance, the allowances of a ten-year-old and a seven-year-old should not be the same. The seven-year-old can accept this if it is clear that when he is ten he will have the same as his brother does now.

Not all brothers and sisters fight each other, nor are all sibling quarrels bitter and serious. A certain amount of bickering is to be expected and may even be healthy. Such disagreements are healthy when the children learn how to settle their differences without bitterness and resentment. This is where the parents can be very helpful, not so much by taking sides or trying to referee disputes as by suggesting ways of dealing with the differences, such as taking turns, making compromises, and similar devices.

There are enormously important lessons the child can learn when he has brothers and sisters. In the intimate, day-by-day necessary adjustments the child can acquire some of the most important social skills: respecting the rights and property of others, taking turns, sharing space and possessions, and cooperation. But these lessons are learned only if the parents make sure that the conditions are right. There must be fairness, no favoritism, and, of course, a good example.

References

Barker, R. C., and Wright, H. F.: *Midwest and Its Children,* Harper & Row, New York, 1954.

Davis, C., and Northway, M. L.: "Siblings, Rivalry or Relationship," *Bulletin of the Institute of Child Study,* Toronto, 1957, No. 74.

Landis, P. H., and Haer, J.: *Helping Children Adjust Socially,* Science Research Associates, Chicago, 1954.

Neisser, E.: *Brothers and Sisters,* Harper & Row, New York, 1951.

Northway, M. L.: "So You Want Your Child To Be Popular?" *Bulletin of the Institute of Child Study,* Toronto, 1952, No. 54.

————: *What is Popularity?* Science Research Associates, Chicago, 1955.

Ojemann, R. H.: *The Child's Society, Clubs, Gangs and Cliques,* Science Research Associates, Chicago, 1953.

chapter 10
The School,
Home and School Relations,
and the Larger Community

The second most important institution in the life of the child is the school. More and more, home and school are thinking of how they can cooperate more closely for the attainment of their common goals and the good of the child.

In the last few decades, school has widened its scope in the modern community. It has moved both downward and upward in the age range as more and more children have the chance for nursery school or junior kindergarten and as the percentage going on beyond elementary school steadily increases. Not only is the age range increasing but the variety and diversity of educational facilities in our communities is rapidly increasing. No longer are our children faced with a single set pattern; on the contrary, in the larger centers especially, they have a variety of choices of courses and kinds of schools.

Education has always been valued in our culture, and today it is held in high esteem. But parents are not uncritical of the school and its program. Nor should they be. From one point of view, the school is an extension of the home, supplementing and extending the training of the child beyond what can be given within the family. Parents are responsible for the total training and education of their own children and should have a voice in how this job is done by the community.

Education is expensive and is a heavy drain on the public purse. But most people today are happy to see their tax money used for this purpose. It is an accepted principle that educational opportunities at all levels be open equally to all children who can profit from them. This principle, although accepted, is not fully implemented at the early prekindergarten age nor in higher education.

When should the child commence school? This question is often answered for us by the school facilities. The school is not prepared to take the child until he is six, for instance. However, where the facilities are available, what is the answer? The best way to get the answer is to think in terms of the child's development and readiness for various kinds of learning. In these terms the answer is clear. He is ready for the wider social group and to start learning to live with his contemporaries at about age two and a half. Those people who still maintain that the child of this age is much too young for school are thinking of school in the narrow sense of a classroom with formal learning tasks.

Nursery Schools

Nursery schools have proved their worth. They provide the opportunities for learning social adjustment, emotional control, conformity to a routine and to group discipline, creativity, and exploration in a way that is impossible in most homes. They do not take the place of the home, rather they help the home to do a better job. They supplement, not supplant. Most good nursery schools draw the parents into the educational orbit. What is being done is explained in detail; the school and home routines and procedures are dovetailed. Discussion groups and individual interviews are provided.

Kindergarten

And now the child is five and ready for kindergarten. If he has been to nursery school this is just a continuation with no major adjustments. If however, this is his first school experience there will be adjustments he will have to make. He can be prepared for these adjustments by previous learning. Here is a sample of the kinds of things he should have learned to be prepared for at this stage of his school experience. He should be able to manage his clothing, being able to dress and undress with very little help; be able to look after his own toilet needs; be able to wash himself; be able to manage the traffic situation, knowing when it is safe to cross the street; be able to play with other children, taking turns and participating in group activities; be able to follow simple directions; be able to conform to a regular routine; have some facility with materials, scissors, paints, crayons, etc. To be ready for kindergarten the child must be accustomed to being away from his mother, and also to the presence of other children. The child who has not had the nursery school experience or something similar frequently has difficulty in adjusting to school.

Kindergarten is a transition year. It is a bridge between the preschool and the school years. It is partly a "play" school and partly a "serious" school. There are tasks to perform and there is much "free" time in which the child can select his own activities. There are rules and there is freedom. There is the necessity for conformity and following directions and there is the opportunity for some initiative and creative activity. There is much learning and some exploration. Use of materials and some of the tools of communication come into the picture without the actual reading, writing, and arithmetic of later grades. There are still a few people who are impatient with the kindergarten and think of it as a waste of time, asking why the child is not taught something. But teaching in the sense of presenting facts and requiring practice in skills is not an essential condition of learning. The child learns much of value even though he does not learn to read and write.

Elementary School

Kindergarten over, the child moves into the grades. And now he is started on his formal education. But "formal" may not be a good label, for in the modern school the formality and regimentation characteristic of earlier days is not very prominent. He is subjected to a planned program of activities. He has "imposed" tasks to perform. He is called on to put forth effort to learn. He is introduced to factual material. He is required to remember. He uses pencil and paper to form letters. But the atmosphere of the classroom is informal and friendly. There are periods of fun and entertainment. School is serious, but school is not a strain or a burden.

There is much that the parent can do to make school the enjoyable, satisfying, valuable experience that it should be for all children. One of the most important of these is to show an attitude of interest, cooperation, and appreciation of the school and the teachers. Of course, parents and taxpayers have the right and the responsibility of being critical of the school and working for its continued improvement. But there is a time and place for this, and it is not when the young students are present. We are not suggesting any insincerity or dishonesty but rather that the parent by his attitude help the child to think of school and teachers as a part of his world not just to be accepted or tolerated, but to be appreciated and valued. We have seen young childen reflecting the complaining, critical, disparaging attitudes of their parents to schools and teachers. Teachers make mistakes, and some teachers should not be in the profession, but it only makes matters worse when parents emphasize these ideas in the presence of the children who are in their classes. Parents can be very helpful by showing to their children a positive attitude of interest and appreciation of what the school and teachers are doing.

Another phase of parental attitude is shown when he takes an interest in the child's progress, activities, and accomplishments in school. This should not be a prying interest, appearing to check up on the child and police his school behavior. Nor should it be a "pressing" attitude, impatient with his apparent slowness, never being satisfied with his progress, and pushing him continually to greater effort. It can be an interested, encouraging attitude which brings his two worlds, home and school, into one orbit and makes it natural for the child to share his school experiences because he knows his parents are both interested and sympathetically understanding of his successes and failures, his progress and his difficulties.

How much help should parents give in the child's schoolwork? This is a difficult question to answer in general. The best kind of help in the early stages is interest and encouragement. Later, more specific help may be required. But if so, it should be given after consultation with the teacher. Homework in most schools has been practically eliminated from the early grades, and is changing in form in the later grades of elementary school. There are large differences from school to school and teacher to teacher, and the only safe guide for the parent is to take direction from the child's teacher. Sometimes, homework in the elementry grades consists of drill in spelling, arithmetic questions to be worked out, or other rather routine drill activities which sometimes require supervision or checking. Sometimes, homework takes the form of some project, collecting materials or ideas and the like. In these the parents may be called on for help in locating materials or finding facts. But may we repeat, parents should provide help with homework in terms of what the child's teacher advises.

Parents and Teachers

We have implied in the discussion of homework in the elementary school that parent and teacher work together. This, we believe, is essential. It means that the parent has to get to know the child's teachers. Some schools make this easy by providing routine machinery to put teachers and parents in touch with each other. Other schools have no such machinery and it is left to parent and teacher to do it or not as they see fit. Also, some teachers welcome contacts with parents while others discourage it. The parent can take the initiative in arranging a chat with the teacher to exchange information about the child. It is much better to do this before any specific problem or crisis arises which would color the discussion.

Effective communication between home and school is one of the pressing unsolved problems of modern education. When the teacher boarded or lived in the small community and visited in the homes of the children, problems of communication and relationship between parent and teacher were nonexistent. But in the larger schools and where the teacher is not necessarily a member of the same little community as her children's parents, the problem becomes acute. The school report sent home four or five times in the year is certainly not an adequate answer. This is true, no matter what form the report takes, whether it provides marks, standing, grades, ratings, or comments, and no matter what categories are used. It cannot adequately communicate to the parents a picture of the child's progress or provide them with the kind of information they need to take their part in the education process.

Reports can sometimes do more harm than good, arousing resentments and misunderstandings. The teacher may write on the report, "Progress is slow in this subject." This comment may mean literally dozens of different things. It can mean that the child is not interested and is not putting forth the necessary effort. Or it can mean that because he is not "ready" for this specific learning his progress is slight. Or it might mean that the child has missed some foundation idea or skill and until this is made up his learning will be slow. Or it could mean any one of many other things. The comment on the report card can easily lead the parents to blame the child and call him names such as stupid or lazy, or it might lead the parents to blame the teacher: why doesn't she make the child work harder? Or the parents may simply be puzzled and because they do not know what it does mean, annoyed at the teacher and the school. And this is true in some form or other with most brief comments made on report cards.

When information about the school is limited to what the child reports and what is provided on the report cards, parents will have a very inadequate picture of the child's adjustment and progress in school. And the picture may be not only inadequate but distorted. To prevent this, ways and means of getting into closer touch with the school have to be found. This is one of the reasons why the parent-teacher or home and school organizations came into being. In some schools this organization serves a very real function of bringing the institutions together and providing opportunities for parents to get to know the teachers. In other schools the parent-teacher association has become a kind of community social group with very little function in the school except to raise money for school extras. It is the parent's responsibility to make full use of the organization that exists in the school and to help make it function more adequately in bringing home and school together.

The parent-teacher association is not a complete solution and needs to be supplemented by individual contacts between parent and teacher, and even visits to the classroom if that is possible.

High School

In some communities the intermediate school or junior high school provides a bridge between the elementary school and the secondary school. When this is the case there are usually facilities for appraisal and decision about the next step in the child's educational career, whether it will be a regular academic course, a commerical course, or a technical course.

Continued interest, encouragement, and sharing of school experiences is the parental role. Discussion of choice of courses, hours for homework, participation in extracurricular activities, sports, drama, music, and social events is one of the best ways the parents can contribute. This is the period when parents can show the young people by example that education is a continuous process and does not stop when formal courses terminate.

The Larger Community

Families do not exist in a vacuum. They are always a part of a larger group, the community. Families depend on the community and of course communities are made up of a number of families. So there are two sides to the picture—the dependence of the family on the community and the contribution the family makes to community life.

There was a time when a family was almost completely self-sufficient. But the time has long since passed, and today's family draws on the whole world for its materials, and through mass communication media is in touch with what is happening everywhere in the world and is affected by it. For instance, thousands of people have contributed to the family meal. The daily activities of the members of the family put them in touch with scores of community organizations for work, education, recreation, culture, religion, and welfare. Community effort pipes water, electricity, fuel, reading material, and entertainment into the modern household. Neighbors are often so close that we can hear their arguments, smell their dinners, be annoyed by their pets and be almost constantly aware of their presence. The schoolboy who insists on blue jeans and a yellow windbreaker is reflecting community pressure. And the complaint from the children that theirs is the only house on the block without television is another indication that no family can be immune to community influence.

The Community

Most families select the community in which they will be located by an examination of schools, shopping facilities, transportation, churches, recreation opportunities, and neighbors. Other considerations limit the choice too, because it is not always possible to find the location for a home that offers all that is desired and still is financially possible. However it is wise, when families have the chance, to find a community which provides as many of the desired features as possible because the setting in which the family functions makes a great difference to family life.

Although the use of community resources and the family's contribution to community life go hand in hand, we'll discuss them one at a time for the sake of simplicity.

Every modern community has scores of organizations to serve the members of the family. Many are commerical organizations whose main reason for existence is profit. Others are nonprofit organizations whose purpose is to serve people. But it is obviously not possible to say that all service organizations are better than all profit organizations. However, it is wise to remember that those which operate for profit will not always give adequate consideration to the welfare of individuals. This can be seen in some motion picture theaters, radio programs, newspapers, poolrooms, and professional athletics. Since profits depend on large numbers of persons using these services (either as participants or as spectators), attention-attracting devices are used widely to create demand. No family can be immune to these appeals and many problems are created by these community influences.

Commercial Entertainment

Should children be protected from commercial entertainment, poor movies, lurid comic books, radio, and television? This question is asked by some serious parents who see all the undesirable features in them. Even if we could exclude these from the child's experience, it is doubtful if we should. Prohibition and censorship are rarely good techniques. To say to the child "You must not see or hear" what other children are experiencing and talking about makes the forbidden more attractive and tends to produce resentment and a feeling of being cheated. Besides, children should have some experience with what is going on in their world. They need to experience a variety of things in order to develop a sense of taste and an ability to discriminate and choose. Of course, the child has to be protected from the terrifying, the indecent, and the obscene. But more important than shielding the child is helping him to understand and assimilate the experiences he has.

Radio and television can be managed so that they do not crowd out other activities. They have their values as well as dangers. For the younger children sensible rules can be formulated by the parents limiting the hours of listening and viewing. With older children agreements can be arrived at through discussion so that they will keep such activities within reasonable bounds.

Clubs and Gangs

The community offers many opportunities for group activity in both organized clubs and in informal gangs. There is a place and value in both for the growing child. In the preschool period the group is not as important to the child as the activity. It does not matter a great deal who the children are as long as they will take part in interesting play activities. Of course, preferences for certain children develop but these are mainly because these preferred children fit in better with the desires and interests of the preferring

child. Later the group itself becomes as important as the activity
and belonging is satisfying in itself. This comes in the late elementary school period. This is the period that some people have
called the "gang age." It is the time when the child joins organized
groups such as clubs and teams. There is value in both the gang
and the club. The gang is free of adult supervision and direction
but is not necessarily antisocial. Belonging to the gang and being
subject to the discipline of the group and free for the time from
adult discipline is an aid to the growing independence of the child.
It is only when children feel that the direction they get from parents
and teachers is unjust and unreasonable that their gang activities
take on the nature of rebellion, destruction of property, and other
antisocial activities. It is not necessary to deplore or try to stop
gang activity or change a gang into a supervised club.

The organized club, planned and directed by adults, is not necessarily better than the gang. It is, however, different as it usually
stresses more formalized programs of activity. Some boys and girls
find in these groups satisfying and stimulating experiences and
leaders who provide desirable patterns to imitate and emulate.
But this is not true of all organized clubs. Just because a club has
a high-sounding name or is linked with a national organization
does not guarantee that it will be a desirable organization for children. It is wise for parents to know what goes on in such clubs,
who the leaders are, and whether they are qualified to provide
the kind of leadership desired.

Companions

Many parents are concerned about what they call "bad companions."
They feel happier if they can choose their children's friends and
associates. But sometimes the children themselves are better judges
of companions than the parents are because they know the other
boys and girls better. When parents try to regulate directly with
whom their children are to associate they may be instrumental in
developing snobbery and intolerance in their children. And they
may also lead their children to adopt deception in order to associate with the forbidden companions. It is better on the whole

to let the child select his own friends. Parents can be more helpful by making the child's self-selected companions welcome in the home and by making it possible for the child to cultivate a variety of companions.

Camps

Summer camps provide for most children a kind of experience which has lasting value. Camps for boys and girls were developed originally for preadolescent and adolescent children. There has been a trend towards lowering the age range, and in most cases trying to adapt a program and a procedure which was suitable for the older child to younger age groups. Camps are not necessarily desirable for all children and especially for younger children. The child can feel that he is being disposed of by his parents, that he is not wanted, and he can be quite unhappy at camp. However, when the child himself wants to go to camp and when he is mature enough for the experience and it is possible for the family to send him, he will probably profit greatly from the experience.

The Adolescent

The adolescent in the main seeks his membership in social groups where he will be with those he likes and admires. Activities take second place to persons. He also likes to have some voice in the organization and group officers and formal structure are important. So is belonging. The mere fact that he is an accepted member of the group means much to him. If he does not find this acceptance and belonging in one setting he will seek it somewhere else. If the community does not provide opportunities for group activity in what are usually called wholesome settings, the adolescent will find other places even if it is the street corner, the poolroom, or the soda fountain.

The older adolescent will be more interested in smaller groups and in "dating." He is less interested in club activities that do not provide chances for pairing off. Now belonging means having a boy friend or a girl friend rather than just being in a group. Now a different set of so-called problems arises. Parents who were a few short years ago concerned about getting the boy to wash a large enough skin area often enough, now find that concern giving place to others. The boy or girl spends what seems to be endless time talking trivialities on the telephone. The adolescent has a "steady" boy or girl friend and parents worry because they seem so young for this adult pattern. But then the "steady" is changed for another one and it is seen that it is a fashion which does not have the same meaning of permanence that the parents had imagined. Hours, use of the family car, and similar problems arise.

What is the parent's role? Many parents of adolescents are puzzled and worried. Perhaps the most important single aspect is trust in the adolescent. He needs to feel that his parents trust him and when he does he usually lives up to the trust. Then he needs advice, suggestions, and borrowed experience. This cannot be imposed on him but should come as an answer to his own comments; it should not be given dogmatically but rather in a friendly "take it or leave it" attitude.

The Adult and the Community

There are many community facilities and organizations for adults. Parents can be better parents if they are in touch with some parts of the world outside the home. Clubs, recreation centers, school affairs, churches, and many others can provide the stimulus for out-of-the-home interests and activities. They lend interest to living and help to make the adult who participates a healthier and more interesting person.

Next to the home and the school, the church is to many people the most important community organization. When the parents are active members of a religious body it is natural that the children should take part in it as well. When it is the accepted thing in the family the children usually take part in the church activities as a matter of course. However, when parents ask us, "Should we make our children go to Sunday school?" we usually find that they themselves do not go to church. Requiring children to be active in an organization which they do not support or whose meetings they do not attend is sometimes difficult and may not be very valuable to the child. The child gets more out of it if he goes because he wants to and not just because he is sent. Most thoughtful parents want their children to receive some exposure to their religious heritage, but forced attendance at a religious service may not be the best way to arrange for this education. Just because it is called a religious education program does not guarantee that it will be a desirable experience for the child. One parent told us about her young school age son who resisted strenuously being sent to Sunday school. When she looked into the situation she found that the reason for his reluctance was the fearful stories about death and torture that were included in the lesson. Parents should know what they require their children to listen to.

The other side of the picture of the relation between family and community is the contribution of the family to community life and activity. An interest and active participation in community activities not only helps to make a better, safer, and more healthy community in which to bring up children but seems to help family life as well. There are two extremes evident: the one is where community activities are so prominent that family life suffers and the other is where there is virtually no interest or participation in the life of the community. Naturally there is a desirable middle course where members of the family take their places in community life without neglecting their family responsibilities. No community is better than what its members want and work for. Here as everywhere else, attitudes are the foundation, and attitudes are absorbed so easily by children from their parents that it is almost certain that children will reflect those of their parents. For instance, if the parents' main attitude toward civic organizations, schools, and churches is one of carping criticism and complaint, the children will almost inevitably show the same spirit. But when parents show pride in their community and are active in making it even better, children will have the same attitude.

The simple facts are that fundamentally the responsibility for the training and education of children rests with the parents. However, in our complex society they receive a lot of help from community organizations. The school, the church, the recreation center, and all the other organizations in the community are extensions of the home, in many cases parent substitutes. That is why it is essential that parents be thoroughly aware of what is done and how, and also that they work with other parents to keep them up to the desired standards. So, participation in community activities is an integral part of parenthood.

References

Bernhardt, K. S.: "Home and School, Two Institutions with the Same Goal," *Parent Education Bulletin,* University of Toronto, Toronto, 1941, No. 13.

Berson, M. P.: *Kindergarten: Your Child's Big Step,* Dutton, New York, 1959.

Fine, B., and Fine, L.: *How to Get the Best Education for Your Child,* Putnam, New York, 1959.

Frank, L. K., and Frank, M.: *How to Help Your Child in School,* Viking Press, New York, 1950.

Hymes, J. L.: *Effective Home-school Relations,* Prentice-Hall, Englewood Cliffs, N.J., 1953.

Mitchell, L. S.: *Our Children and Our Schools,* Simon and Schuster, New York, 1950.

Warren, V. B.: *Tested Ways to Help Your Child Learn,* Prentice-Hall, Englewood Cliffs, N.J., 1961.

chapter 11
Work—Home Chores, Working for Money, and Preparing for a Career

What is the difference between work and play? If you ask a group of people this question, you usually get as your first answer, "Play is fun, work is a burden," or "One is pleasant and the other is not." But a minute's thought changes this, for work can be very pleasant too. Work is something we do because we have to, play is done only because we want to. Of course, we can want to work too, but there is always some compulsion about it—a compulsion from outside.

Work need not be a burden. It can be pleasant and satisfying. It can yield enduring rewards in feelings of achievement, creation, and worthwhile accomplishment. It is work because it is necessary; it must be done for some reason. And our society is so organized that practically everyone has to work.

A superficial view would seem to indicate that work is for adults and that children are exempt from it. But a more careful look shows that work starts very early in the child's development and continues to an increasing extent throughout childhood. Nor should this be hidden from the child. It is possible to camouflage the child's work by making it look like play and thus trick him into doing the things that living requires of him. But it does seem more sensible to keep work and play separate and distinct and to help the child learn that life does consist of two kinds of activities: those he must do whether he wants to or not (work) and those that he can do or not as he likes (play). The sooner the child discovers this fact about the world in

121

which he is living the better. There has been an unfortunate tendency recently to try to remove from the life of the child all compulsions and requirements, to work entirely through interest and wants. If the child does not want to do something, the suggestion has been, let him alone until he does; you must not take the chance of damaging his delicate personality growth by requiring him to do what he does not want to do. Of course, interest and self-motivation is a good avenue of approach, but it is also true that the child has to learn to accept and perform tasks in which he has no present interest, in other words, to submit to the sensible requirements of living.

In infancy there is very little that can be called work. However, there is a beginning of at least the idea of external compulsion or requirement which is the basis of work. Even the infant has to accept control and manipulation in dressing, washing, being put to bed, and similar routines. The routines in the life of the infant and preschool child correspond to work in later periods.

Work in the Preschool Period

The preschool period is the time when learning to satisfy needs in a socially acceptable way has a central place. Considerable time each day is spent in the routines of eating, sleeping, washing, and dressing. These are areas of work, activities in which there is an element of external compulsion. Most preschool children conform readily to the demands made on them. They find the activities themselves interesting at first and later accept them as a to-be-expected part of each day. They can learn to conform to "what is done" and need not come to think of these activities as the whims of their parents.

The preschool period is not too soon to start the principle of the child taking part in the work of the household. Of course, what he can do is really very little but the important thing is for him to get the idea that all members of the family do their share and contribute to the common, necessary work. But not as "mother's little helper." He is not doing mother's work but his own. And this idea continues and expands as he becomes more helpful. We want him to feel that he belongs, that he is a member of the family, and that all members take their share of the load. There are many little responsibilities that the preschool child can assume and every month can add something new. He can put his own things away. He can be responsible for clearing his own dinner table and stacking up the dishes. He can hang up his clothes. He can deliver little messages, and so on.

It is important that these little jobs be started in the right atmosphere as *his* jobs and therefore not paid for, as his responsibility and so not taken over by anyone else too readily.

Work in the School Age Period

When the child starts at school a new area of work opens up for him, schoolwork. We expect him to enjoy this and to get a good deal of satisfaction from his achievements. On the other hand, we expect him to accept schoolwork as something that must be done, not play but serious business. We expect him to put forth effort, to develop a sense of responsibility: "This is my job, I must work at it and make a 'go' of it."

There will be many times when he will need encouragement, even help, over the difficult places, but this encouragement and help should not diminish in any way the main or central idea that it is up to him, that it is his job, that this is what is required of him.

Home chores will continue along with his schoolwork and will even increase as he grows older and more competent. It is wise to give the child some "say" in the planning and allow some variety, so that the jobs that are his may change from week to week. It is a very different feeling to be doing work that you have had some part in deciding on from doing what someone else has decided and demanded of you. It makes for a better feeling when the child takes part in the discussion of who does what each week. Some way of arranging things so that constant reminders (or nagging) are unnecessary also helps a lot. A family notice board on which the plan of work for the week is posted is such a device.

Some parents say that it is easier to do the work themselves than go through the annoyance of talking, coaxing, or threatening the child to get him to do it. But the point is, such a procedure is not necessary. There are other ways of managing.

The problem of pay for home chores is frequently raised by parents. On the whole it is best to keep home chores and allowance separate and not pay the child for doing his share of household work. If, however, there are extra jobs, these can be offered the child; he can contract to do them and be paid at market rates or he can decide not to do so. These are, however, different from the regular jobs which are his share and which he does as his contribution to the family work.

The problem of outside jobs also arises. It is sometimes a very difficult decision whether the school age boy should or should not take a part-time job, a paper route, a job as delivery boy at the store, or similar work. Many things have to be considered: his health, his other interests and activities, his schoolwork, family activities, and so on. It is a decision which should be made only after thorough discussion in which the boy himself has had a part. Should it be decided that he take the job, adjustments have to be made in other activities. If it is an early morning paper route, his bedtime has to be adjusted. If it is an after-school position, arrangements have to be made to allow time for both schoolwork and play. In general, it is best to postpone outside jobs until he is about fifteen.

Work in Adolescence

The boy and girl at high school present a different picture. Now club activities, sports, and even dating take up much time. Homework calls for more attention than previously. Part-time jobs are possibilities. Theaters, concerts, church work, all make their demands. Home chores may be pushed in the background. This is the time for discussion and compromises. The young adolescent wants and should have quite a bit to say about the use of his time. He will resent commands and pronouncements. He will be amenable to guidance and will profit from understanding sympathetic treatment. He can be led where he can't be bossed. It is difficult to keep the program within sensible dimensions. However, careful planning can find a time for schoolwork, home chores, extracurricular activities, hobbies and interests, and even part-time work.

Vocational Choice

During adolescence the problem of vocational choice becomes prominent. Decisions must be made in regard to school courses—academic, commercial, or technical. At sixteen the law allows a boy or girl to stop school. So even if it is not the final decision about the child's ultimate vocation, some choices have to be made. There are a number of important points to keep in mind. Just as much as possible it should be the child's own decision, not that of his parents or teachers. Decisions should not be hurried or forced. No choice should be considered final and unchangeable. Whatever facilities are available for help should be utilized.

As wide a knowledge and experience of different kinds of work as is possible should be provided. There is no perfect fit of people and jobs. Most people could be equally happy and successful in a number of vocations. Now let us look at some of these considerations in more detail and do so in the context of a developmental picture of vocational choice and adjustment.

Learning to Work

First, we should say that work is such a central aspect of living that a good adjustment to work is an important aspect of the happiness and mental health of the individual. The person who is unhappy in his work is likely to be unhappy and discontented with life as a whole. Work should yield satisfactions which make life worth living.

Another general point has to do with the individual's general attitude toward work. This is, of course, a product of many experiences in the home, school, and community. It is possible for the child to learn that work is evil, a necessary evil but still evil, and therefore something to avoid as much as possible and to do as little as possible. Or the child can develop the idea that work is a burden, to be put up with but never to be enjoyed. There are many other similar attitudes but these will serve to make the point that attitudes can develop which make it difficult either to enjoy work or be very efficient in it.

It is equally true that healthy attitudes toward work can be produced. It is largely a matter of example and the contagion of attitudes. What are desirable attitudes toward work? Here are some suggestions: a willing acceptance of the necessity for work and the responsibility for doing one's share; an attitude of cooperation or willingness to work with others; an attitude of interest and understanding of the meaning of the work and how it fits into a larger pattern of living; an attitude of contribution or thinking of work in terms of contributing rather than what you get out of it; and an attitude which indicates an absence of work snobbery—no work is too menial.

Another important preparation for life work is the development of good work habits such as concentration or working while you work, intelligent persistence or staying with a task long enough to make some progress, the quality of the work or doing the job well enough for the purpose involved, dependability or carrying through with a task without the necessity of constant supervision or checkup, and enjoyment or having feelings of satisfaction in accomplishment. These and other similar habits are developed in the day-by-day home and school situations if the child receives the kind of leadership and guidance conducive to such learning.

Vocational Guidance

Both healthy attitudes toward work and good work habits are preparation for happy vocational adjustment. The problem still remains, what will the choice of a vocation be and how will the decision be made. This is a problem that is best met over a long period of time. Boys and girls can be helped to get to know about the world of work and the great variety of occupations. They should see many kinds of work as they grow up and become familiar with quite a few of them. They can meet and talk with friends of the family. They can read stories about various people in various occupations. The main point here is that as the boy or girl is going to have to make the choice some time, it is wise for them to have a background of knowledge to use.

Few parents, today, try to steer their children into a particular occupation, although some do. But many parents do try to influence their children indirectly by stressing the values in specific vocations and deprecating others. This is one place where parents should tread lightly. The child should feel no pressure from his parents to follow any particular career. We sometimes meet young people who tell a story similar to a student who had started in a medical course but was very unhappy with it. When he was asked why he did not change to another course, which he both wanted and was better suited for, he answered that if he did it would break his parents' hearts. We believe that no child should be made to feel that he must choose any particular vocation because his parents want him to.

Most schools have vocational guidance departments and guidance teachers whose function is to help boys and girls make vocational choices. Some of these guidance people are very helpful and view their place as that of providing help, but not telling the boy or girl what he should do. When any of them do try to make the decision for the child and tell him what he should do, then it is no longer guidance.

The guidance teacher can provide two very important services: (1) the chance to study occupations and (2) the appraisal of the child's ability, aptitudes, interests, personality, and so on. These two kinds of information can be very helpful to the youth in his thinking about his future career and in deciding on educational courses.

During adolescence there is usually the opportunity to have work experiences during the summer vacations. These can be valuable to the boy or girl whether he needs the money or not. The relatively impersonal relationship with an employer who is not a member of the family provides a new kind of situation and stimulus to responsibility. The chance to learn to contribute effort for a money return as well as the discipline of a work situation with its demands for punctuality, initiative, and dependability should all contribute to the growing-up process. And it is another step in emancipation from parental control. Besides these values, there is the chance to see a segment of the world of work and experience at first hand in at least one occupational area.

Leaving School

It frequently happens that the boy or girl becomes "fed up" with school at about grade ten and wonders if it is worthwhile. This is the time when many boys want to quit school and go to work. Some parents meet this situation with an emotional appeal or storm, ending in an unfortunate threat that if he stops now he need not expect support later if he changes his mind. It should seem to be much better to try to talk the matter over and bring sympathetic understanding to the discussion and even suggest that he might try a job for a year with the understanding that, if and when he changes his mind and wants to go back to school, he will get every support from his parents.

Sometimes this desire to leave school can be met in a different way. It may mean that a careful appraisal of the whole educational program of the youth is in order. It may be that a different course, school, or objective should be arranged. Sometimes, this loss of interest in school is an indication that the boy or girl needs help in thinking about his future plans. It may be that he has gone on from year to year in regular high school courses with no very clear idea of what he is working toward and now needs to evaluate the whole situation in terms of specific goals.

In adolescence there are a number of aspects of work to be considered: schoolwork with increasing amounts of home study, home chores, part-time employment during the school term and vacations, and preparation for and getting started in his work career. Let us summarize each of these with the parents' role taken into account.

Schoolwork is pretty much his own responsibility. However, the parent is naturally interested in his academic progress and wants to contribute to his success in it. This sometimes leads parents to a kind of futile nagging or close supervision that is resented. To avoid this, other parents try a "hands-off" policy which is interpreted by some adolescents a meaning that their parents are not interested in their school progress and do not care how well or poorly they do. Obviously, there is a middle course in which parents express their interest, provide encouragement and moral support, indicate their faith in the youth, and also provide the setting for efficient work and discussion about details which include hours of study, nights out, and so on. Here again, we can see the value of indirect control in the provision of an atmosphere conducive to study both in the stimulation from interest and encouragement and in the providing of the physical setting: a place, a desk, materials, and uninterrupted time.

Home chores are sometimes a storm center, but they need not be. With adequate regular planning and discussion and sufficient flexibility in the plan, most young people are prepared to do their reasonable share. Again the important thing seems to be that the atmosphere of all working together (not necessarily together in time) is the feature that makes all the difference. The adolescent is jealous of his time and his self-management. He resents being "pushed around" too much. He does not like to be treated like a child even though his behavior and attitudes are at times childish. This means that when and how he does his share of the household chores have to be left to him to a large extent. His way of making a bed, cleaning up the basement, or cutting the lawn may not be exactly the same as his parents'. But the main thing is that he does his share even though he may do it in his own time and in his own way. And like anyone else, he feels important when his ideas are solicited and his suggestions listened to.

Another aspect of home chores during adolescence is the expansion of the scope of the work. Girls can be given opportunities to do more than just the routine chores. They can plan and prepare meals, start making clothes, rearrange and decorate rooms, and so on. Boys can branch out into minor plumbing, electrical work, carpentry, and painting. They are now doing more than just helping with the monotonous routine tasks.

Employment outside the home has to be considered carefully. Its values have to be balanced with its disadvantages. Matters of health, school progress, and disruption of home routines have to be considered. But in the home in which there is a real attempt to understand each other, such problems can be solved through discussion.

Now to return to the preparation for a career. We have indicated that in early adolescence the problem of vocational choice arises and usually some preliminary decisions have to be made in terms of school courses. Now in later adolescence more specific decisions are called for. Is education to be continued beyond high school? What course should be taken? At what institution? How is it to be financed? If his formal education is to end at high school graduation, what kind of work is he to seek? How can he get started? and so on.

These and other related questions must be answered. In the main they have to be answered by the adolescent himself. But he needs help from his parents and possibly the help of other people too. He must know without a shadow of a doubt that you stand behind him, that you will help him when he needs you, and that you have confidence in him. This is a delicate matter, for it is easy to give too much help, just as it is easy to convey the impression that you have washed your hands of the whole affair.

The adolescent, let us say, has decided to go on to college. It now becomes a matter of cooperative planning. It is cheaper to stay at home and go to the nearby college. On the other hand, a more remote and therefore more expensive college has a better course. How much can the family finances stand? How much can the youth earn himself? What are the possibilities of a scholarship or a grant-in-aid? These problems can all be worked out, provided the parents and the adolescent can together thrash them out in discussion.

There are many possible problems involved in prolonged education, and in vocational choice and adjustment. All these problems can be resolved in some way if the lines of communication between parents and adolescents are kept open and if parents remember that it is the adolescents' lives that are being planned. Emancipation without economic independence is possible and indeed necessary. The old principle often invoked by parents, that as long as they pay the bills they also call the tune, has to be discarded.

References

Humphreys, J. A.: *Helping Youth Choose Careers,* Science Research Associates, Chicago, 1950.

Johnson, F. L.: "Learning to Work," *Bulletin of the Institute of Child Study,* Toronto, 1952, No. 52.

Osborne, E.: *How to Teach Your Child about Work,* Public Affairs Pamphlet No. 216, New York.

chapter 12
Possessions,
Ownership,
and Money

Possessions can dominate life or take their place as valuable servants. It depends on the kind of experiences the child has and the kind of example he lives with. There are three possessive pronouns which the child learns eventually and which express important differences in the meaning of ownership. They are "mine," "yours," and "ours."

Even the infant has things which belong exclusively to him even though he does not as yet have any conception of ownership. The care of these is someone else's responsibility at this stage.

Ownership

The preschool child begins to learn the meaning of ownership and respect for the property of others. He has his own clothes, furniture, and play materials. He can be helped to look after his belongings, hang up his clothes, and put his toys away. This is done by arranging that the physical facilities are suitable: low hooks, toy boxes, and shelves. He learns slowly to put materials in their place after use. He may have to be helped in this learning by being deprived of some of his possessions that he has left lying around. But in most cases simply providing the suitable place and making clear to the child what is expected of him is enough.

The child can learn the meaning of ownership more easily and quickly when he owns things himself and his ownership is respected. If we do not think about what is involved we may do things like the mother who in her housecleaning zeal threw away what was to her "junk" but which was to her young son prized possessions.

There are important but subtle differences in ways of thinking about possessions. Obviously, ownership has its values. One of these is free use of possessions to bring satisfaction to the possessor and others. Another is the enhancing of prestige and power through possession. This can become dangerous to the individual's development and should not be encouraged. The child who depends on ownership of play materials for social acceptance is hindered in his development of more valuable and permanent personality characteristics. And when he extends this to the use of possessions as a means of power or dominance over others, he has fallen into a pattern which has brought many unfortunate results in our society.

What we are trying to express is that possessions and ownership are not the simple situation they may appear. They have many overtones and undertones in personality development. The child who feels deprived and inferior because his possessions (clothes, house, play materials, and so on) are inferior to those of his companions can easily develop compensatory patterns of behavior which can be detrimental. On the other hand, the child whose abundance of possessions leads him to use his plenty to dominate or control has slipped into an equally unfortunate pattern.

It is possible for the child to learn to value things without such evaluation being out of balance. The value is in terms of use and appreciation without making the possessions take the place of personal contribution. Care of possessions without hoarding, pride of ownership without gloating, sharing without use of things for coercion, are some of the healthy patterns indicated. These healthy patterns emerge partly as the result of example and expressed attitudes in the home. And they result partly from an emphasis on values other than ownership so that possessions do not dominate the atmosphere of the home. For instance, the evaluation of people by criteria which stress the personality and character of the individual rather than the extent of his possessions is one of these positive emphases.

Common ownership is another important phase of this area. The home is a made-to-order situation for communal ownership and cooperative use of possessions. Unfortunately it is very easy to develop a pattern in which the house belongs to father and most of the furnishings belong to mother and the children are led to feel that they are living not in their own home but in that of their parents. In other words, in our culture individual ownership is much more prominent than communal ownership. So, it is father's car and not the family car. And those are father's books, mother's dishes, and so on. But it is just as easy, if we wish to do so, to give the impression that house and car, furniture and materials belong to the family and are for use not by one but by the group. This pattern has its very distinct values, not the least of which is that the children feel themselves a more intimate part of the group.

Protecting Possessions

When the children are young there are at least two possibilities, one of which can be followed. One is to leave all the prized possessions within reach of exploring fingers and erect a barrage of pro-hibitions and "mustn't touch" and "no, no" and punishments. The other is to put such perishable possessions out of sight and reach until the children are old enough to be able to navigate among the *objets d'art* without disaster. Or there may be a sensible com-promise between these two extremes. Certainly the young child cannot be allowed to destroy valuable objects, but equally certainly it is undesirable continually to prohibit and punish. When the child has his own possessions to use, the temptation to use or misuse the family possessions is not so great.

Money

Money is one kind of possession which is so universal and important in our part of the world that it can serve as an example of training in the use of possessions. In considering this training, it is wise to look first at what objectives we have in mind. These can be simply expressed as the fostering of desirable attitudes and the develop-ment of the ability to use money wisely. But these objectives need some elaboration.

Desirable attitudes express values. As attitudes are more caught than taught, it is almost inevitable that the child will develop the attitudes prominent in his family. One exception to this is where the child experiences the unsatisfactory results of a parental attitude and therefore builds a contrasting one as a consequence. Sometimes the child's experiences lead him to adopt attitudes which are different from family attitudes but not necessarily contrary to them. Attitudes are reflections of feelings and tendencies to behave in specific ways. For instance, the child who has a hoarding attitude toward money has some underlying feelings which lead him to try to pile up money and gloat over its mere possession.

One very valuable attitude is that money is for use. There are still traces of the older idea that money is something to be saved and parted with only reluctantly. In most homes today the emphasis in training is more on use than saving. Even when the child is helped to save it is done in terms of future spending, not saving in general but saving for a specific purpose such as skates, a bicycle, or a vacation. This basic attitude accepts the idea that money is a medium of exchange and not primarily a means of control of others or a source of prestige.

We hope the child will come to recognize that there are many values which cannot be estimated in dollars and cents, and that there are some things that money cannot buy. Because money provides such an easy standard to use, some people employ it as the sole standard of value. So people, objects, and experiences are judged by price tags. Even affection, respect, and the like are given a price. The child picks up this idea when he is paid for goodness and when he sees his parents estimating the worth of people by the extent of their possessions.

Money and its use provide an example of the delicate balance between self-interest and a social sense. Sharing what one possesses with others is an expression of a social sensitivity that is valued in our society. To manage one's money wisely looks like self-interest but need not be selfish. True sharing that is not buying the favor of others, purchasing prestige, or exerting control over others is an adult characteristic and does not appear in the child without the slow accumulation of values and a social sense which takes years. However, it is an objective that parents can keep in mind if they agree that it is important.

If the child is to learn to use money intelligently and to acquire the attitudes which are considered healthy, he must have money of his own in terms of a regular income. This allowance can start as soon as the child has learned to recognize coins and has opportunities to use money for his own purposes. The age of the child when he is thus ready for an allowance varies with the child and with the community in which he lives. The amount of the allowance is determined by the child's wants that can be satisfied this way, by his present ability to manage, and by his chances to spend it. The amount is adjusted periodically as he grows and his wants increase. The allowance is his own money, for him to use as he wishes. What is included in the allowance is determined by discussion, and this too is adjusted from time to time so that both the amount and scope of the allowance increase as the child learns. By the time the child has reached adolescence the allowance can cover most of the things that are individual and the child is handling for himself the share of family finances that applies to him.

The child's income will probably be more than his regular allowance. It will be supplemented by gifts from relatives, extras from his parents for special requirements, and what he may earn himself. All these should be integrated into the plan of training. His gifts can be designated by discussion and agreement for special uses, for instance.

Problems of borrowing, instalment buying, and similar problems may arise. Borrowing money or receiving his allowance or part of it ahead of time may hinder the kind of learning we hope will take place. There will be times when he will need to experience the results of his thoughtless spending by having to do without something. This is hard for parents to enforce. But it does seem necessary at times to resist generous tendencies so that the child can learn that if he uses up all his weekly allowance early in the week he has nothing left for the things he wants until the next allowance day. An exception to this is when the child wants something that is desirable for him to have but which is beyond his meager resources. Parents can help him find a solution by advancing the total amount and arranging that he pay it back week by week from his allowance. A very useful principle is that such borrowing be allowed only when the purchased object will last longer than the debt.

The problem of accounting sometimes arises. Should the child be required to account to his parents for the use of his allowance? There are a number of factors to consider in finding an answer to this question. One thing is clear and that is that we think of the child's allowance as his own. He is not spending his parents' money; he is using his own money. This would seem to point to not requiring the child to account for it. On the other hand, discussions of adjustments in allowance and decisions about an increase in scope and amount will have to draw on the child's demonstrated ability to manage. Also keeping a record of what is done with his money is a very good way for the child to learn to choose wisely and manage intelligently. So the child can be encouraged to keep accounts but the accounts are not examined or audited except when the child himself introduces his records into a discussion.

The child's use of his income usually includes spending, saving, and giving. At least in the early stages, spending or using his allowance is the most prominent. Let us look at a number of examples to see some of the details.

Here is a boy of nine. He belongs to the Cub Scouts and goes to Sunday school and he needs money for these and his other activities. After careful consideration it is decided that for the present year he should have 50 cents a week and out of it look after Sunday school collection and his Cub fees.

A girl of thirteen in first-year high school has demonstrated that she can manage money fairly well. It is decided that her allowance should cover her carfare, school lunch, recreation, social activities, and "incidental" clothes (not including coats, dresses, and shoes). And because she has learned much about managing, the allowance is arranged on a monthly basis; $20 is deposited in her bank account each month.

A boy of seventeen, who works in the summer vacation and who is planning to go to college next year, presents a more complicated picture. After discussion it is agreed that what he saves from his summer job will be used for fees next year. His allowance is to cover his bus fare to school, lunch, social and athletic activities, and his school books, supplies, and clothes. The monthly basis is decided on and a special amount added in September for the books. It is agreed that the larger clothes items will be discussed and extra amounts provided as needed. It is further agreed that he will keep a rough record of expenditures, and the amount deposited in his account each month will be approximately what he spent the month before. He is fully aware of the family income and expenses and knows that there is not an unlimited supply, but he also appreciates that his parents are prepared to trust his judgment and to support his reasonable requests.

These brief pictures indicate that the allowance should be determined realistically and by mutual agreement with all factors considered. As the child acquires more judgment and ability to manage, the scope of his management increases, so that, by the time he is ready to leave home to strike out for himself, he has had plenty of practice in managing an income which covers more than just incidentals.

Family Finances

Another phase of this training program is participation in family finances. Our observations would lead us to conclude that very few children have any very detailed knowledge of the complexities of family finance. They see father hand over an amount each week or month to mother for household expenses. They get their allowance from the same source. They hear rather vaguely about debts, mortgages, instalment payments, insurance policies, and the high cost of living. But none of these are discussed with them in anything but very general terms or through puzzling comments such as "Do you think we are made of money?" "Of course we can't have a second car, we're not millionaires." "If you had to earn it you wouldn't be so free in spending it."

Somewhere along the line as the child grows up, he can be introduced to the details of managing family finances. He can be introduced gradually and as his knowledge and understanding increase he can share in family discussions about choices between a new car and another insurance policy, or a television set or a new rug for the living room. He can know about provision for retirement, financing a new house, saving for a special trip, and all the thousand and one details of running a household and making a budget cover the wants of the family.

A very dramatic example of lack of knowledge of family finances came to our attention recently. A university student came to tell us she was leaving college. When asked why, she said simply she could not afford to go on any longer and let her mother sacrifice for her. Further discussion revealed the whole story. Her father had died some years ago and her mother had carried on in the family home in the same way as when her father was alive. She had started to college under the impression the family finances were plentiful. She had spent money, not extravagantly but without much restraint. She had written home when she needed more money and it had always come. She had had a very pleasant summer vacation but had not taken a job and earned money as she supposed that was not necessary. But one day she overheard a comment of someone from her hometown to the effect "Isn't it a shame Mrs. —— has to sacrifice so much to keep Mary at college?" This came as a real shock to Mary and when she investigated she discovered that her mother was actually depriving herself and had put a mortgage on the home to raise money for her fees and expenses. As Mary herself put it, "If mother had only told me I could have worked last summer and earned enough for my tuition fees." When asked why she was withdrawing now and why she was not applying for a grant-in-aid to carry her through the rest of the year, she said her mother was too proud to have her daughter "take charity." Mary was anything but grateful to her mother for her sacrifices. She resented the fact that she was not taken into her confidence. She was determined to never take another cent from her mother and to pay back all she had spent on her at college. All the hard feelings, the tragedy of an unfinished course, and the feelings of guilt could have been prevented by the simple method of honest discussion.

There are many features of family finances which children can and should become familiar with as preparation for the establishment and management of their own homes. Some of these they can learn by direct experience in managing their own income. Banking, interest, budgeting and accounts, saving for special purchases, getting value for money spent, anticipating future wants are just a few of these. They can learn other aspects by participating in family discussions and decisions about matters that involve the whole group—financing a house, fitting the purchase of a new car into the budget, money for continued education, balancing one want against others, even instalment buying and bank loans, insurance and investments.

The Family Court provides many examples of young people whose family life has come to grief because they had not learned how to manage finances. Young husbands complain bitterly that their wives squander their hard-earned money. Wives accuse their husbands of being stingy and not giving them enough to "run the house decently." Managing finances of the home is not, of course, the whole story of homemaking but it is a central and important part of it. That is why all boys and girls should have some knowledge and experience of it in their parents' home before they can be expected to set up their own.

Happy, efficient adults are those who have learned to put money and possessions in their place as aids to living and not the whole of life. They have learned to make "things" work for them rather than dominate their lives. They have learned that money is for "use" and have learned how to use it to further their own ends. Whether the amount at their disposal is great or small or just adequate, they are intelligent masters of it. Fortunate are the children who grow up in a family in which money and possessions are subordinated to human values, who live with a pattern of mutual trust, understanding, and cooperation in the management of money, and who have plenty of practice both in managing their own limited but regular income and in participating in the larger picture of family finances.

References

Foster, N.: "The Child and His Money," *Bulletin of the Institute of Child Study,* Toronto, 1953, No. 59.
Gruenberg, S. M., and Gruenberg, B. C.: *Parents, Children and Money,* Viking, New York, 1933.

chapter 13

The Family Council, Planning Together

Families, like states, have to be governed; decisions have to be made, rules formulated and enforced, work assigned, finances administered, and so on. There was a time when all this was handled by the "head of the household." But the family pattern has been changing. The dictatorship in family organization has gone out of fashion. We are moving toward a more democratic method of family government. But old patterns take time to change and the present picture seems to be partway between the traditional head-of-the-household kind of family and a new model which is more democratic in nature.

The way the family is governed depends on the relationship of the husband and wife. This in turn depends on our social concept of the place of women in the world. During the last century women have made rapid progress toward emancipation, and today the idea of equality of the sexes is pretty well accepted. Marriage is being thought of as a partnership of equals. When "obey" was dropped from most marriage rituals it indicated a recognition of our progress away from the dictatorship family. No longer are women content to be submissive to their lords and masters. All this is having a profound effect on family life.

Head of the Household

The traditional method was much easier to manage. All that was necessary was that both parties accepted the idea of a dominant head. There could be no conflict as long as both parties accepted their respective roles. Dictatorships are efficient even though unacceptable to us for other reasons. As long as the wife was ready to accept direction from the husband, allow him to make all major decisions, and "obey" his dictates then there was no reason for conflict or disagreement. But that day has gone and, within the framework of modern democratic ideas, wives can no longer be content to accept a submissive role. They want and should have a position of equality.

Partnership in Marriage

The equality relationship is much more difficult to manage. As long as the husband was accepted as a final authority and his decisions were "law," there was no room for conflict even though there might be resentment and even rebellion. In an equality relationship there is plenty of room for conflict, for it means that differences of opinion have to be taken into account and resolved, and the resolution is no longer as simple as a decision by the dominant member. An equality relationship means that both partners have an equal voice in what is to be done. For this to work, there must be a resolution of differences of opinion and values. This requires discussion and compromise.

We do not seem to be well prepared for these techniques. For one thing, we have been so well trained in wanting and trying to win. An effective equality relationship is difficult if not impossible if the partners are in competition with each other. What is needed is discussion in which the participants are not trying to dominate or win out against each other. Discussion of partners in marriage must be based on another kind of a foundation. Discussion and compromise depend on the elimination of the competitive spirit and the presence of a desire to achieve the best solution irrespective of whose idea it may be. This assumes a common purpose and mutual respect and confidence. At the present time most families show a picture which is a mixture of the authoritarian and the partnership patterns. Our progress toward effective partnership depends on the development of the ability to adopt common goals, to iron out differences through discussion, and to be satisfied with compromise in which each partner gives up a little in order to move nearer together and achieve a workable agreement which can then be put into action. The foundation for this is mutual trust. If this kind of foundation is present then it is possible to build a democratic family and a family "council" or forum for the discussion of family affairs. It is only when the parents have managed to make the discussion method work that it is possible to bring the children into the family government picture.

The Democratic Family

We should be clear, however, that a democratic family is an impossibility if we mean by that term that all members of the family have an equal part in the management of family affairs. To have an equal vote implies at least near equality in maturity of experience, skill, and knowledge. But a family is a group of individuals who are not equal in these ways. For a six-year-old to have an equal vote on matters of family finance with his parents is obviously silly. Yet there are features of the democratic idea which have real value as applied to the family. The idea of the worth of the individual is one of these: that the family or state exists to serve the person, not the person to serve the family or state. Another is that it is possible for people to work together for a common good and not just for their own selfish ends. So there is sense in talking about a democratic family, and it is possible to think in terms of a family council.

The Family Council

The main idea of a family council is to provide an opportunity for all the members of the family to talk over and work through discussion the details of the family living together as a group. It is a forum for both the communication of ideas and feelings, and the making of decisions. If the parents have had some success with this method themselves, then it will be possible to involve the children in it as they become older.

As in most family matters, there is no one single right way. There are many possibilities and each family can find the method which best suits its own situations. In doing so it should be possible to take into consideration all members of the group and their own peculiar requirements, needs, and abilities. It is possible, also, to develop methods which will provide the best learning possibilities for the children. Whatever method is adopted should take into account that the family meets many problems and needs to have an easy way of solving them. All families have problems and the main difference between adequate and inadequate families is simply that the inadequate family fails to meet and deal with the daily difficulties as they arise.

The family council has its beginnings in husband and wife discussions. This discussion, sharing ideas and searching for solutions to problems, is the core of cooperation in building a happy family life. This father-mother discussion group later grows into a family council in which the children participate. This can start in a small way as the young children are given a chance to voice their ideas and wants and have them dealt with. As the children grow older the council extends its scope to include most of the decisions and planning, and the children feel that they are very much a part of it all.

There is no one pattern for a family council. The form that it takes depends on the family circumstances. The same pattern will not be suitable for all families. Some families will find that a high degree of formality is desirable: a chairman, a secretary, and rules of procedure. Other families will prefer a more informal way of carrying on, with no set meeting time, very little formality, a minimum of rules, and much more spontaneous discussion. Whatever form it takes, the important thing is some way for the family group to get together to talk over their common problems and to plan their activities.

When the children are very young the parents decide about bedtime, mealtime, and other routines, about what the child should wear, where he plays and with whom, and all the thousand and one details of everyday living. But soon some of this responsibility must be passed to the child. The family council can be a very useful method of making this shift.

Almost anything can be the subject of discussion by the council. What is discussed will depend on the nature of the family itself. Routine activities, individual bedtimes, mealtime, the use of common family possessions, radio, television, and car, the management of the family income are but a few of the topics that can be discussed. The planning for vacations, holidays, special events, indeed anything that affects the whole family is a legitimate subject for discussion.

One of the values of family discussions is that they do provide opportunities for members of the family, both adults and children, to express their grievances, feelings of injustice, and unsatisfied wants. Sometimes there is a very real basis for the grievance and if so, it can be rectified. Sometimes the grievance is only imagined and can be removed through expression and discussion. It is rather important that the council does not become a kind of court. That is why routine decisions and planning should make up the bulk of the agenda. The function of the family council is not just to make decisions and solve problems, although such decisions and solutions are important. The main function of the council is to provide all members of the family, young and old, with opportunities to express their ideas, make suggestions, and listen to what other members of the family think. By this means, each person should get the very definite and important feeling of being a wanted, accepted, and important member of the family group.

One very useful function of the council is to plan regularly for the distribution of the work of the household. In this way, each child can be helped to accept the idea of doing his share of the necessary work of the household and not think of it as helping mother or doing some of her work for her. Responsibility is that ability to accept one's share of group activity and to carry through without the need for reminder, supervision, or checkup. This kind of responsibility is fostered by the group planning of a family council. When the chores for the coming week are decided in the family meeting, then it becomes the responsibility of each individual to carry out what was agreed upon. He knows that if the division of labor seems a bit unfair this week it can be adjusted in the discussion the following week.

No family can get along without rules and regulations. When the rules are made by one person and imposed on the rest of the group it is not easy for them to accept the rules and abide by them. But when the rules are made by all members cooperatively, then the rules are better understood and more easily accepted and lived up to. So the council can make the rules and also amend them when necessary. Sometimes rules persist long after they are needed, but when the whole group participates in making the rules then those which are unnecessary are soon disposed of.

A discussion is not easy to manage. It can so easily deteriorate into argument and be spoiled by emotional elements. The atmosphere is set by the parents, but the discussion is not dominated by them, because it is necessary for them to listen to what the children have to say. This requires some practice, as the usual procedure is for the adult to do the talking and to expect the children to listen. But an effective discussion is an exchange of ideas and opinions so that members of the group understand each other better. Family discussions usually require more than just mutual understanding; they require decisions and agreement on practical matters. Frequently this is something in which all are emotionally involved and prepared to fight for their ideas. Sometimes a discussion has to be postponed until emotions cool and a more objective attitude is possible.

The family council can be a valuable preparation for the establishment of a new family by the children when the time comes. Many young people enter marriage today with only a vague idea of what is involved in family finance, household management, and group living. But the child who has been a member of a functioning family council for a dozen years and taken part in the discussion of all the details of family life will have a very good start when he takes part in the establishment of a new family.

We have had parents say to us, "I can't talk things over with my children. I always get mad at them and say things I regret later. They are so immature that there is no common ground for understanding. And anyway it's a lot easier to decide what is best for them and just tell them what to do and see that they do it." There is no doubt that it is much easier to be a dictator than a leader. Discussion takes more skill, patience, and much practice to make it work. But there are two very good reasons for trying. One is the training it provides the children and the other is that it helps to produce that feeling of group membership which is so important in the family.

Some families have what is in effect a family council but have not named it or thought of it in such formal terms. Sometimes this informality is an indication of the mutual trust, common purposes, and attitudes of cooperation that are the foundation of effective family life. But other families have not been in the habit of discussing their common plans and aspirations. In fact, some parents believe that it is a mistake to bother children with such matters. But the children are being robbed of both the chance to feel that they are full members of the group and also the experiences that can be such valuable preparation for their own families.

What we are working for is a setting in which the ideas and opinions of all ages are respected, where it is possible to disagree and work through to an agreement, where the atmosphere is one in which everyone is trying to understand the others while expressing his own peculiar point of view. Children who grow up in such an atmosphere should be well prepared to take their places in society and participate in democratic processes of government.

References

Beasley, C.: *Democracy in the Home*, Association Press, New York, 1954.
Levy, J., and Munro, R.: *The Happy Family*, Knopf, New York, 1956.
Osborne, E.: *Democracy Begins in the Home*, Public Affairs Pamphlet No. 192, New York.

chapter 14

Fathers
and Other People
in the Family

Father's role in the modern family is not a clearly defined one. But one thing is sure: fathers are parents too. They can be left out of the picture very easily. Some fathers want to be left out, others regret the fact that they do not have more to do with their children, and still others have found it possible to be active, participating parents. There are some fathers who keep promising themselves that when their children are older they will be "pals," but the years quickly slip by and the children seem to become almost strangers to them. Then there are those fathers who see their role as the provider and the "last court of appeal in matters of discipline." They seem to be content to bring in the money to run the family and to be a kind of remote figure of authority. When difficulties arise they may step in to scold, punish, or "lay down the law." The rest of the time they stay pretty much outside the day-by-day family activities. Occasionally we find the father who has tried to take a hand in the daily routine of the family but found that he was so awkward and unskilled that he retired from the scene and has been content to leave it all to mother.

Fathers as Parents

As we have said, fathers are parents too. They have a part to play in the rearing of the children and this part should be a great deal more than just being a provider and policeman-judge. Parenthood is a partnership. It is something of an accomplishment in our culture to be a good partner. Most of us have been so well trained in

147

competition that we are not as good at cooperating as we might be. Yet, ready or not, we must be fathers and this means, among other things, being a partner with the other parent.

There is a myth in our society to the effect that being a father means being a "he-man," thoroughly masculine and never a sissy. This myth has held back many a father from the fun, thrills, and satisfactions of taking part in the intimate, everyday lives of his children. What we fail to realize, sometimes, is how strong these folkways are and how difficult it is to break with them. But there is nothing sacred or compulsory about folkways. We can chart our own course and let the neighbors raise their eyebrows if they like.

Of course, mother's part in the bringing up of children is necessarily more intimate, continuous, and detailed than father's can be. It is usually her responsibility to look after the feeding, bathing, dressing, putting to bed, and all the hundred and one daily activities that go to make up the care required by the very young child. She almost certainly becomes more emotionally involved and the baby becomes very attached to her. Even in these early months father can, and we believe should, have a part in it. He can learn some of the skills necessary to change diapers, bathe the baby, and give him his bottle. And this is not just to relieve mother but to get to know his baby better and to have the baby accustomed to its father.

When the child is a bit older father's part can become even more prominent. He can take his turn in looking after the bedtime routine and perhaps reading or telling a bedtime story. He can have a play time with the toddler. He can try to answer some of the many questions that the child asks once he has mastered language. There can, also, be special times when mother is relieved of the care of the children completely for a time and father has to struggle on alone. Being a father in the full sense is only possible if there is this kind of participation in some of the little details of the daily activities. Nowadays most fathers have a long weekend and it should be possible for them to devote some of this time to getting acquainted with their children. Young children change rapidly; new phases of development are taking place nearly every week; and father can be right in the middle of such interesting events as they occur.

The school age boy or girl both need a father's companionship. He brings a different point of view and can provide a kind of link with the world outside the home. So often we meet adolescents who have lost touch with their parents and even though they live in the same home have very little communication with each other. In nearly every case the gap between parent and child started to develop in the preadolescent period. We are not suggesting that companionship with parents should in any way exclude the desirable social contacts of the child with his own contemporaries, but there is a place also for companionship with his parents and especially father. The school age child needs the support, affection, acceptance, and dependability of an understanding, sympathetic adult. And this is what parents are for, fathers as well as mothers. Some children have really splendid people for parents but they have never discovered this because the only contact they have with these parents is when they are being directed, regulated, or punished.

As implied already, adolescents need parents, not just to provide board, lodging, and an allowance, but to give advice, moral support, and stimulation. Daughters can learn to appreciate male companionship from their relationship with father. Sons can find in their father a pattern of male maturity. Fathers usually have a wealth of experience that they can lend to their children. A word of caution may be necessary. When advice is offered we must not be surprised when the youth exercises his option to disregard it. If it is advice it can be taken or not by the recipient. If we mean something as a direction or a requirement we should not disguise it as advice.

It is a fortunate child who has two functioning parents, especially when the parents have learned to work together. Consistency in the basic requirements and restrictions is important. Otherwise it is easy for the child to learn to "play one parent against the other." Parents need to get together on the important routine things. But this does not mean that there should be uniformity in interests, tastes, preference, and the like. In fact, it is well that there should be differences so that the child sees in his home the importance and value of individuality in likes, dislikes, and ways of looking and thinking about things.

One of the most valuable ways in which father can be a useful

member of the parent team is through discussion and exchange of
experiences and observations with his partner. They can help each
other greatly. Perhaps it should go without saying that these discussions need never descend to blaming each other for mistakes in
dealing with the children. Sometimes they solve their differences
of opinion about routine requirements and techniques by finding
a compromise. Thus mother may think father is too strict and too
demanding in some regards and father may think that mother is
too meticulous about what he sees as unimportant things. Such differences can become bones of contention or they may be merely
starting points for helpful discussion. It depends on the attitudes
the parents bring to such discussions. When two people are truly
partners in the adventure of parenthood and sharing the joys and
disappointments of the process, they can usually bring helpful attitudes to the exchange and automatically exclude any attempt to
blame each other. Mother can realize that she is so closely and in-
timately related to the annoying details of the daily routine that
she is sometimes incapable of taking a very objective view of what
goes on and needs the more detached attitude that father can bring.
Father, on the other hand, can realize that he knows less about the
details of child management and care. The point is that both mother
and father have an important contribution to make but that each
is different and can be complementary to the other.

"Other People" in the Family

What is a family? Mother and father and children? Sometimes, but
frequently other people are included, such as grandparents, other
relatives, boarders or roomers, and servants. And sometimes even
pets are included in the select group we call family. In some homes
visitors, whether for a meal, a week, or longer, are treated like family members.

As we see it, the main principle is that the child's parents have
the responsibility for the care and training of the children, the
management of the home, the major decisions, and the general
atmosphere of the home. The "other" people must accept this and
fit in with it.

Grandparents

Grandparents have a place in the home which can be very valuable but which can also produce problems and difficulties. One of the sources of difficulty can be incomplete emancipation of one of the parents from parental control or domination by a grandparent. For example, the father in the home may be still dominated by his mother who as grandmother is a member of the family. This is a situation which can be a source of difficulty even when the grandmother does not live in the home, but when she does it becomes an almost impossible situation. Even worse is the wife's mother who still directs her daughter's life. These are, of course, examples of the notorious mother-in-law problem. Resentments, hurt feelings, conflict, and even family breakup can result.

There is only one solution—complete emancipation. Sometimes, unfortunately, this cannot be achieved with the grandparent in the same household. If this is so, it is certainly the part of wisdom to make some other arrangement, so that the divided authority and parental domination of wife or husband does not ruin the family.

Grandparents have much to offer both to parents and children. Their long experience and perspective, their less involved attitude, their freer time are real assets. Their presence provides a greater variety of adult companionship for the children. They are available as "sitters" to relieve the parents and allow them greater freedom to continue their interests and social activities. And they can be a source of information and moral support, standing by in emergencies and providing valuable help and advice.

Consistency in Discipline

One of the most important principles of discipline is consistency, in requirements and their enforcement. This means consistency by an individual, consistency between mother and father, and also among all the other people who participate in the control. This is not easy to achieve. There are always differences of opinion and values and different interpretations put on situations and requirements. For instance, fathers tend to be more demanding and require more prompt and immediate obedience. Mothers tend to be more patient, to overlook some things and stress others and to be more personal, depending on appeals to affection for results. Grandparents tend to be more indulgent and have the reputation of "spoiling" children.

Young children can soon learn to "play one adult against another," to get what they want by selecting the "right" adult. But all these schemes can be taken care of fairly easily if a clear-cut plan of what is to be required of the child in the essentials of the routines and how it is to be enforced is worked out and agreed on by the parents and made known to the "others." This is to make sure that no matter who is in charge the same basic requirements are made on the child and the same consequences result for his nonconformity.

This implies that whenever a person is supervising the child's activities he has full responsibility for following through with the reasonable requirements of the situation. It is undesirable to have a grandparent or sitter use the common, "I'll tell your mother when she comes home if you do not do what I say." And it defeats the purpose of an adequate scheme of discipline to have the results of nonconformity delayed.

It may seem as though we are advocating a kind of adult united front arranged against the child, a kind of battle. But that is not what we have in mind at all. Rather we view the family as a group of people living together in relative harmony, learning to meet the daily problems of living in cooperative ways. Children are members of this group, but members who are still immature and in need of guidance. What we have in mind is the kind of guidance which is most conducive to learning and progress toward maturity. When grandparents protect the child from "facing the music," it retards this development.

Visitors

Visitors can be very valuable to the child's progress. There are some features which can be avoided. One of these is putting the child on display. Most parents are naturally proud of their children and like to have other people admire them, so they are often tempted to make the young child the center of attention and have him do his tricks. A moment's thought will indicate how undesirable this is. For one thing the young child can very easily become self-conscious and shy. He can get a distorted view of his importance. He can over-step the bounds of adult propriety and precipitate a scene ending in tears, disapproval, and so on. It is much better to have young children meet the visitors for a brief period and then be allowed to retire to their own play place and go on with their own activities.

As the children get older they can take a larger part in the enter-tainment of visitors but still without being on display. If they have skills which are of interest and want to contribute to the group, they can do so within limits set by the situation and interest of the group. They can gradually develop a liking for some of their parents' friends and acquaintances but children should not be forced on the visitors, nor the visitors on the children.

The atmosphere that we strive to create is acceptance for the time being of the visitor into the family. He is virtually a temporary member of the family group and sharing the life of the home while he is there. When we think of it this way some things fall into place. The children are treated the same way as usual—and requirements are enforced without change. It must be confusing for some chil-dren to be treated one way when the family is alone and a very dif-ferent way when visitors are present. Perhaps this is a good test of parental practice. If what is done needs no change when there is an audience it may be fairly adequate. But when we think we have to act differently toward the child when others are present, it may be that appraisal and revision are called for. It cannot be anything but confusing to a child to be spoken to with honeyed tones while the visitors are there and then to be the target of a torrent of dis-approval and name-calling as soon as the door closes on the visitors.

Manners

Another aspect of this is the contrast the child may see between the courtesy shown relative strangers and the lack of it for members of the family. It is a puzzling fact that the more intimate we are with people the less we seem to think courtesy is needed. Perhaps this is because we have developed distorted ideas about courtesy and politeness and think that their function is to hide rather than express our feelings. But actually the more intimate the relationship, the less need there is to try to hide feelings; as courtesy is an expression of consideration of the other person, the place where it should be most prominent is in the home and within the family itself. Children often reflect this peculiar reversal by being on their best behavior when visiting other homes and on their worst behavior when alone with the family. Of course, the family is a place where everybody should feel at home, where they can let down, drop the mask of social veneer, and be themselves. But the point we are trying to make is that true consideration for others need not be absent when people are at home.

Baby-sitters

"Sitters" are important. When there are no regular members of the household such as grandparents or other relatives available, parents should not be completely tied down while their children are young. Because it is good for both parents and children to be away from each other some of the time, a sitter is necessary. As the sitter is a parent substitute, she should be selected with some care. It should be someone in whom the parents have confidence so that they can leave with a free mind. The sitter should be well briefed as to what to do, where things needed are to be found, and how to contact the parents in an emergency. The sitter should not be a stranger to the children. This may mean that an opportunity for them to become acquainted should be made before the "sitting" starts.

A question frequently asked by parents is whether it is better for young children to know they are going out or whether they should plan to get the children asleep and then leave. Obviously, the possibility of the children waking up and finding someone else there in place of the parents must be considered. It is better therefore that the children know that the parents are going out but that they will be back. Children get feelings of being abandoned not so much from knowing that parents are going somewhere but from discovering that they have gone and not knowing where they are or when they will return.

The sitter must not only know the routine to be followed but also be given full authority to enforce the routine requirements and know the methods used by the parents. This substitute parent must be prepared for the kinds of situations that may arise and know the methods of dealing with them. It may require considerable searching and some time to train an adequate sitter but it is well worth the effort. Even if it means going out less frequently because of the extra cost of an adequately trained person to act as a substitute parent, it is well worth it in freedom from worry and the feeling of confidence that the children are in good hands.

Pets

Many homes include in the family circle pets—dogs, cats, or other animals. Besides the pleasure (and nuisance) they provide for the adults, they can be very valuable for the children. Even at an early age children can learn to take some responsibility for their care. And they can learn a great deal about biological functions from observing animals.

The variety of family patterns is enormous. Relatives, boarders, servants, sitters, visitors, and pets may be involved. No matter what the constitution of the group, the family can be a group of people who are enjoying life together and learning from one another, meeting common problems, supporting each other in disappointments and failures, and rejoicing together over successes. Even though it is a cooperative group, the key persons are the parents, for it is they who must accept the responsibility for the management of the home and the training of the children. They can have all kinds of help and advice, but in the last analysis the major decisions must be theirs. There is nothing quite so important in life as effective personal relations, and it is a very fortunate child who is brought up in a group of people who can manage to live together smoothly and enjoy each other in the process.

References

Albrecht, R.: "The Parental Responsibilities of Grandparents," *Marriage & Family Living*, 1954, **16**, 201–204.

Bartemeier, L.: "The Contribution of the Father to the Mental Health of the Family," *American Journal of Psychiatry*, 1953, **110**, 277–280.

English, S., and Foster, C. J.: *Fathers Are Parents Too*, Putnam, New York, 1951.

────── and ──────: *A Guide to Successful Fatherhood*, Science Research Associates, Chicago, 1954.

Kellogg, R.: *Babies Need Fathers Too*, Comet Press, New York, 1954.

Neisser, W., and Neisser, E.: *Making the Grade as Dad*, Public Affairs Pamphlet No. 157, New York.

chapter 15

Special Family

Situations

No two families are alike. They differ from each other in every conceivable way. In this chapter we shall look at some examples of special family situations which can be sources of difficulty even though they need not be. For every potential difficulty or source of trouble there is a possible compensation. No matter how different a family may be from the usual pattern, it is still possible to make that family a happy effective setting in which children can grow up and achieve maturity. We shall pick out a number of kinds of special situations for discussion, and what we say about these will indicate how other situations may be met.

Broken Homes

Perhaps the most obvious special family circumstance is where one parent is missing for some reason. This is commonly called the "broken" home. The main danger here is that the children will miss and feel cheated of what other children have. They may feel insecure, different, even inadequate. They may be jealous of other children not so deprived. At the same time the remaining parent may try to make the children fill the emotional vacuum left by the absent spouse. There may be anxieties and worries which will be communicated to the children. Not only will the children experience a loss or lack of a parent but also the strains and stresses of an abnormal situation. When we are thoroughly aware of the dangers and undesirable aspects of such a situation, it is usually possible to arrange to safeguard it. The boy who has lost his father can be provided with settings in which there are good father substitutes, such as summer camps, community recreation centers, or schools where there are good men teachers. Relatives, aunts, uncles, and others can sometimes partly fill the gap.

Stepparents

Another of the so-called special situations is the introduction of a stepparent to repair the broken family. Some thought and planning are necessary to make this work. The children can be prepared for it by becoming acquainted with the new family member ahead of time so that it will not be a stranger who comes to live with them. The parent can take pains to make sure that the children do not feel left out or supplanted in affection by the new stepparent. And the stepparent should not expect to be completely accepted immediately but must be patient and wait for the children to become accustomed to the new regime. It is wise also that not too many changes in family routine, rules, and activities are introduced all at once. It sometimes happens that the time just before the stepparent arrives has been unusual or disorganized, and the children may have become accustomed to lax control and so the introduction of more adequate supervision and control needs to be gradual rather than abrupt.

Adopted Children

The home with an adopted child or children is another special case. Usually adopted children are wanted children so that the atmosphere is good to start with. The problem almost always arises as to whether the adopted child should be told that he is adopted and if so, when. The answer to this question is usually quite clear. If there is any danger (and there almost always is) that the child may learn of this, it is better that his adoptive parents tell him in a matter of fact way as soon as he is able to understand. It may be something of a shock to him and he may want to be by himself to think about it. He may even appear sulky, sullen, or absent-minded. He is digesting the news. Do not hurry him. It is best to let him work it out in his own thoughts. He can be reassured that his parents love him just as much, that he is a *real* member of the family. He is almost sure to be curious about his own parents and wonder if he will ever meet them. Let him talk about it and get it out of his system.

It sometimes happens that there are both adopted and nonadopted children in the same family. The danger here is that the parents may show favoritism, not necessarily to their own offspring. Sometimes they will be so anxious to be fair to the adopted child that they will be unfair to the others. Requirements, control, and affection can be impartial to all but it takes care and thought to do it. It is natural that there be preferences for one child but such preferences can be kept from making the parent unjust or unusual in treatment of the children.

The Only Child

Then there is the only-child family. Of course the oldest child is an only child for a time. Only children have the reputation of being spoiled and some undoubtedly are, but it is not inevitable. The danger is that parents will concentrate too much attention and emotional attachment on their only child. They may expect too much of him. He may have to carry the whole weight of their family ambitions and hopes. He may also miss the give-and-take, sharing and adjustments which are necessary between brothers and sisters. The only child can profit greatly from the nursery school and later summer camp, and possibly boarding school. If these are not possible, the parents can see that he has companions of his own age. They can also make sure that the child does not get too much adult attention and that there is not too much pressure on him to succeed.

Working Mothers

Another special family situation is the home with the mother who works at a career outside the home. In some cases, this is done for financial reasons but in many others it is because the mother wants the satisfaction of being involved in what are to her more important things than housekeeping. The danger is that the children may feel neglected even though their physical needs are taken care of. They may feel the lack of parental affection and companionship. Sometimes the mother is too tired from her work to be able to deal with the little details of home life and her relationship with the children without irritation. And frequently the little important things that make home life happy and relaxed become lost or neglected. Family living can be pushed into second place and the home becomes a kind of boardinghouse, physically comfortable but emotionally incomplete. If mother is to work, it is essential that an arrangement be made so that the younger children will not feel neglected or abandoned, so that there is daily contact with a mother who is not at that time an efficient career woman but a warm, motherly mother. With older children plans can be made so that they take part in the housework but do not have so much responsibility that they feel cheated of the normal play activities of their age. It is possible for mothers to have a career outside the home, but it is not easy to do so and still maintain the kind of home that is conducive to the healthy development of children. Homemaking is a career that takes a lot of thought, planning, and hard work. When it is combined with another career something is usually neglected, and what is left out is frequently the more important but less obvious aspects of the situation—the little daily attentions which help the child to feel secure and wanted.

The Itinerant Family

Sometimes it is necessary for the family to make frequent moves. When this is the case it is difficult for the young child to get the feeling of permanence that is so helpful for his healthy development. He is faced with the necessity of making new friends and getting established in new play groups. Frequent changes of school interrupt the continuity of his education. On the other hand, the child in the family which changes location frequently can learn to lean on the permanent features of his world, such as the family itself. He can feel that there are some dependable things such as parental affection and consistency.

The Crowded Home

Perhaps the most difficult of these special conditions to deal with adequately is the home which is crowded into insufficient space. This means no adequate play space, and not much chance for individual privacy. When the crowded living space is further complicated by nearness to the next family unit, such as is the case with flats and apartments, it becomes extremely difficult to manage. When the noise of the children's play annoys the neighbors, when the family activities are constantly restricted by the possibility of disturbing neighbors, the freedom of family life can be lost. But compensations can be found. More careful planning for the use of the space available so that every member of the family can have at least a corner of a room for his belongings, greater use of outdoor play space, and more dependence on community resources such as nursery schools for the preschool children and community centers for the older ones are some of these necessary adjustments. More careful planning of the use of radio, television, and other family possessions will be necessary, so that the family can function as a happy group and all members will have a chance to carry on their individual activities without disturbing the others too much.

Deviant Children in the Family

Some families have a child with some kind of disability which calls for special handling. The variety of disabilities is great but some of the more common ones might be mentioned. Physical defects including both motor and sensory handicaps; the relatively permanent illnesses such as rheumatic heart disease, tuberculosis, and diabetes; the child who tends to be obese; the left-handed child; the child with speech disorders; and the child who is mentally backward—these are some of the more common disabilities calling for careful handling. There are two aspects of the problem: the treatment of the child and the effect on the rest of the family.

When there is some kind of disability there have to be modifications in the routines and the requirements, but these modifications should not destroy the basic discipline. That is, the principle of consistency, or progressive shift of responsibility to the child, must be maintained as the details of the supervision are modified to fit in with the present abilities and conditions of the child. The differences between the child with the disability and the other children need not be emphasized. However, he has to learn to accept his disability and realize that there are some things he cannot do. He can be helped to find adequate substitutes. That he will envy other children is almost inevitable, but if he is helped to find satisfying activities to replace those he is denied this envy should not be too serious. There is the very real danger of the child with a weak heart or a crippled leg or a speech defect developing a feeling of great difference from others and feelings of inadequacy and insecurity which may lead him into patterns of undesirable behavior. What we have to try to help him to do is to accept his limitations without regret or without feeling too different from others. An emphasis on the fact that every individual is different and that everyone has assets and something unique to contribute should help.

Perhaps the biggest parental temptation with these children is to overprotect them. This makes them even more conscious of their disability. Even though it may be necessary to set limits to activity, the positive features can be emphasized also, the things the child *can* do. The child may need a greater amount of encouragement to try what is within his ability and a greater amount of recognition for his efforts.

Most of the situations we have mentioned and similar ones are special in the sense that they are different from the usual run of families. However none of them need spoil family life or lead to undesirable features in the developing personality of the child. They do, however, call for special attention, thought, and planning. Some of the happiest and most effective families have been those in which special circumstances have called for greater effort.

References

Cutts, N. E., and Mosely, N.: *The Only Child*, Putnam, New York, 1954.
Despert, J. L.: *Children of Divorce*, Doubleday, Garden City, N.Y., 1953.
Egleson, J., and Egleson, J. F.: *Parents without Partners: A Guide for Divorced, Widowed or Separated Parents*, Dutton, New York, 1961.
Langer, M.: *Learning to Live as a Widow*, Copp Clark, Toronto, 1957.
Neisser, E. G.: *The Eldest Child*, Harper, New York, 1957.
Stewart, M.: *Problems of Family Life*, Harper, New York, 1956.

chapter 16
Emotions,
Danger, and
New Experiences

Emotions are a part of human nature. Life would be pretty dull without them. But emotions can be masters or servants. They can be controlled and used to serve life's purposes, or they can control the person so that he is a slave to his own emotions. What happens depends on the kinds of experiences the child has and the kind of treatment he receives. There was a time when emotional education was mainly a matter of training in hiding emotions. However, as our knowledge of human nature has expanded we have come to see that there are other important considerations.

The Nature of Emotions

Basically an emotion is a response to some kind of an emergency or novel situation. For instance, when the individual perceives some situation as containing a threat to his safety or well-being he is aroused to activity. If he finds some way to deal with the threat he is not greatly disturbed. However, if he has no method of coping with it he may become more and more disturbed and we say he is afraid. If the disturbance is extreme we call it terror. Also, if he perceives a situation as being a hindrance to the satisfaction of his desires he is aroused again and the same principle holds: if he is able to solve the difficulty adequately the disturbance is not serious. If not, then the emotional disturbance is called anger, and if extreme, rage. Along with these basic emotions of fear and anger there are many varieties of emotional experiences. There is the condition

of excitement which results from situations which are at least partially unpredictable. Excitement changes to joy when it is seen
that there is no threat or thwarting or when the threat is adequately
safeguarded. Jealousy is a combination of fear and anger, fear that
the individual will lose his place in the affections of someone and
anger at the person who seems to threaten that place. Moods are
emotional conditions, often the aftereffects of emotions or the pre-
cursor of an emotion. Sentiments are more or less permanent emotional attitudes directed toward persons, objects, or institutions. We
have sentiments of love and hate, patriotism, and so on.

All behavior is emotional to a certain extent. It is when the emotional component becomes prominent that it is noticeable and when
it becomes the central feature of the behavior it is disruptive or
the main controlling feature of the person's experience and activity.

Children's Emotions

Now we shall look at some of the practical aspects of emotion in
the life of children and some of the things we need to consider in
guiding children's learning. In infancy there seem to be no specific
emotions but the infant can be emotionally disturbed. This disturbance results from intense stimuli, discomfort, or pain. The usual
response of the infant when emotionally disturbed is a kind of all-
over reaction which includes crying and what looks like struggling.
The infant who is too frequently disturbed in this way seems to develop a kind of underlying insecurity which makes him more easily
disturbed (more emotional). On the other hand the infant who has
a more serene, comfortable existence seems to build up a kind of
security which makes him less susceptible to emotional disturbance.

As the child's experience brings some meaning into his environment his emotions become more definite and specific. He now has
fears and is angry, experiences joy and disappointment, jealousy and
grief. Many of his fears are the result of ignorance. He knows enough
to recognize threats but his recognition is not always accurate. He
sees threats where none exist. Or he is afraid because he has so
little skill and cannot protect himself or cope with the situation.
These fears normally disappear as he learns more so that he under-

stands situations better and can deal with them more adequately.
At first his method of coping is to seek protection and haven with
his parents. Later he is helped to cope with the situation for himself with the parental haven as a place of retreat when it is too much
for him. Although "familiarity breeds contempt," the repetition of
a fear-provoking situation does not automatically reduce fear. It
only does so if the child's understanding is increased and he learns
what to do in order to deal with it. To tell the young child there
is nothing to fear often says to him that it is a fearful situation. It is
usually better to recognize that there is fear and to stress what to
do and what to expect.

Fears in Children

Studies of fears in young children show that strangeness, noise,
the unexpected, and objects and people associated with pain or
fear in the past are frequently fear-producing situations. This means
that the child needs to be prepared for some new and strange situations not by vague statements that there's nothing to be afraid of,
or that everything will be all right, but by specific information about
what will likely happen. Visits to the dentist, the doctor, or the hospital are examples. Trickery and deceit are never wise. The young
child who started out to visit his grandmother but ended up at the
hospital was so disturbed and afraid that an examination was impossible. The child who was prepared for what would happen—the
doctor in white, nurses in uniform, looking down his throat, the
slight pain of a needle in his arm, and so on—found it an interesting excursion and submitted willingly to all that was done to him
even though the needle did hurt a bit. The child who feels he can
trust his parents and can believe what they tell him and who is intelligently prepared for what will happen can face the dentist's chair,
the barber's scissors, the doctor's office, and even the operating room
with courage and little disturbance. But the child who cannot trust
his parents because they have misled him or tricked him into strange
and fearful situations may be so fearful that every such visit is a
major crisis.

Shyness

Shyness and self-consciousness are a mild kind of fear. Most babies, when they have learned to distinguish familiar from unfamiliar people, act suspicious, that is, shrink from the strange person. Normally, this is of short duration if the baby is given a chance to become familiar with the unfamiliar from the safe haven of his mother's arms. Soon unknown persons become interesting rather than fearful. Later the same pattern of shyness may reappear when the toddler is put on display before visitors and expected to "say hello to Mrs. Smith" or "shake hands with Mrs. Jones." Here the shyness is usually a result of not knowing what to expect. The child who is gradually accustomed to adult society and who is not put too much in the spotlight soon gets over this shyness. This is especially true when he is fortunate enough to meet adults who can be natural with children and not subject them to a barrage of silly questions.

Self-consciousness and stage fright are not problems when the child has had opportunities to participate in concerts, plays, and the like in simple situations at first, and when he is sharing something he enjoys. The child can learn to participate in situations where he shares his skills with others rather than being put on display or coaxed to show off his bag of tricks.

Disappointments

Disappointments can be very intense in childhood, but some disappointments are inevitable and the child needs help in learning how to adjust to them. There are some occasions when it seems desirable to soften the blow for the child by providing some substitute for the anticipated pleasure which is impossible, but it hinders the child's learning when this becomes routine. He can be helped to see that everything cannot happen the way he wants or expects. One aspect of this should be mentioned. Parents can be careful about making promises because it is important that such promises be kept if at all possible. It is better not to promise the child something if there is a possibility that the promise cannot be kept.

Excitement

Excitement and joy are usually prominent emotions in childhood. The child bubbles over with excitement and sleep and other routines become difficult. Exciting movies and television programs can interfere with sleep. Some planning is required to see that children are not exposed too frequently to the excitement of highly stimulating movies, the circus, and the like. But these joyful, even exciting experiences have a place and do not need to be excluded entirely.

Jealousy

Jealousy is a sign of feeling insecure in a personal relationship. The jealous child feels vaguely that a new brother or sister is taking his place in the affections of his parents. When there is favoritism or comparisons between siblings jealousy is the usual result. Jealousy of the new member of the family can be prevented by having the child help prepare for the new baby. He is kept in the picture rather than being shipped off, to return to find he has lost his crib and, he thinks, his place in the attention and affections of his parents. Rather, he can be given a place of importance in helping plan and get ready for the expected arrival. He can have a feeling of advancement rather than deprivation. Jealousy from favoritism or comparisons can be prevented by simply making sure that there is neither.

Children's Anger

Anger and temper tantrums are inevitable in young children. They are the natural result of frustration. When the young child cannot have what he wants when he wants it he may lose control, kick, scream, and even hold his breath until he is red in the face. The main thing is to see that the temper tantrum does not succeed; otherwise he will learn to use this display of anger to get his own way. But when it fails he will find other ways of adjusting to frustration. Of course, if temper tantrums are frequent this is an indication that there are too many demands and restrictions, and a modification of the routine is called for.

One sign of growing up is a continued reduction in the volume of tears and the frequency of emotional explosions. The usual picture is one of gradually increasing emotional control. If there is not this increase then a careful scrutiny of the methods being used is in order. The school age child makes a greater use of language in his emotional expression. He may shout, argue, and hurl words in place of the temper tantrum. He will put his disturbances into words rather than tears. But the general principles are the same; he needs to be helped to increase both his understanding of the situation and his skill in dealing with it, so that he can divert the energy generated by his emotional disturbances into solving his problems.

Emotional Maturity

Emotional maturity takes a long time. The adolescent will show immature patterns at times. What we are working toward and helping the child eventually achieve is a maturity in which emotions serve the individual. Poise is harnessed, used emotions, not repressed, denied emotions. Emotional control means not the removal or denial of emotions but their use as a source of energy in meeting and dealing with life's problems. The emotionally mature person is not devoid of emotions but one whose emotions work for him. Such emotional control is not to be expected in the child or even the early adolescent. It results from a long series of experiences in meeting and dealing with threatening or frustrating situations. A large part of the learning comes from the child's absorbing patterns of adjustment from his parents. He learns slowly and gradually to struggle with his problems rather than to run away or deny their existence.

Emotions are in bad repute. At least our social norms seem to indicate that a blasé, sophisticated attitude is cherished. It does not seem to be fashionable to be enthusiastic about anything. This is unfortunate and unnecessary. People are more interesting and more healthy when their emotions are not hidden but channeled.

Danger and Safety Education

Every newspaper has its quota of gruesome reports of accidents. We live in a dangerous world. Our problem as adults is to be relatively safe without too much restricting or limiting the scope of our activities. And our problem with children is to help them to learn to be intelligently cautious without becoming timid, to teach them how to cope with the many potentially dangerous situations without developing fear.

Knives cut, water drowns, fire burns, cars knock people down, poison kills, are simple facts of life which children can learn. And they can learn also that knives are very useful instruments when properly used, that swimming can be fun, that fire warms people and cooks meals, that cars are comfortable vehicles, and even that poison has its uses. The basis of effective safety education is understanding, not fear.

Safety in Early Childhood

With the infant, safety, like nearly everything else, is the responsibility of the parents. The infant must be protected; later the child will learn how to avoid danger himself.

The creeper and later the toddler must also be protected as he learns. His ignorance, curiosity, and desire to explore can get him into trouble. Some of the least serious results such as bumps on hard floors and furniture will provide some of the lessons he needs. But some results of his explorations may be serious and he should be protected from them. Hot stoves, boiling water, open fireplaces, unscreened windows, open stairs, sharp knives are some of the serious hazards from which the toddler must be shielded. It is not enough to say "No, no, mustn't touch" because this may merely sharpen his curiosity and lead him to explore when our backs are turned.

It should not be overlooked that exploration and curiosity are valuable assets which should not be curbed too much. In our anxiety for the safety of young children it is easy to go too far in protecting the child so that he is denied the chances he should have to explore his world. The child's little world can be made safe without restricting his activity too much.

The most available method of restricting the child may be the poorest one. This is verbal warning, "Don't run, you'll trip," "Don't climb, you'll fall," "Don't touch," "Be careful." Such warnings can have either one of two results, either of which is unfortunate. The child can learn to turn a deaf ear and to disregard these warnings. Or he can take them all seriously and become a timid, inhibited individual who is afraid of anything new or different.

If fear is an undesirable method of training in sensible caution and verbal warning is often unsuccessful, how can the adult handle the many situations in which the immature, exploring, and impulsive child may be in danger? The answer includes two features. First, by a sensible reduction in serious danger: by barred windows, sharp knives always out of reach, hot stoves and boiling water blocked off, poisons and medicines locked up, and so on. Second, by training the child how to cope with situations which may be fraught with danger.

Training is both general and specific. The general training comes in all kinds of situations in which skills, initiative, and ability to think and act quickly have a chance to develop. One example of this is the provision of climbing apparatus such as the jungle gym for preschool children so that, rather than prohibiting climbing, the child is provided with chances to learn how to climb safely. The principle is to provide chances to learn how to manage himself in situations which have an element of danger but which are not beyond his present abilities. Instead of removing scissors entirely from the child's experience until he is older, it is possible to provide blunt-nosed, relatively dull scissors for him to use and become proficient with.

The traffic situation is one which naturally causes many parents a great deal of worry. The number of young children who are killed or injured each year by traffic points to the seriousness of the problem. As soon as the child is ready for it, parents can provide a carefully planned program of training. This training is positive: when to cross the street rather than the merely negative, "You must never go on the road." Training is given in watching the traffic signals, where to cross the street (at the corner, not the middle of the block), how to judge when it is safe, and so on. This training can go on every time the parent takes the toddler for a walk. But one or two occasions will not be sufficient. It will take many, many repetitions before the training is complete. If it is started at about two the child should be able to manage for himself by the time he begins kindergarten.

Fire is another danger situation about which many people are worried. Fire is fascinating to most people, children and adults alike. Some children want to play with fire just as most adults run to see a building ablaze. Because of this attraction a training program which is negative is not likely to be successful. In fact, it may produce unfortunate results such as the young child who was forbidden ever to start a fire, who waited until he had the chance and then lit a bonfire under the porch. Other examples can be given of the desire to experiment with fire leading children to do so when they were unsupervised, with disastrous results. All this points to the importance of training in how and when to use fire and a development of understanding of what is involved. Some parents have been successful in showing their children how to light matches and at the same time making it clear that there is a time and place and a way of doing it.

The child takes his lead from the adult when there is a real emergency. If the parent becomes excited and disturbed the child will also. If the parent remains comparatively calm and controlled the chances are the child will follow his example. The idea that the child must be trained in instant unquestioning obedience so that when an emergency arises he will follow commands, leaves out of consideration the fact that some emergencies arise when the parents are not there. This requires that the child deal with the situation himself, which of course he will be unable to do if all his training has been to follow commands. When commands are necessary and obedience is required to ensure the safety of the child, the best guarantee is that the child has developed confidence in the adult and recognizes that the tone of voice indicates something serious.

Safety in the Older Child

As the child grows older and acquires the knowledge and skill necessary to manage the usual danger situations other problems arise. These have to do with such things as driving a car or taking part in strenuous games such as rugby and hockey. Life is never free from danger no matter how sheltered the individual may be. Parents have to be prepared to have their active children take the normal risks of athletics, play, and childhood adventure. It is more important that they learn to face situations than to be shielded from danger, even though it may mean cuts, bruises, and even broken bones.

There are some children who need special training because they seem to belong to that group of people who have been called "accident prone." They may have slower reaction time, less adequate muscular coordination or some sensory defects, or they may be more impulsive and thoughtless. But even these children can be trained to take the necessary precautions, understand the ordinary dangerous situations, and be able to cope with them.

One of the difficulties in our usual thinking about danger is that we have tended to stress the negative side and to try to devise ways to restrain children rather than the more positive approach of training in understanding and in learning how to behave. The child who is shown how to manage tools in a safe way, for instance, is much better prepared for life than the child who has been protected and forbidden ever to use anything sharp.

We cannot be completely safe as long as we are active but we can be comparatively secure. Safety depends on some factors that are beyond our control. Security is a feeling of confidence based on knowledge and skills. The child can be safe from drowning if he never goes near water, but the child can be secure when he has learned enough about the dangers and has acquired skills which allow him to feel "at home" in or on water.

When the child has had the kind of training we have sketched he grows into an adult who is neither foolhardy nor timid and who can face danger and cope with it without losing his head. He has learned to think and act quickly when necessary, and he does not take unnecessary chances; on the other hand, he does not shrink from situations merely because there is some element of danger in them.

Preparation for a New Brother or Sister

Mary had been such a charming, happy little girl, but now everything seemed to have gone wrong. She exploded in temper tantrums with very little provocation, she fought against bedtime, she wet the bed, she sometimes clung to her mother and wouldn't let her out of her sight, other times she refused to do anything she was told. How could she manage to change so quickly from a happy, contented, healthy three-year-old to a fussy, irritable, unhappy little girl? The answer was obvious when the story of the last few months was told. Mary had a new baby brother but she had not been prepared for it. In fact nearly everything that had happened contributed to Mary's unhappiness and bewilderment. For some reason Mary's parents had not told her of the coming event. Mary was sent away to stay with grandmother for some weeks. She was fond of her grandmother but after all it wasn't home and she was lonesome for mother and her little playmates. When she arrived home she found that her baby brother was in *her* crib and that she was to sleep in another room. Her mother seemed to be always busy with the new baby and even daddy did not seem to have much time to play with her. Mary was no longer the center of attention as she had been for three years. It is not surprising that Mary was an unhappy girl. When Mary's parents realized what they had done to her, they tried to make amends. It took some weeks to get back their happy little girl again. Even now there are scars, and Mary will probably never feel as warm and loving toward her little brother as she might have.

It is so easy to neglect the simple, common-sense things in dealing with children. It is so easy to think, they are just children, it doesn't matter. But of course these seemingly small things do matter; sometimes they matter a great deal. For instance, there is a world of difference to the three-year-old between being promoted to a larger bed because she is a big girl now and being deprived of the old familiar crib and pushed into a strange bed. Perhaps the easiest way to put it is that parents sometimes take too much for granted. Children need to be prepared for new experiences such as a new baby, the first visit to the dentist, barber, or nursery school.

Not many parents are as thoughtless as Mary's parents. But many do seem to fail to prepare the child for the new role of older brother or sister. The main feature of this preparation is making sure that the child does not feel left out of the important event, or deposed from his place in the affections of the parents. First and foremost, he should know what is happening and should have a part in it. The details do not matter so long as what is said and done makes the child feel that he is still as secure in the family as before. He can help in the preparations. He can be taken into the discussions about furniture, sleeping arrangements, and other necessary changes because there is to be another member of the family. He can feel some of the thrills of anticipation as the day approaches. He need not feel that he is being deserted as mother is rushed off to the hospital, for he knows what is going on. He does not feel neglected when mother has to look after the baby because he is in the picture too and not left out. He doesn't feel that there is any less love for him because the baby is loved too; rather he is in the circle of love. He is a part of it.

New Experiences

Of course the child cannot be prepared for every one of life's new experiences. But he can and should be helped to meet some of them. Sometimes the unusual or extreme case helps us to see what may happen in the more ordinary situations. I watched one day a boy about eight become completely paralyzed with terror in a department store riding on an escalator. Evidently this boy was visiting the big city and was riding this moving stairway for the first time.

I do not know what produced the fear but there was no doubt that it was a terrifying experience for him. How different it might have been if someone had prepared him for it.

What the young child needs in meeting new experiences is support and some understanding. Strange, unexpected, and sudden happenings can be fearful to the child. Preparation can reduce the elements of novelty and the unexpected and enable the child to meet and cope with the new experience. Vague, general statements such as, "There's nothing to be afraid of" are often of no help. In fact, to tell a child, "There is nothing to be afraid of" usually means to him just the reverse. Nor does preparation mean that the event or situation is given an importance it does not deserve. Simple matter-of-fact statements about what will happen are what are needed.

Visiting the Dentist

Little Tom was being taken to the dentist for the first time. At first it was a great adventure. He didn't know much about dentists. His mother had told him that they fixed teeth, but this did not mean much to him; fixing meant mending things that were broken and his teeth were not broken. Tom was puzzled and a little apprehensive, but mother seemed busy with other things and didn't even hear some of his questions. When they arrived at the dentist's office they had to wait and Tom was told to sit still and not bother mother. As the minutes passed and Tom tried hard to sit quietly he became more and more disturbed. What happened behind that door? What were those funny noises he was hearing? Then at last the door opened and a man in a white coat came out and he was saying to the other person, "That didn't hurt very much, did it?" And Tom caught a glimpse of a funny looking chair with strange instruments on a little table in front of it. He was really afraid now. Then the man in the white coat turned to Tom, and said, "Come with me, sonny, and I'll see what your teeth are like." But Tom had had all he could stand so he burst into tears and clung to his mother. It was quite a scene. Mother couldn't understand it; Tom had never behaved like this before. Why, she had told him that dentists fixed teeth and that there was nothing to be afraid of. But

Tom was not prepared for this new experience. It was too strange and different, and he did not understand it, so it was frightening.

Going to the Hospital

Susan was a timid little girl. Her mother had protected her as much as possible. Nearly every day Susan was warned about dangers and terrible things that might happen to her. So Susan was afraid of many things but mostly of things that might happen but never did. The doctor told Susan's mother that Sue would have to have her tonsils out. Mother decided that Susan would be too worried and afraid if she told her about it, so on the appointed day she got Susan all ready and told her they were going to visit grandmother. But instead of arriving at grandmother's Susan found herself being led into a big building. She was dragged into a strange room and a strange woman in white started to undress her. Susan was terrified and screamed and fought. Later when the operation was all over and Susan came to in a strange bed and saw her mother sitting there she turned her back on her mother and in a pathetic little voice she said, "I'll never believe anything you tell me again." Need we say that children should never be tricked by adults. Children must be able to trust their adults.

The best preparation for new and strange experiences is some knowledge of what is to happen and why. Of course babies and little toddlers cannot understand such explanations but they do understand the comforting presence of someone like mother. When they are a little older they can accept both the explanations and the support they can have from someone they trust who has never let them down. Such explanations must be specific and within their ability to grasp.

When Children Are Ill

Illness is an experience that comes at some time or other to all children. Colds, measles, mumps, and the like visit nearly all children. Some children have more serious and prolonged periods of illness.

And practically all children have cuts, bruises, or broken bones. So every child has to learn to accept and tolerate illness. How the child will face illness and adjust to it will depend to a large extent on the attitudes of his parents and how they behave when the child is ill.

Illness is bound to be distressing, and it is sometimes quite painful. The child's activity will be curtailed, the usual routines upset, and new demands and restrictions made of him. Being sick is no fun for the child so we must help soften the blow for him. Of course, we may spoil him a bit but when he is well again we can get back into the usual routine without too much trouble. He can and should have our sympathy, extra attention, and even special treats; and he should realize that these go with the illness and are not to be expected when he is better again. There is one danger that we must be aware of: that sickness may become so pleasant that he will learn to exaggerate illness and even play sick. But this is not too prominent a danger and not very likely to happen unless we overdo the special treatment during real sickness.

When it is a minor illness the degree of sympathy and extra treatment is also minor. The child takes his cue from the way the parents behave. When a great deal of fuss is made over a mild cold the child soon learns to put more emphasis on minor ills than he should. In fact, he can easily learn to capitalize on his illnesses. But this only happens when the child feels inadequate or insecure to start with.

When the child is ill there are various details that become necessary. The child must submit to examination, have his temperature taken, and the like. He may have to take medicine regularly, have a change in his diet, have more rest than usual, and may even be completely immobilized. These can usually be managed fairly easily if they are approached by the parents in a calm, unemotional manner without fuss or overemphasis. Of course, the reason for the various forms of treatment is explained simply to the child and his desire to get well promptly is assumed.

When the child is not too sick but still must remain in bed, special play materials can be provided for short periods, with something new and different brought out when the child becomes bored with what he has. He can be read to, have records played for him, and have someone nearby to converse with. We all like to have special treatment when we are ill and children are no different. As he gets better the special treatment is gradually withdrawn and the requirements and responsibilities are restored.

There are some parental attitudes which should be avoided if at all possible. One of these is the attitude of exaggeration, when even a minor ailment is a serious calamity and given an importance quite out of proportion to its seriousness. This has two results in the child's experience. He accepts his minor illness as serious and does not seek to get better. And he may also learn to fear illness.

Another parental attitude which is unfortunate and should be avoided is looking for blame. Parents may blame themselves or they may blame the child or someone else. Such assigning of guilt does not help and it may do harm. For instance, the child may take it seriously when mother blames herself for letting him play with other children from whom he may have caught the measles and he too blames her. Or he may learn to think of illness as being caused by many things that really have nothing to do with it at all. Sometimes parents tell the sick child that his sickness resulted from his disobedience or badness and a feeling of guilt is added to his discomfort.

Sometimes parents emphasize the nuisance to themselves of the child's being sick. They even act as though the child had got sick on purpose to keep them from going out or doing something else they wanted to do. The fact is that parents do not realize how seriously children take their only half-meant comments. Of course, we know that Johnny didn't get the mumps on purpose but in our annoyance at the disturbance to our plans we may act as though he did and Johnny takes us seriously. When children are ill they need all the sympathy, love, and understanding we can provide. Their resistance is lowered and they are very susceptible to feelings of injustice and disapproval. And the memory of these casual comments lingers.

When the child is ill parents need to walk a middle road between too much fuss and attention and too little. The child needs to feel that we are sympathetic, ready to provide extra attention and care, but we do not want him to think that his illness is some kind of major calamity. What we are helping the child to do is to meet such experiences with courage, tolerate unavoidable discomfort and pain, and cooperate in those measures designed to aid speedy recovery.

Sometimes serious and prolonged illness requires special measures such as a stay in a hospital, difficult treatment, long periods of immobility, and other conditions difficult for the child to take. These situations call for special handling. When the child must be left in a hospital, he should be made to know that he is not losing his parents, that they will be in to see him as often as circumstances permit, and that they are looking forward to the day when they will have him home again. It seems easy for some children to get the idea that they are being abandoned by their parents.

Illness inevitably requires changes in the plan of discipline. Some of the usual requirements have to be forgotten for the time being. But this does not mean that the child's every whim has to be pampered or that all controls have to be discarded. Nor does it mean that we have to resort to coaxing and bribery to get him to do what is necessary for his recovery. The same calm expectation of acceptance of those things that must be done and the following through with the important, necessary activities, is used with the sick child as well as those who are well.

References

Bernhardt, K. S.: "Children's Emotions Can Be Respectable," *Bulletin of the Institute of Child Study*, Toronto, 1959, No. 82.

————: "Feeling, Affection and Happiness in Children," *Bulletin of the Institute of Child Study*, Toronto, 1961, No. 89.

Blatz, W. E., and Millichamp, D. A.: *The Development of Emotion in the Infant*, Child Development Series, University of Toronto, Toronto, 1935, No. 4.

Bley, E. S.: *Your Child Steps Out*, Sterling, New York, 1961.

Goodenough, F. L.: *Anger in Young Children*, Institute of Child Welfare Monograph Series, University of Minnesota Press, Minneapolis, 1931, No. 9.

Hoch, P. H., and Zubin, J.: *Anxiety*, Grune and Stratton, New York, 1950.

Jersild, A. T., Markey, F. V., and Jersild, C. L.: *Children's Dreams, Fears, Wishes, Daydreams, Likes, Dislikes, Pleasant and Unpleasant Memories*,

Child Development Monograph, Society for Research in Child Development, 1933, No. 12.

—— and Holmes, F. B.: *Children's Fears,* Child Development Monograph, Society for Research in Child Development, 1935, No. 20.

—— and ——: "Methods of Overcoming Children's Fears," *Journal of Psychology,* 1935, 1, 75–104.

Redl, F., and Wineman, D.: *Children Who Hate,* Free Press, New York, 1951.

chapter 17
Myths and Facts

What should we tell our children about life and death, sickness, abnormality, religion, sex, and all the thousand and one areas that they may be curious about? Some people have a simple and easy answer—"Why, the truth, of course!" But it isn't as simple as that for a number of reasons. The child may not be capable of understanding and assimilating the "truth" about everything yet. We do not know the truth about everything. The bare, bald truth may be too frightening or gruesome. And anyway our world of ideas and thought is made up of much more than facts. There are opinions, judgments, beliefs, fiction, and myths as well as facts, and to restrict our telling to facts would be unfortunate. Among other things we want the child to learn to distinguish between facts and myths and to value both in their right places.

Children's Questions

Almost as soon as the child has acquired some language facility he asks questions. Sometimes he asks because he wants to know and sometimes his questions are used as a device to gain attention or feel important. The child's search for knowledge obviously calls for response by the adult. In the early stages, most of the questions just ask "What's that?" and the child is accumulating names for objects in his environment. Later he asks the when, how, and even why questions. His curiosity covers all kinds of things and until the difference in the response of the adults indicates to him that some topics are different from others, his questions may be about everything. He may want to know where daddy goes, where the water comes from that comes out of the tap, why it gets dark, where babies come from, and so on.

Parents will answer many of the young child's questions but may hesitate with others. As much as possible, the child when answered should be given accurate and understandable answers. At this stage the parent is the source of all knowledge and in the mind of the child knows everything. A silly, flippant remark may be taken seriously. When his questions about sex differences or where babies come from are met by a very different attitude than his other questions and he is put off or told that he should not ask such questions, his curiosity does not disappear but he classifies that topic as different or bad, and a twisted unhealthy attitude may be born. In answering the young child's questions it is very easy to try to give the child more information than he wants or can take in at the time. Usually a simple, straightforward, factual answer is all that is needed. Further questions and answers will help him to build on the small beginning.

The young child has difficulty keeping fact and fancy, memory and imagination, truth and myths, separated and distinguished. He may confuse what he sees and hears with what he imagines. He may think of stories as actual events. He needs help to develop the ability to make this important distinction. Some very simple method such as to name the nonfactual "just pretend" may help.

Sex Education

All preschool children are curious about sex differences, birth, and reproduction and practically all of them ask about such matters. The kind of answers they receive determines to a large extent the kind of attitudes they will develop. It isn't surprising that most parents are embarrassed by these questions, it is such an intimate, personal subject. On the other hand it is so terribly important that the child get started right. It is not just a matter of answering the child's questions and providing him with factual information. It involves attitudes, feelings, values, and the way he thinks about life, marriage, and the family. The young child who trusts his parents because they are dependable and who feels secure in their love has a solid foundation on which to build. He can even later assimilate the gutter talk he is sure to hear if he has this solid, healthy foundation. But no matter what the atmosphere of the home may be, he is certain to be curious and want to know. Parents must meet this curiosity somehow, and the way they do so will be important both for the present and the future.

One of the most important features is the retention of the child's confidence. We want him to think that the very best place for him to get information and to resolve his confusions and worries is in his own home. For this to happen he has to feel that no matter what he asks he will get an honest answer and that no one will blame him for being curious and expressing his curiosity. This is one of the main reasons why parents have to be careful that they do not postpone answering or give silly answers. To tell the three- or four-year-old that the doctor brings babies in his little black bag, that the stork delivers them, or that the hospital provides them may stop the questions but may also lead to loss of confidence in the parents as a good source of information. To tell the child that when he is older he will find out about such things will not reduce curiosity but will direct it to other sources of information. Over 90 per cent of good parents believe that the preschool child's questions about sex should be given straightforward, true answers but less than 30 per cent of the same parents give such answers.

When does sex education begin? One father answered this by telling of doing his duty in giving his fourteen-year-old son the "facts of life." But how this boy could live in a modern city for that long and be unaware of sex and some of its significance, he did not say. Others think of sex education as beginning with the preschool child's questions. Actually sex education begins in infancy and continues throughout the whole lifetime of the individual. Actually boy infants are treated differently from girls right from the beginning. Sex education starts with parental attitudes, the way they feel about having a boy or girl baby. Even when parents do not have a decided preference and are ready to accept the infant whether boy or girl, they still treat girls as girls and boys as boys. Little boys do not play with dolls. Girls are not noisy and do not get dirty.

The child's body is an object of interest to the young child. He discovers his fingers as pleasant objects to suck, his toes to play with, and his genitals to handle. The reaction of the parents leads him to realize that the genitals are very different and in some way disapproved of. But it is possible to allow the child to go through this stage without being made to feel that there is something "bad" about parts of his body. When he has learned to talk he will want to know the names of parts of the body and he should be given the correct names for all parts.

Learning the correct vocabulary of sex is desirable for boys and girls. It keeps sex from being furtive and shameful. Using the right words makes a lot of reteaching unnecessary later. The same is true of factual information. When the preschool child asks his inevitable questions he should get truthful answers; but he is not asking for the whole detailed story of human reproduction and needs only a little bit at a time.

One mother had determined she would do her "duty" so she kept listening for her child's questions. One day a question was asked so she cleared her throat and started to tell the story of birth which she had prepared. Before she was half through with it she had lost her audience. A few days later another question was asked. So she learned what the preschool child wants and requires is a little simple information at a time and that it takes many occasions to build anything like the complete story.

Sometimes young children show their curiosity by direct exploration rather than questions. This too is normal behavior. This is one reason why in the modern nursery school boys and girls use the same washroom. And in many homes today children see other members of the family in various stages of undress and no one is embarrassed. All of this helps the child to think of the body as a natural, ordinary part of living and not something shameful and to be hidden. The following little scene illustrates an attitude which is still too common. Two little three-year-olds were playing happily together in a back garden on a hot summer day. They became bored with play and the little girl suggested they undress and soon the boy and the girl were running around naked. The boy's mother discovered them and in a highly emotional way ordered the girl to go home and not come back and carried the boy into the house and made it clear to him by a spanking that he had done something terribly bad. Of course, children have to learn that clothes of some kind must be worn in public, but they do not need to learn at the same time that bodies are shameful and that curiosity is a sin. Modesty is sensible and privacy is desirable but social customs such as clothing and closed bathroom doors do not need to mean anything bad, disgraceful, or undesirable.

The school age child will almost inevitably hear much about sex, love, reproduction, and marital relationships. But what he hears may be very confused and distorted. He needs to have more straight-forward information from his parents. He has many gaps in his knowledge which should be filled. Sex education is a continuing process, going on all through the growing-up period. It is during this period some time or other that the child meets various kinds of distortions and abnormalities. He reads in the papers or hears dis-cussed sex deviates, homosexuals, prostitution, illegitimate children, masturbation, and so on. He needs help to understand and assimi-late these new ideas. And the best place for him to get this help is from his own parents if they are capable of talking about them without too much emotion. Failing this, it is wise for parents to see that the child can get the chance to discuss them with other com-petent adults: teachers, club leaders, or family friends.

Preparation for Puberty

As adolescence approaches the boy and girl have to be prepared for the dramatic events in their own development. Preparation means understanding. They need to know what to expect. Otherwise fears, worries, and unnecessary feelings of shame and guilt may arise. It isn't enough to give the child a few facts of life. An informal, con-tinuing discussion in the family in which no subject is taboo pro-vides a better foundation. Books and pamphlets, special lectures, and moving pictures can aid but cannot adequately substitute for a family setting in which the child can get his distortions straight-ened out and his fears and worries dissipated.

Is There a Santa Claus?

Another area that seems to give some parents concern are such legends as Santa Claus. Some people say that a legend like this has no place in modern society, that it is a form of deceit that is undesirable. They would insist that the child must be told nothing but fact, and that myths are dangerous. The Santa Claus legend is firmly embedded in our society and even though it has been grossly over-commercialized it has its place. There is a grain of an idea at the center of the legend which is valuable. It is the idea of anonymous giving. The jolly old man with the whiskers is a concrete representation of this idea of giving without thought of credit or return. No one would deny that life would be poorer if all these legends and customs were removed and life were ruled by cold logic and fact. But the problem remains for parents as to how to keep the romance and thrills of fiction without doing an injustice to fact and logic. Or to be more specific, the question is, should children be led to believe in Santa Claus?

Like all similar questions, this must be answered by each parent for himself. However, should a parent decide to have Santa Claus as a feature of the family Christmas, it will be wise to prepare for the day when the children decide there is no "real" Santa, for it is then that they can be helped to understand the meaning of the legend. They will be ready then to get the idea by playing Santa Claus to some children not so fortunate as themselves.

What about fairy stories? Should children be exposed to this land of make-believe? Again we suggest that the world of imagination is a part of life. Young children can enjoy the world of "pretend" and have no ill effects from their excursions out of reality and into fiction.

Religion

Religion is another area of parental concern. Perhaps this is the best topic in which to make the point that life cannot be understood in terms of just logic and facts. Religion takes us out of the world of proved fact into the universe of belief. And life cannot go on without belief. How do we know that there will be a tomorrow? Only on the basis of the many todays we have experienced and the faith that things will go on much as they have been. How do we know that there is anything more in life than matter and motion? Only because we believe (not know) that there is purpose and meaning to living. Why do our children trust us? Because they have learned that we are that kind of people. Society can only function when people have faith in each other and in the values and goals that are implicit in society itself.

What should we tell our children about religion? That, of course, depends on the kind of religion we ourselves have. Should we insist on their accepting and believing what we believe? That again is a matter of choice, but when all things are considered it does seem best not only to let but to expect them to develop their own life philosophy. However, we do think that children should know what we value and what the nature of our faith is and at the same time be exposed to that of other people as well.

The Sordid

There are many ugly and sordid facts which children may encounter. In most cases it isn't so much a matter of trying to protect the child from these as helping him to understand and assimilate them. He is almost certain to hear about and even see at first hand evidence of crime, mental illness, sex deviation, meanness, injustice, and so on. The child can accept the facts as they are if he is given some help. It is never wise to say to the child, "We don't talk about such things." It is usually better to talk about them and help the child get them sorted out, than to shut off any discussion and thus let fears and distortions plague the child.

Superstitions

One of the things that children need help with is to avoid superstitions and false beliefs and to develop the ability of straight, accurate thinking. There is an important place for opinion, judgment, and belief but these should be distinguished clearly from fact. Young children, because of their lack of knowledge and experience, are incapable of very clear thinking. But in the process of growing up they should be helped to avoid the common errors in thinking. This does not mean that we have to correct every error directly. But it does mean that we help the child check his thinking against facts so that he can avoid wishful thinking, exaggeration or sweeping generalizations, thinking in terms of extremes, and quoting an "authority." Perhaps the best thing for parents to do is to keep asking about many situations, "Let's see how it works."

It is a fascinating study to watch and participate in the development of children in their progress toward objective thought. At first nearly everything has a self-reference. "The sun rises so that I can go out to play." Slowly, experience helps the child to realize that he is not the center of the universe and that everything is not arranged for his personal satisfaction. Slowly, he learns about cause and effect and the hard facts of living. This is a process which takes years and which cannot be hurried although it can be helped.

What we are working toward is an individual who can think for himself, who can weigh and evaluate and choose. He will become a person who can avoid the pitfalls, who will be neither too gullible nor too skeptical. His skepticism will be intelligent in that he will want evidence for conclusions. He will have learned to be relatively objective in his appraisals and his opinions will have a better basis than just that he wants it that way.

References

FOR CHILDREN AND ADOLESCENTS

Bibby, C. L.: *How Life Is Handed On,* Nelson, New York, 1946.
Corner, G. W.: *Attaining Manhood: A Doctor Talks to Boys about Sex,* Harper, New York, 1952.
————: *Attaining Womanhood: A Doctor Talks to Girls about Sex,* Harper, New York, 1952.
De Schweinitz, K.: *Growing Up,* Macmillan, New York, 1953.
Duvall, E. G.: *Facts of Life and Love for Teenagers,* Popular, New York, 1954.
Fedder, R.: *A Girl Grows Up,* McGraw-Hill, New York, 1957.
Gruenberg, B. C., and Gruenberg, S. M.: *The Wonderful Story of You,* Doubleday, Garden City, N.Y., 1960.
Gruenberg, S. M.: *The Wonderful Story of How You Were Born,* Doubleday, Garden City, N.Y., 1952.
Landis, P.: *Your Dating Days,* McGraw-Hill, New York, 1954.

Levine, M. I., and Seligman, J. H.: *A Baby Is Born,* Simon and Schuster, New York, 1949.

────── and ──────: *The Wonder of Life,* Simon and Schuster, New York, 1952.

McKown, H. C.: *A Boy Grows Up,* McGraw-Hill, New York, 1958.

Strain, F. B.: *Love at the Threshold,* Appleton-Century-Crofts, New York, 1939.

──────: *Teen Days,* Appleton-Century-Crofts, New York, 1946.

──────: *Being Born,* Appleton-Century-Crofts, New York, 1954.

FOR PARENTS AND OTHER ADULTS

Bernhardt, K. S.: "Sex Education," *Bulletin of the Institute of Child Study,* Toronto, 1954, No. 60.

──────: "Family Life Education," *Bulletin of the Institute of Child Study,* Toronto, 1962, No. 94.

Bibby, C.: *Sex Education: A Guide for Parents, Teachers and Youth Leaders,* Macmillan, New York, 1948.

Bro, M.: *When Children Ask,* Harper, New York, 1956.

Child Study Association of America: *Facts of Life for Children,* Bobbs-Merrill, Indianapolis, 1954.

──────: *What to Tell Your Child,* Permabooks, New York, 1954.

Crow, D. L., and Crow, A.: *Sex Education for the Growing Family,* Christopher Publishing House, Boston, 1959.

Hymes, J. L., Jr.: *How to Tell Your Child about Sex,* Public Affairs Pamphlet No. 149, New York.

Levine, M. I., and Seligman, J. H.: *Helping Boys and Girls Understand Their Sex Roles,* Science Research Associates, Chicago, 1953.

Mooney, B. S.: *How Shall I Tell My Child?* Cadillac, New York, 1944.

Strain, F. B.: *New Patterns in Sex Teaching,* Appleton-Century-Crofts, New York, 1951.

Swift, E. H.: *Step by Step in Sex Education,* Macmillan, New York, 1953.

Wolf, K. M., and Auerback, A. B.: *When Children Ask about Sex,* Child Study Association of America, New York, 1953.

chapter 18
Books and Reading,
Radio, Television,
and Motion Pictures

It may not be out of place in a book on discipline to have something to say about books and reading. If for no other reason, it gives us a chance to emphasize the fact that every experience the child has leaves him a different person. This is true whether the experience is a social contact, taking part in some strenuous activity, or a vicarious experience he finds between the covers of some book. Books are a mine of knowledge, information, imagination, fancy, adventure, and beauty. They provide expanding horizons, stimulation, ideas, and escape from humdrum reality. In books the child can find heroes, patterns to copy, and values to adopt. He can find answers to his curiosities and solution of his problems. He can fly through space, explore the ocean depths, sail the seven seas, climb the high mountains, and penetrate the jungles. He can meet strange people, thrill to high adventure, or learn about man's long struggle up from savagery to civilization. Every child should be introduced to this limitless store of fact and fiction that is a part of his heritage.

Reading Readiness

The child who has enjoyed picture books and stories read to him from books and who has seen his parents and others deriving much pleasure from reading, looks forward eagerly to the time when he too can read. The printed page is almost as much a part of the modern home as the kitchen table was in the home of our grandparents. One indication of the importance placed on reading today is the large number of parents who are asking why children have to wait so long to start learning to read. They are wondering if the nursery school child or at least the kindergarten age child could not be started on this important learning.

Perhaps some educators have put too much emphasis or at least a misplaced emphasis on reading readiness. This is an important concept but it can be oversimplified. For instance, it has been said that the child is ready for learning to read when he has a mental age of six and a half and not before. But mental age is only one indication of readiness and a rather crude indicator. Some children are reading fairly efficiently before they have a mental age of six and a half, while others have passed that mental age but are still not reading. Neither mental nor chronological age tells the whole story. It is not so much the number of years the child has lived that counts so much as what has happened in those years. Mental development as measured by an intelligence test is a better predictor but it is far from perfect.

Reading readiness depends on a number of factors. The child's spoken vocabulary is one. The more words he has at his command the more ready he is to discover these words in print. The richness of his experience is another factor. When the child has seen trains, boats, cows and horses, lakes and rivers, stores, firehouses, and hundreds of other parts of his world and when he knows the words that stand for these objects and events, he has the necessary materials for reading. Speech is another of these foundation factors. Pronouncing words clearly and correctly is a great help in learning to read. "Baby talk" may be cute, but the sooner the child leaves it behind the sooner he will be ready for reading. Still another factor is a wealth of experience with different shapes, sizes, and forms. It is from this experience with various materials that he builds his ability to perceive differences in form that is necessary if he is to learn to pick out various letters easily. So even though the four- or five-year-old may not be learning to read, he can be learning much that he will need for this skill.

Introduction to Books

Long before the child reads for himself he can be introduced to books and discover the pleasures that are between their covers. As a little toddler he can have books of his own, both picture books and storybooks. The picture books he can use himself, recognizing and naming the objects, animals, and people he sees. The storybooks he can have read to him, becoming familiar with the fact that books are interesting.

Reading pictures is the first kind of primitive reading. The picture stands for the object or event and when the little child reads the picture accurately he is able to say, "That's a dog (or house or man)." Later the words will enable him to do the same thing, to know that the print stands for something. So, the two-year-old who reads the pictures has started on his career of reading. And most toddlers love to read pictures of familiar things, to recognize and name familiar things. Every child should have picture books.

Mother Goose and her nursery rhymes have an almost universal appeal to the little child. Perhaps it is the sound of the rhythms rather than their meaning that is the basis of their appeal for young children. They love hearing them over and over again, until they can repeat them from memory. If the adult shows the child where the words are in the book he begins to get the idea that the printed squiggles stand for something. He may even learn to recognize some of the squiggles. And if he is shown his own name in large print often enough he learns to recognize it and even copy it. Meanwhile he has been moving from the simple picture books and nursery rhymes to longer stories such as "Three Little Kittens," "Ask Mr. Bear," and "Angus." Stories with simple plots, much repetition, simple language, and many pictures are what he likes best. As he gets older the stories can be longer and more complicated. Preschool children like stories about familiar things, but even at this age tastes differ widely. The great variety of literature for young children provides an opportunity both to cater to the child's likes and to widen his interests. Most public libraries offer a wide selection which can be sampled in order to decide which books can be bought for the child's own library.

Choosing Books for Children

In choosing books for children there are a number of things to be considered. We should ask:

1. Is it well written? Is the language clear and are the ideas well expressed? Does it provide a good model to imitate?
2. Is it suitable for the child's level of mental development?
3. Is it likely to fit in with the child's present interests or develop those interests?
4. Is the content wholesome and worthwhile?
5. Is it well printed and bound, well illustrated and durable?
6. Is it something you want your child to treasure, read, and reread?
7. Is it something the child wants himself?

Children should own some books, ones they can treasure and read over and over again. They need a place to keep them so they can get at them whenever they want. A desire for the new and scorn of the old should not be allowed to keep each generation of children from discovering the treasures in some of the classics. Some parents have the thrilling experience of seeing their children discover books that they themselves loved as children. But age is no guarantee of either worth or appeal. The Horatio Alger books that were read by tens of thousands of boys fifty years ago have very little appeal to modern boys who may revel in science fiction and space travel.

Learning to Read

When the child is ready for the first grade he is often told, "Now, you'll learn to read." The child may expect some kind of magic and that he will be able to read in a day or so. How discouraged he must be when days, weeks, and months pass and still the printed page is a mystery to him. It is better that he realize that it will require much effort and considerable time before he will be reading. The time required will vary greatly from child to child. Some children will make rapid progress and will be well on their way to reading simple material before the year is over. Other children will take much longer. Here, as in most learning situations, comparisons are undesirable and pressure on the child hinders rather than helps progress.

While the child is learning to read it is wise to continue reading to him. Some parents feel that as long as they read for him he will not try to read for himself. But the best stimulation for learning to read is the constant reminder of what interesting things are to be found in print. There is often a fairly long period when the child is making slow progress in reading mastery. During this time his interest and enjoyment of books can be maintained by continuing to read to him.

For some time now learning to read has been the subject of much study and some controversy. The "look and see" or word recognition method has been contrasted with the "sound it out" or the phonetic method. Perhaps we shall find eventually that a combination of both phonetic and recognition methods will be best. In the meantime, tens of thousands of eager children each year master the printed page and learn to read. Teachers are trained to teach the skill and parents must be careful that they do not confuse the child too much by introducing different methods. This does not mean that they have to keep hands off entirely. They can help a great deal with their interest and encouragement. But, if they are to participate in the details of the learning, they should take their lead from the teacher and fit in with the method employed.

Reading is such a complex activity that it is not surprising that difficulties often arise. Most school systems have persons who have specialized in these reading difficulties and stand prepared to help when needed. Tests of reading readiness, of the level of reading skill, and for the diagnosis of difficulties, have been devised. Remedial reading programs are employed when necessary. Even though parents may not understand all the technical details of these activities, they should be prepared to support and cooperate in them when called on to do so. Of one thing we can be sure, and that is that not all children will make the same progress; some will be fast and others slow in developing reading skills. Parents must be prepared to accept their child's rate of progress, whatever it is, without blaming either the child or the teacher.

Good Literature and Trash

When the child has learned to read and feels comfortable with the activity he may become an avid reader. This is the time when some parents become concerned about what the child reads. They may succumb to the temptation to exhort their children to read good literature and not trash. The difficulty is that the children may be enjoying what the adults label trash and the exhortations may succeed in making the good literature forbidding. It does seem to be important that the child sample a variety of books so that he may gradually develop his own standards of taste and preference. He may concentrate on the comic book for a time, but if other types of literature are readily available he will try them too, and the chances are that he will discover much of interest and pleasure. Reading good books should not be a duty or a burden but a joy.

Kinds of Reading

There are many reasons why people read and there are several kinds of reading. We shall distinguish the two main ones, reading for information and reading for pleasure or appreciation. Of course, reading for information can be enjoyable and satisfying but the attitude of the reader is different. Reading for information implies a search for facts and ideas and a serious attempt to remember what is discovered. Reading for pleasure or appreciation has a different approach. Here we are being entertained, appreciating the author's creation. Naturally, we learn something in the process and remember some of what we have read, but this is more in the nature of a by-product rather than the main purpose. The child can be helped to adopt these differing sets of approaches to his reading.

In reading for information there are a number of suggestions that have been found to be helpful. An answer-seeking attitude is conducive to learning and remembering. With a few questions in mind as he reads, if the answers are in the material the child discovers them, and remembers them. Most of us have had the experience of reading something and remembering practically nothing of what we have read. Part of the reason has been that we have not posed any questions for the author to answer, and we have not had any very strong curiosities leading to discoveries. When we are reading for information we need to have an active, seeking attitude; we want to know, to discover facts, and to assimilate ideas. We read to discover, to find out, to acquire knowledge. We have the remembering set. We are not just being entertained; we are actively seeking knowledge. It helps a great deal if we test ourselves. When we finish a section we say to ourselves, what has the author told me? What have I learned? And we make ourselves recite or recall the main points we have learned, and we check back to see if we are right. Of course, it will take time for the young child to acquire this reading for information skill. However, his natural curiosity will give him a good start and with some help from parents and teachers he can learn this kind of efficient reading.

Reading for pleasure or to appreciate is rather different. Now facts and information and acquiring knowledge and remembering what is read is not as important as enjoying the plot of a story, the beauty of the language, and the pictures painted in words. Too much concern about remembering details, analyzing construction, or "memory work" can make it difficult for the child to enjoy or appreciate literature. Reading can be a very healthy form of relaxation, a way of using part of leisure time, and a habit which can be continued throughout life. Living can never be dull and commonplace for the individual who can explore new realms of human experience through the pages of books. Reading stimulates intellectual growth and provides material for thought as well as for the building of ideals, ambitions, and attitudes. Reading should make schoolwork more interesting and meaningful for the child. It is well that the child learn to read both for information and for appreciation.

Some parents worry when their children "always have their noses in books." Some children become so interested in books that other things get crowded out for the time being. With most children it is usually only for a time and other activities usually take their place again. It is nearly always a healthy sign; it means that the world of books has become a thrilling one to explore. Generally, the best way is just to let it run its course and hope that when the reading binge is over there will be a continuing interest in the treasures of literature. Once in a while, we meet a child who has learned to escape from the world of reality, responsibility, and problems into the pleasant universe of books. Here we tread lightly and do what we can to redirect him to everyday matters by making his world of reality more pleasant and still not spoil his pleasure in reading.

Radio, Television, and Motion Pictures

Within the lifetime of some of us the miracles of the telephone, motion pictures, talking pictures, radio, and television have transformed our world. Of course, they are not miracles for our children. They are simply a familiar part of their world. As far as they are concerned they have always been there and are as taken for granted as running water and electric lights are by their parents.

Most parents are aware that motion pictures, radio, and television have an effect on their children and some are quite concerned about it. They are a part of the multitude of influences that make up our complex modern civilization. Sometimes we wonder if the so-called civilization is ruling our lives or if it is possible to be master of these powerful influences. But that is exactly what we must do: make these modern inventions work for us rather than become their slaves.

Some parents have met the challenge by pretending that they do not exist. For instance, one parent stated that he would not allow a television receiver in his house. He said he was protecting his children from the trash that was being sent over the air. And he had turned a deaf ear and a blind eye to his children's resentment that their home was different from those of their playmates. Whether he knew it or not, his children were not protected after all, for they were viewing some of the "trash" in neighbors' homes and trying to keep this from him. Maybe the trash was not as detrimental as their feeling of guilt because they were doing something their father disapproved. To make it even worse, mother was a part of the conspiracy of deception.

Of course, these inventions are a mixed blessing, but they are very much a part of life as it is lived today in our part of the world. There is no use trying to pretend they do not exist or trying to banish them in a vain attempt to return to the "good old days."

There is little doubt that there are good movies and bad movies, good radio programs and poor ones, television programs worth viewing and others that are a waste of time. To the thoughtful parent this means choosing and selecting. And to the serious parent it means control and supervision of the child's viewing and listening activities. If this sounds like censorship, perhaps it is a form of censorship, but we hope the kind that will help the child to develop his own standards of taste. This control and supervision is not so much in terms of content as in time and amount. The greatest danger is that movies, radio, and television will monopolize the child's time and shut the door on other kinds of activities that he needs to maintain a balanced program of leisure-time pursuits.

At the present time television has taken first place over radio and movies in the leisure-time activities of children. It has decreased movie going, radio listening, and comic book and magazine reading. It also reduces the time for play, tends to disrupt routines, postpones bedtime, and dominates the child's leisure time. It has been estimated that about one out of three three-year-old children watch television. By age five, four out of five, and at age six, nine out of ten children are television viewers. Perhaps the most serious feature is the amount of time these children spend with their eyes glued to the screen. The school age child spends about two hours a day viewing programs. (See the reference for Schramm, Lyle, and Parker at the end of this chapter.)

What do children see and hear over television? Some good programs, of course, but on the whole what they see is at a fairly poor level. The school age child has for the most part turned from children's programs to westerns, adventure, crime, situation comedies, and popular music and variety shows. In spite of the fact that much has been said about the great educational value of television, for the most part children use television for entertainment and escape. One could certainly wish that it were better entertainment and that our children did not spend so much time in just being entertained.

Television viewing is not all bad. The child does learn something from it. He increases his vocabulary, for instance. And he can find, if he looks for them, programs which are informative and which increase his knowledge of the world. There is no doubt that television is a medium of information and education with a great potential, but a potential that is not being used very adequately as yet. If viewing conditions are properly controlled there is very little danger of any damage to vision.

Radio, television, and motion pictures all have two functions in our culture. They are used for entertainment and for education just as books are. But the entertainment function dominates. This has meant that when children are listening to radio or viewing television or motion pictures their attitude is one of expecting to be entertained. This approach has hindered the educational use of these media. Instead of viewing or listening in order to learn and remember, they look and listen mainly to be entertained, whether the program is informative or entertaining. Family discussions about what is seen and heard may help the child to take the learning and remembering set.

Children usually adopt the attitude toward things that they see in their parents. It is not surprising therefore that children acquire a nondiscriminating listening and viewing habit. So many adults have this rather unfortunate habit of turning on the radio with no knowledge of what programs are available. It does seem better to help the child to develop an attitude of discrimination and choice so that he is not looking at or listening to just anything that happens to be on the air at the time.

There are a number of things that parents can do about motion pictures, radio, and television. Let us summarize them.

1. The amount of time spent on these activities can be restricted. Just how much time is to be spent on movies, television, and radio is a decision that each parent should make in terms of the age of the child, the opportunities for other activities, and the indications from the child himself as to the effect the viewing has on him.

2. These activities should be regulated so that they do not interfere with the important daily routines, schoolwork, home chores, and sleep. Of course compromises will have to be made to take care of the fact that some desirable programs occur at awkward hours.

3. Some attention should be given to helping the child to adopt

different approaches to different programs. Some he will learn to think of as a chance to learn and remember, while others he will think of as entertainment.

4. Parents need to be on the alert with some children to see that they are not exposed to too much excitement or to frightening programs. This is especially true of very young children and those who are disturbed by such programs and have nightmares and other sleep disturbances.

5. Most children need help in assimilating what they see or hear. There is a very important place for family discussions of programs so that children may place what they see and hear in perspective.

6. Children can be helped to develop taste and preference and standards of what is worth spending time on and what is a clear waste of time. Of course, the child's taste will not be the same as that of his parents but the important thing is that he choose rather than be dominated by the machine. Radio, television, and movies can be very useful servants of mankind but they should never be allowed to become the masters.

References

"The Child and Books," *Bulletin of the Institute of Child Study,* Toronto, 1952, No. 55.

Clark, W. K.: "Radio Listening Habits of Children," *Journal of Social Psychology,* 1940, 11, 131–149.

Coffin, T. E.: "Television's Effect on Leisure Time Activities," *Journal of Applied Psychology,* 1948, 32, 550–558.

Frank, J.: *Comics, T.V., Radio, Movies—What Do They Offer Children?* Public Affairs Pamphlet No. 148, New York.

Gates, D.: *Helping Children Discover Books,* Better Living Booklets, Science Research Associates, Chicago.

Grossman, J., and Le Shan, E.: *How Children Play for Fun and Learning,* Better Living Booklets, Science Research Associates, Chicago.

Larrick, N.: *Parent's Guide to Children's Reading,* Pocket, New York, 1958.

Schramm, W., Lyle, J., and Parker, E. B.: *Television in the Lives of Our Children,* Stanford, Stanford, Calif., 1961.

Shayon, R. L.: *Television and Our Children,* Longmans, New York, 1951.

Witty, P., and Bricker, H.: *Your Child and Radio, T.V., Comics and Movies,* Science Research Associates, Chicago, 1952.

chapter 19
Current
Worries
of Parents

Most parents worry about their children. Some worry more than others. And nearly every parent has his own pet worry of the moment. The trouble is that most worries lead parents to do and say things that would be better left undone and unsaid. But isn't worry a part of parenthood? Don't parents *have* to worry? Well, let us see.

What do parents worry about? Almost anything: the child's health, safety, growth, learning, what he will do for a living, whether he will be liked, whether he will make a good marriage, whether he will disgrace the family, and so on. Practically all parental worries can be classified under one or other of the following: (1) success in life, vocation, income, prestige; (2) sex and marriage; (3) position and social acceptance, what people will think and say; (4) religion and morals; and (5) safety and well-being.

In the early years of the child's life his parents are mostly concerned about his health and safety. Here as in all other areas concern which leads to sensible precautions is healthy and desirable. But when the concern becomes worry which produces emotion and senseless, fussy behavior, it is definitely unhealthy and undesirable. The mother who sterilizes every plaything and who has a horror of dirt in any form is showing a pattern of behavior which cannot help but be harmful to the child's development. And when the concern makes the mother hover over the child and hang on every spoonful of food, what she is doing is making it almost certain that the child will refuse new foods. If the child is to grow and learn he cannot be protected from all germs, dirt, and the possibility of accident. Young children can be very quick to sense and take advantage of parental concerns, especially in such situations as mealtime.

What the neighbors think can be a constant source of concern and worry. It is not surprising that it is, because social approval or disapproval is one of the most powerful kinds of social control. Most of us are only vaguely aware of how much our behavior is influenced by this. And we can very easily become slaves to what the neighbors may think. For instance, several parents have told us that they want to tell their young children about "where babies come from" but hesitate to do so because their children may talk about it and the neighbors hear them. Or there are parents who can't stand being the only people on the street without a television aerial.

This concern about family position can cause parents to be so concerned about their child's progress as to push the child at school and to expect the impossible from him. It can affect nearly every aspect of development. The mother who hears that Mrs. Boastful has "trained" her six-month-old baby in toilet habits, tries to hurry the training of her child. Walking, cutting teeth, starting to school, obtaining grades, skipping grades, are just some of the features of the child's development which can be the subject of concern lest the neighbor children get ahead of our children. There would be nothing very much wrong with this if it did not have an adverse effect on the child, which it almost inevitably has. Many children are made to feel unhappy and inadequate by overambitious parents who are never content with the child's rate of progress. Worry, concern, and the consequent pressure on the child are far from being a healthy atmosphere for the child's development. When parents realize that every child has a different rate of development from every other child, they see that it is unfair to compare children and to expect their child to be always faster, brighter, more successful than other children.

This desire to win, to get ahead of other people, never to take a subordinate position unless forced to do so, is one of the prominent features of our present society. It is one aspect of the idea of competition which produces more harm than good. Most of us have been so well trained in it that we hardly realize how prominent it is. But it is not a desirable way to train children. When we make it a central value—the importance of winning—we automatically doom most people to failure and a feeling of inadequacy. Competition has a place but not so prominent a place as we have given it. Taking the neighbors into account and being aware of how they feel about us also has a place, but that place is not as the main director of our behavior.

Religion and morals also generate concern and worry in many parents. This can be seen in the amount of preaching that many parents indulge in. "You must never tell a lie for only bad people lie," may be said just a few minutes before the child is instructed to answer the door and if it is Mrs. Smith to tell her that mother is not at home. Honesty as the best policy may be preached by the parent who is heard telling how he fooled the customs man. Worry and preaching, which often go together, are a poor approach to character education. One father was heard to say in the presence of his ten-year-old son, "I'll never be able to trust him again." Of course, he really did not mean it, but his son thought he did. The boy had been caught pilfering money from his mother's purse. The father was worried for he had visions of his son starting on a criminal career which would end behind prison bars. It is natural that he should be concerned but the important thing is that his concern does not lead him to do and say things which would make matters worse. He, as a parent, has a problem which he must solve. His problem is how to help the boy to learn better ways of meeting his problems. Worry and emotional reactions are liable to result in solutions that are not very intelligent, such as the father's remark about never trusting his son again.

Perhaps parents worry more and do less of a constructive nature about morals than any other area. And perhaps the reason why they worry so much is because they do so little of a positive nature to help their children learn to develop desirable forms of behavior. It does seem easier to restrict and punish than to help the child learn by experiencing the results of his own behavior. In the example given above, for instance, it never occurred to the father to see that the boy paid back what he had taken and to go on from there to see that he had a regular allowance.

In talking with many adolescents, one finds that their most frequent complaint about their parents is lack of trust. This is another way of saying that parents of adolescents do not have enough confidence in their own training and the influence of the home. When adolescents are on their own, as they are today a lot of the time, all the parent who lacks this trust can do is to worry. Not all mothers of adolescent boys and girls lie awake until their sons and daughters return home, but many do. Not all parents demand that their teen-age children account for every minute of their time, but we know that some do. Some adolescents have told us frankly that the only way they know to do the things they want to do is to deceive their parents. Deceit and underhand practices are at least one result of the worrying parent who tries to check up closely on the child's activities. It is our observation that when young people feel that they are trusted by their parents they rarely let them down.

The most extreme parental worry is about sex. This is not sur-prising because of the central importance of sex in human life and the customary emotional coloring with which it is surrounded. We have seen parents and teachers who are usually sensible and effective in dealing with other misdemeanors in children become violently disturbed by some sexual immaturity. The most severe punishments are usually reserved for this area. Masturbation is still treated by some adults as a serious crime even though it is well known that practically all boys experiment with it at some time or other. When sex is treated as a normal, healthy part of human life and given its proper place in home conversation so that the child develops healthy understanding and attitudes, none of the so-called sex problems are serious or the source of parental worry. It is when sex is thought of as shameful and nasty and no effort is made to help the child un-derstand what it is all about that the parents must worry.

Parental worry about the success of their children, their occupa-tional choices, and their advancement, like other worries can be unfortunate. Such worry usually leads the parent to try to steer the child into a particular vocation. It makes it difficult for the parent to keep from trying to manage their children's lives.

It is easy to say to parents, "You should not worry." But what should be more valuable is to say that worrying does not help; it usually hinders. In place of worry, parents can take thought about what can be done. Finally, parents must have faith in the home atmosphere, in their methods, and in the children themselves. We get from children (and adults too) about what we expect. When we expect a battle we usually have it. When we expect difficulties we almost always find them. And when we expect (and are reasonable in our expectations) that the child will behave in an appropriate way, he usually does.

Reference

Bernhardt, K. S.: "Help for Confused Parents," *Canadian Welfare,* 1957, 32, No. 7, 334–340.

chapter 20
Common
Behavior
Problems

It would be surprising if a boy or girl grew up without presenting the challenge of behavior problems in some form or other. Such problems can be nearly anything, for behavior is problem behavior depending on how adults look at it. It might be difficulties with the daily routines of eating, sleeping, elimination, and the like. Or it might be temper tantrums or fears. It could be resistance to direction, rebellion, or negativism. Or it might be some form of dishonesty, stealing, lying, or cheating. It could be shyness or social withdrawal. On the other hand it could be fighting, quarreling, or overaggression. Or it might be any one of dozens of other forms of deviant behavior. One thing is sure, there will be some kind of problem behavior, or what adults call problem behavior, for children are children and thus immature.

Incidental or Chronic?

There is one judgment about problem behavior that is useful. This is whether it is incidental or chronic. If it is incidental it is merely a phase of growing up, an incident in a complex picture of development, something that happens once or twice and then is left behind as the child learns better. If it is chronic, a pattern of adjustment that is more or less permanent, it is a recurring behavior. The incidental problem behavior can be safely handled in the routine manner, with the logical consequence applied, and, if the child is old enough, with explanations and discussions. However, the chronic problem behavior needs more study and a program of reeducation that may take months or even years.

Problem Behavior as Badness

The usual approach to most problem behavior is to think of the child as bad, naughty, and sinful. Therefore he should be punished, made to feel sorry for what he has done, repent, reform, and promise never to do it again. The main trouble with this simple formula is that it rarely gets to the root of the difficulty and leaves untouched its cause. It may succeed in removing the undesirable behavior, but just as likely another form of problem behavior will take its place. It may be that conviction of sin, repentance, resolving to do better and thus reform may be effective with adults, but it seems out of place with children. Their problem behavior is not the expression of badness; it is often the expression of ignorance and immaturity. There are no bad children, merely misguided or ignorant ones.

Recognizing Symptoms

The first step is to recognize that the problem behavior, whatever it may be, is a symptom or indication that something is going wrong in development. Of course, we have to be careful that we view the behavior in its developmental context. A temper tantrum at three is not the same as one at twelve. Telling untruths at six may be very different from lying at fifteen. A one-year-old baby sucking his thumb may mean something very different from thumb sucking by a seven-year-old. Some forms of behavior may be quite normal and to be expected at one age but clearly an indication of maladjustment at another age. So in assessing behavior as a problem we do so in terms of the state of development of the child and the time and opportunities he has had for learning.

Problem Behavior Is Learned

Problem behavior is best thought of as the result of learning gone astray or failure to learn. The child has so much to learn that it is not surprising that there are failures and difficulties. All children are faced with at least six areas of adjustment. The child must learn to adjust to people, both adults and children, so as to enjoy their companionship and be able to participate in group activities. He must learn to adjust to the world of things, to master materials and his physical environment sufficiently. He must also learn to adjust to the world of ideas, to acquire enough facts and knowledge as to feel at home in this area. He must learn to be able to weigh, choose, and discriminate among the opinions, beliefs, superstitions, and judgments that he encounters. He has the difficult job of adjusting to a complex set of customs, folkways, laws, taboos, and mores that make up the organized society into which he was born. And there is the difficult adjustment to the emotions that tend to disturb him. This is not merely trying to deny or repress these strong forces but using them in coping with a world in which there are threats and frustrations. And finally there is the problem of growing up, of building self-confidence, of achieving independence and self-regulation. So what we mean by maladjustment is simply that one or more of these general problems of adjustment have been more than the child can handle.

Motives

Related to this learning approach to problem behavior is thinking in terms of motivation. Nothing happens by chance, everything has a cause, or more accurately, a set of causes. Although we may make many mistakes, it can be very helpful to ask ourselves, What want or desire is the child trying to satisfy by his undesirable behavior? How can he be helped to satisfy this want in a more socially acceptable manner? Or sometimes, how can he be helped to modify his wants so that he will want the right things? For instance, why does Harry distort the truth? Is he afraid? Of what? Is he seeking attention? If so, why does he feel the need of more attention? This search for the reasons for problem behavior, if successful, will provide the clues for dealing with it.

Causes in the Environment

The causes of problem behavior will be found to be not so much in the child as in the child's environment. This will be true of most cases. This means that the cure will also come from a modification of this environment. In some cases this will be a change in the scheme of discipline. And in others it will mean that the child will have to be made to feel that he is wanted, accepted, and loved. In still other cases it may mean a program of reeducation of the child which will enable him to learn how to find his satisfactions in better ways.

Of course, some so-called behavior problems are such because the parents think of them that way even though the child may be merely acting in a way natural for his age. There is a tendency today for many parents to look for problems and expect difficulties. This is often accompanied by a reliance on other people and a desire for experts to solve their problems for them. They expect some kind of magic cure or simple formula to set matters right. But there are no magic cures or simple formulas. When things are not going well in development they can only be set right by insight and understanding, a rearrangement of environment and methods of handling the child. Of course, parents can get help in achieving this understanding and planning of better regimes, but in the last analysis they have to do the job for themselves.

Problems rarely occur in isolation; they usually involve not one area but a number. The individual is a unity and when things go wrong in one sphere it usually affects other areas as well. In the preschool child difficulties show up in the routines of eating, sleeping, and elimination. In the school age period the most sensitive indicator of difficulties is school achievement; in adolescence it is in social relationships that difficulties may be indicated. However, behavior difficulties may become evident in almost any area. The important point to keep in mind is that the cause of the difficulty may not be in the area where the undesirable behavior is seen; for instance, the child who is insecure and unhappy at school may take it out on mother by being negative and uncooperative.

Symptoms

Almost anything can be a symptom of maladjustment. It is necessary to recognize the symptoms, but it is rarely wise to treat the symptoms themselves. It is wise to get behind the symptom to the causes. There are many symptoms or indicators of developmental difficulties. Some of the more common are social withdrawal, as when the child shuns contact and would sooner be by himself all the time; overaggressive behavior including constant bragging, bullying, fighting, and the like; excessive emotional disturbances such as frequent fears, much crying, and violent temper tantrums; retreat from reality in daydreaming, avoiding situations, and frequent forgetting; various kinds of dishonesty, lying, stealing, and cheating; underachievement in schoolwork and other activities; persisting negativism, nonconformity to necessary rules, and evasion of responsibility; and speech difficulties, enuresis, and nervous tics.

The Search for Causes

When we recognize any such symptom, the next step is to search for the reason for it. There is very little use in asking the child; the chances are he does not know himself. However, careful observation over a period of time usually provides clues as to what is at the root of the difficulty. If the parent feels that the difficulty is serious it is wise to seek help. Sometimes some physical condition needs attention. The child's doctor can advise. Sometimes the main cause is in the school situation: the child may have missed some basic knowledge or skill which makes failure inevitable, or he may be bored because of too little challenge for him, or he may be faced with work beyond his ability. The teacher and school authorities may be of help here. And again the cause may be in the home situation: the methods of discipline used, the presence of favoritism, un-realistic expectations, too much pressure, or a lack of full acceptance of the child by his parents. It helps if the parent can adopt a kind of outside observer attitude and try to view the home situation in as objective a manner as possible.

Common Mistakes

There are some common mistakes and situations which frequently lead to difficulties. These conditions do not always produce behavior difficulties immediately, but they cannot help but have some adverse effect on the child's development and thus should be avoided if at all possible.

1. Insufficient parental affection and acceptance. Of course most parents love their children but some parents manage to hide this affection so completely that the children cannot feel that they are loved and wanted. Sometimes children are aggravating; parents show their annoyance and the children may feel insecure.

2. Misused or smothering parental affection. This is when the parents try to control the child by the use of affection and appear to withdraw their love when the child misbehaves. Sometimes parental affection leads to overdependence when the parents really hinder the child's growing up.

3. Parental anxiety. This may show up in an overemphasis of the child's mistakes, or in too much pressure for perfection.

4. Parental compensations. This is when the parent tries to have the child achieve what they themselves could not achieve. It is a form of unrealistic parental expectation that makes the child feel inadequate or insecure because he is unable ever to satisfy the parent.

5. Unreasonable demands and requirements. This is sometimes thought of as a too strict discipline. It is not so much the strictness as the multiplicity of requirements that produces a feeling in the child of being hemmed in and of having every detail of his life managed for him. When the child cannot meet all that is required of him he has a feeling of failure and inadequacy.

6. Inconsistency. This leads to confusion and uncertainty. The

child cannot learn what to expect or what is required of him. He may develop a feeling of injustice when he is punished one time for something that had just been laughed at previously.

7. Irregularity, disorder, and confusion. Children can only feel secure if there are sufficient order and regularity in their world that they can feel that there are some things on which they can depend. Not only is learning hindered but a child's basic security is threatened by confusion and disorder.

8. The use of various undesirable techniques. Perhaps it will be enough merely to name some of these: the use of fear, nagging, fault-finding, disparagement, threats, coaxing, extracting promises, bribery, physical punishments, and any other technique that is unfair or violates the essential dignity of the child.

9. Highly emotionally charged situations. When the child is living in a home where there are constant tensions, conflict, strains, and worries it is very difficult for him to have that feeling of stability that is conducive to healthy development.

One of the features of the make-up of most children is their resiliency. They usually do recover fairly promptly from disturbing situations. However, there is a limit to this and when the unhealthy situation is constant or recurs frequently it is more than most children can tolerate and they begin to show the effects in their behavior. It is the persisting, constant, or frequently happening conditions in the home that have their effects on the child. Of course, a single experience, if it is vivid enough or frightening, can also leave its scars and start trends in development. But, in general, if the background picture is sound, occasional mistakes by the parents are not too serious.

Dealing with Problems

Perhaps we can illustrate how most behavior problems in children can be handled by taking a few examples. Billie is three years old. His mother reports that nearly every meal is a difficult time. He dawdles. He plays with his food. He refuses to eat some foods. When Billie's mother was asked to keep records of what happened at every meal and a record of all eating both at meals and between meals, she called to say that her problem was solved and she would not need to come for help any more about this. What had happened was very simple; when she kept records she had seen just what was actually happening, and what needed to be done to clear up the difficulty. She discovered that Billie was eating more between meals than at mealtime. She also saw that she was coaxing Billie, even bribing him, and that he was enjoying the attention he was getting this way. She decided that there should be more attention to the planning of when Billie should have food and that the eating between meals must be controlled. She also saw that Billie was getting too much attention and too much pressure at mealtimes, that he needed to be left alone to eat without coaxing or bribing. She instituted a time limit for a meal, placed the food before Billie, and left him alone for this time. Then when the time was up she removed the food. Of course, Billie made a big fuss about it but Billie did not get his own way and after a few days was eating what he was given and even seemed to enjoy it. Not all behavior problems are as easy to handle as this one, however.

Little Johnny came home from a birthday party with his pockets full of miniature doll furniture. When asked about it, Johnny said he was told he could have it. It was obvious that Johnny had taken what did not belong to him and had distorted the truth. Johnny was a thief and a liar—the usual adult labels for such behavior. But Johnny had understanding parents. They did not accuse him of stealing and lying. They simply explained to him that the miniature furniture belonged to someone else and that he would have to return it. So he was taken back and his father explained to his hostess that Johnny had made a mistake and wanted to return the toys he had taken home with him. A brief discussion when they returned home helped little Johnny to know more about the meaning of ownership of property and the necessity of respecting the property rights of others. Of course, Johnny was not a thief and a liar, but just an immature little boy who needed (and received) help in understanding about ownership.

Mary was a charming little girl eight years old. But Mary seemed to like being by herself. She did not seem to have any friends. Whenever she had the choice, she played alone. At recess she was off in a corner alone. After school she walked home alone and seemed to be content to engage in solitary activities. Whenever suggestions were made about playing with other children, Mary would always have some excuse. Naturally, Mary's parents were worried and wondered what they should do. Mary was an only child and Mary was fast becoming a "withdrawn" child. Why? This was not easy to answer and it took some time for Mary's parents to discover what was wrong and what they could do to help. Mary just did not have the skills the other children possessed. She was always left out of games because she did not know how to play. She felt slighted and inadequate, and to protect herself from these feelings of inadequacy she had avoided social contacts as much as possible. Mary's parents were able to help her to acquire the skills she needed, then gradually arranged to have other children visit. They made sure that Mary had a good time and before very long they were glad to observe Mary seeking other children's company. Soon Mary was a happy outgoing child who enjoyed companionship although she was still capable of entertaining herself.

Harry was a seven-year-old who always seemed to have a chip on his shoulder. He was mixed up in quarrels and fights almost daily. He resented any adult interference or direction. Although he was above average in intelligence his schoolwork was poor. He rarely finished a piece of work assigned to him. The other children avoided him and he was hardly ever chosen for games. Harry was becoming more and more sullen and unhappy. The more his parents tried to help him the more negative he became. His teacher tried to "shame" him into working harder. He was kept in after school but this seemed to make him worse. He was fast coming to hate school, and one day he played truant. It was not easy to find out what was Harry's difficulty. He lived in a comfortable home, he had plenty of play materials and equipment, and he had a regular allowance. But it was clear that Harry felt inferior and seemed to be trying to prove to himself that he was important, but the more he tried the more trouble he got into. Harry was small for his age and his muscular coordination was poor. He loved sports but try as he might he was never successful; there was always someone who could do better. Somewhere he had got the idea that academic success was "sissy" stuff and not for big tough boys so he worked hard resisting work at school. Harry needed help, for he was well on the way to becoming an unhappy, maladjusted boy who was beginning to think all adults were his enemies and even the children were against him. It took nearly a year to bring Harry back to normal. His parents needed quite a bit of help to see that their methods of handling Harry were just aggravating the situation. Harry was helped to feel important in acceptable ways. His teacher was drawn into the picture and helped to see that she would get further with him if she discarded her negative approach and found ways to give him some praise and approval if he showed any signs of effort or responsibility. Harry's father took him to some hockey games, fixed up a small gym in the basement, and taught him some skills. Mother stopped telling him that he was small because he did not eat enough of some kinds of food. Harry was drawn into family discussions and activities. His mother arranged a surprise birthday party. And slowly Harry began to enjoy life, his home, and even school.

Similar stories could be told about Betty who bit her nails, Susan who refused to do anything her mother asked her, and Anne who sulked. In all three cases there was a reason for the problem behavior. It wasn't easy to find the reason but when the cause was ferreted out it was pretty clear what had to be done. A direct attack on the nail biting, resistance, and sulking had not helped at all; in fact in every case it just made matters worse. To help children it is necessary to know the reason for the undesirable behavior.

For some reason or other, boys present far more behavior problems than do girls. This is partly because we expect girls to be more conforming and they tend to live up to our expectations. But one could guess also that girls on the whole receive more gentle treatment than boys do and thus develop less resentment and hostility. And perhaps we have left the supervision, teaching, and direction of children pretty much in feminine hands and boys may resent this and rebel against it.

In thinking about problem behavior in children, we are tempted to put the emphasis on the kind of behavior that is annoying, disturbing, or disruptive. And high on the list of misdemeanors are such things as sex, disobedience, and "talking back." But some of the less disturbing kinds of behavior may be even more serious. The "good" child who never gives any trouble may be seriously withdrawn, overtimid, or acutely unhappy. So we should make sure that we are alert to signs of developmental difficulty even though the child may not break rules, resist direction, or make a nuisance of himself.

References

Bakwin, H., and Bakwin, R. M.: *Clinical Management of Behavior Disorders,* Saunders, Philadelphia, 1960.
Bernhardt, K. S.: "How to Behave When Children Misbehave," *National Parent-Teacher,* 1960, **54,** No. 5, 10–12.
English, O. S., and Finch, S. M.: *Emotional Problems of Growing Up,* Science Research Associates, Chicago, 1951.
Griffiths, W.: *Behavior Difficulties of Children as Perceived and Judged by Parents, Teachers and Children Themselves,* University of Minnesota Press, Minneapolis, 1952.
Gruenberg, S. M.: *Parents' Guide to Everyday Problems of Boys and Girls,* Random House, New York, 1958.
Leonard, C. W.: *Why Children Misbehave,* Science Research Associates, Chicago, 1952.
MacFarlane, J., Allen, L., and Honzik, M. P.: *A Developmental Study of the Behavior Problems of Children between Twenty-one Months and Fourteen Years,* University of California Press, Berkeley, Calif., 1954.
Odenwald, M. D.: *Your Child's World,* Random House, New York, 1959.

chapter 21
Emancipation from
Parental Control

Both the goal and the method of discipline are contained in the idea of emancipation. If it were possible to sum up in a few brief words what parents are trying to do with and for their children, it would be: to produce men and women who can run their own lives. Emancipation is that slow process which moves the child from dependency to independence. The reason we choose one technique rather than another is because it contributes more than the other to this progress toward maturity. One indication of success of parents is that the children need their direction, control, and supervision less and less each year as they get nearer to adulthood. And it is an indication of how effective parenthood is if parents are able to let the child be more and more on his own.

Emancipation Starts in Infancy

Emancipation is not a sudden launching of an individual on the world after long years of protection and detailed direction. It is a process that starts in infancy and slowly and gradually brings about a change in the status of the child and his relationship with his parents. Emancipation is not a sudden giving up of power over the child, "You are old enough now, and you are on your own." Nor is it a thrusting of the child out of the nest to fend for himself, ill-prepared though he may be. Nor is it something that happens automatically with the passage of time, "You are now eighteen (or twenty-one) so you must now fend for yourself. I have fed you, clothed you, protected you, supervised you all these years, now you must do it all for yourself." Rather we think of emancipation as a slow, gradual, cumulative process by means of which the child learns, step by step, to manage his own activities and his own affairs. And as he learns he takes over or is given the responsibility for his own actions. As he learns he becomes less and less dependent on others to decide things for him, to do things for him, and to control and direct his activities.

Emancipation is a very complex business, but it becomes more complicated and difficult when the two parental functions of affection and discipline are not kept separate. Because of the child's immaturity he needs discipline and because he is a human being he must have affection to become a happy healthy person. If emancipation is to progress effectively, affection should continue undiminished while control gradually decreases, so affection should not be used as a method of discipline. To make parental love a reward for good behavior is not only to cheapen love but to hinder the emancipation of the child.

Everything the child learns makes him less dependent on others. When the preschool child learns to hold a cup and to move it to his mouth, when he can handle a spoon, when he can walk by himself, he is on the road to emancipation. That is why it is important that help be gradually withdrawn when the child shows signs of readiness to do anything for himself. When he can feed himself, then that responsibility becomes his and his parents leave it to him. It is not only the skill that is so important but also the feeling that the child can have of being less dependent and more of an individual in his own right.

Just as the acquisition of self-help skills brings about the beginnings of emancipation so does the development of knowledge and thought. When the child begins to learn the connection between what he does and the results of it, he can begin to anticipate or foresee the effects of his behavior and to control his own activity in terms of these consequences. He learns that stoves are hot or the floor hard, by touching stoves and falling on floors. His learning about the physical world is usually faster than that about his social environment since there is more consistency with things than with people. When he becomes aware that water is always wet he can begin to control his behavior with this item of knowledge as a guide. Later he will learn that if he behaves in a certain way, other children will not play with him. He can learn that temper tantrums will not get him what he wants, that if he doesn't eat he will be hungry, and that if he spends all his weekly allowance on Monday he will not have any for the rest of the week.

Human beings have two very important assets: to be able to remember and thus profit from experience and to anticipate the future and thus shape their activities in terms of their possible consequences. It is these two assets that we make use of when we try to guide the child's development toward maturity. We help him to profit from his experiences and to practice controlling his behavior by the anticipation of the results of that behavior. So progress toward maturity is indicated by an increase in self-controlled behavior rather than impulsive activity. As modern living is so complex and there is so much to learn, it takes years for the child to be able to choose wisely and be responsible for his own affairs. While he is learning, parents have to take the responsibility for him and direct what he does. But as the child can only learn to be responsible and self-regulating by practice, the parents must provide the practice in areas that are not too serious or dangerous and gradually increase these areas until the individual is finally managing all his own affairs.

Besides the two assets of memory and foresight, the child will gradually acquire another aid as to how to behave. This consists of his beginning awareness of standards, values, and what is acceptable and what is not. He is developing what is usually called a conscience, which really means that he is becoming aware of what other people approve of and disapprove of. He now feels guilty when he behaves in a way he knows is not acceptable to his parents or teacher or other people in his life. He is building his inner controls. He is becoming socialized. And all of this is essential to his progress in emancipation.

In infancy the parent provides for the child, protects him, meets his needs, and shields him from the consequences of his behavior. The parent is dependable and consistent in the treatment of the child and thus trust in the parent is born. Because his needs are met regularly and because he has developed very few wants as yet, he has no real problems and need not make any decisions. This is complete immature dependence. The infant's awareness of what happens to him and his feelings of comfort and satisfaction when his needs are satisfied are a part of his accumulating experience. He develops both trust and affection for his mother who is associated with these pleasant experiences. As his muscles and nerves grow and develop, he begins to acquire control of some of his activities and with every increase in skill and accumulation of experience he moves away from his dependence. So even in infancy a start is being made on the long journey from helplessness and dependence to independence and self-discipline.

Emancipation in the Preschool Period

During the preschool period there are great strides forward in emancipation. This is a period of an enormous amount of learning. The child quite literally changes from a helpless, dependent individual to one who can manage many of his own daily activities for himself. He has acquired control of his large muscles; he is now able to feed himself, wash his hands, and manipulate materials, and he is acquiring mastery of language and elimination. Every skill he develops makes him that much less dependent on others and makes him capable of more responsibility. His play is becoming more ordered and meaningful and through play more skills are developed. Along with the skills there is an increase in self-reliance and initiative. He soon learns to accept the necessity for routine requirements and because he has trust and confidence in his parents he accepts their direction and guidance. Each new situation is a challenge to be met and some insecurity is inevitable. This insecurity is met sometimes by retreat to dependence on the parents and sometimes by attack on the problem and learning. It is wise to help him meet these new situations without too frequent retreat to the previous dependency. However, he still needs the comfort and security of being dependent, for this is the safe base from which he can launch out to meet the challenge of new learning. When he gets too much help and protection he does not have enough chance to learn. On the other hand if there are too many of these new experiences without some support, he can develop fear and timidity. So it is a matter of finding a wise balance between letting him struggle and providing help over the difficult places.

In this preschool period the child is becoming more and more aware of himself as a person. He is building self-esteem, self-confidence, and a feeling of personal worth. But this is a delicate growth and easily blighted. The parent can help the child's progress by consistent, just, understanding treatment, by an attitude of acceptance of the child, and by clear indications of interest in him and affection for him. In other words, he is helped to feel that he is respected as a person, that his parents have confidence in him. This is the kind of environment in which he can learn, explore, try out his developing abilities, and yet have a dependable background of adult support and even an emotional haven to run to when things get too difficult for him. Now that he has language there is much that can be explained to him, and with his accumulating fund of experience there is much that he can now understand. He is well started along the way toward maturity but there is still a long road ahead.

The School Age Child

When the child starts to school, emancipation enters a new phase. He now has to accept a new authority. He will discover that the school and the classroom have their own rules and requirements. There will be new demands made of him and new responsibilities added. He will be less supervised than previously in his free time and will have more opportunities to control his own behavior. He will be less protected from his mistakes. But the parental functions of discipline and affection are still needed. He will meet the new challenges better if he knows that he has the understanding of those he trusts, his parents. Neither his skill nor experience is yet great enough for him to manage everything. There must still be external control and a planned discipline. This will provide the chances to learn as it sets the boundaries, limits, and guidelines and at the same time protects him from those situations that are still beyond his competence.

The school age child should be advancing from the stage of accepting rules and requirements because adults formulate them to the stage of understanding the necessity and reasonableness of these rules. If there is the trust we mentioned previously, the child will be ready to accept what the adult says about the value and necessity of certain patterns of behavior. Of course, the rules and requirements have to be clearly necessary and reasonable or else the understanding is impossible. Then parents and teachers have to fall back on "You do it because I say so and I'm your parent (or teacher) and you have to do what I say, or else. . . ." One of the best ways to help this developing understanding is to have the child participate in the making of the rules.

The Final Stage in Adolescence

Adolescence is the time when the parents have their last chance to complete the process of emancipation. Just how the adolescent will meet and deal with the serious problems he faces will depend on a number of things. Chief among these are: how far he has already progressed in self-reliance and responsibility, the nature of his relationship with his parents, and the kind of help and support he gets now. Some of his most difficult problems are his adjustments to the opposite sex, the selection of a career and the preparation for it, and the formulation of a philosophy of life. All these are related to his emancipation from parental control.

As one views the development of children, it becomes clear that it is a unity in which one stage builds on all that has gone before. So how the adolescent will deal with his present problems and react to his present situations will depend to a considerable degree on his previous experiences. For instance, the boy or girl who has had plenty of opportunities to associate with members of the opposite sex before adolescence will probably have an easier time managing this kind of relationship now when both biology and custom push him into it. And the child who has had reason to trust and appreciate his parents in the years of childhood will be the adolescent who will still retain a healthy respect and affection for his parents. All progress in development and learning builds on what has gone before. Final emancipation is neither difficult nor painful for child or parent if it has been a continuous cumulative process.

Having said all this, we should emphasize that what has gone before does not make it impossible to compensate for things that have been missed or neglected earlier. The adolescent who has been brought up by an extreme authoritarian method can still learn how to be a self-disciplined, responsible, independent adult. It may, however, be more difficult, for he has to telescope years of practice into a shorter time.

In later adolescence direct parental control has given place to moral support, sympathetic understanding, adult example and advice. Emancipation is nearly complete even though the adolescent may be still economically dependent, as he is still completing his education or training for his career. In some ways this may be a difficult stage. As one parent expressed it, "As long as I pay the bills he has to do what I tell him." An adolescent said almost the same thing when he insisted, "I can't accept my parents' support without taking their advice too." But it should not be necessary or desirable that submission to control be the price paid for economic support. It is not fair for the parent to say to his grown son, "I'll support you for a medical course but I will not for a course in fine arts." Perhaps the core of the matter is the amount of faith or lack of it by the parents in their own children.

What adolescents frequently miss is this confidence, faith, and trust in them by their parents. That must be the meaning of the attempt on the part of some parents to continue to try to control their adolescents long after the time when the adolescents should be able to make their own decisions and manage their own affairs. It may be that this lack of trust in the adolescent is in effect lack of confidence in their methods of bringing him up. Whatever it means, it can have unfortunate results. In some cases adolescents learn ways of deceit—doing things behind their parents' backs in order to get the feeling of being grown up and in charge of their own lives. But they are rarely happy about doing it and frequently feel guilty for what they are doing. Adolescents still need parents, but not to direct their activities, rather to provide the moral support and backing as well as the chance for discussion and advice. It does seem too bad that some adolescents have to rebel in order to have their chance to practice self-discipline, but rebellion may be better than continued dependence.

There are several things that can be done by the adolescent to aid his own emancipation. He can get away from home for periods when he will be on his own to a large extent. Going away to work for the summer, or to take a course, or to summer camp or a trip, may give him a chance to try himself out and to demonstrate to himself as well as others that he can be responsible and self-regulating. He can accept responsibilities at home or school or community. He can show that he has mature interests as well as standards of behavior that are no longer childish. The more the adolescent demonstrates his maturity the more his parents will be ready to reduce their direction and control.

Parents of adolescents can aid the emancipation in a number of ways. They can indicate their readiness to allow the youth to grow up. They can show their faith and trust in him. They can make opportunities for the adolescent to take responsibility. They can treat him as a near-adult, talk to him as an equal, and in many subtle ways make it clear that they are aware of his changing status.

Completed emancipation means emergence from parental supervision. In place of dependence on the parents there is a reliance on inner resources and inner controls. There is a changed attitude toward the parents; instead of thinking of the parents as disciplinarians, providers, and protectors, parents are now thought of as friends, guides, and advisors. This emancipation goes hand in hand with the achievement of an all-round maturity including physical, emotional, social, intellectual, and psychosexual maturity. A brief word about each of these may help us to see what is involved.

Attaining Maturity

Physical maturity is fairly automatic. It is taken care of by the growth process and very little can be done about it except to understand it and plan for it. Physical maturity should bring with it a respect for the body and sensible care of it. It should include also a realization of the great individual differences in size and body shape and an acceptance of one's own physical characteristics whatever they may be. A mature attitude puts the body in its place as something to take care of and not something to be flaunted or to be ashamed of.

Emotional maturity means mastery of the emotions, rather than being at their mercy. This requires adequate emotional expression, but expression that is socially approved. It means the elimination of childish fears and insecurities. It includes an ability to deal with worries and vague fears. It means being able to face unpleasant situations without either escape or rationalization. It means that the individual has learned how to have his emotions work for him instead of being a disruptive influence on his experience and activity.

Social maturity means skills and knowledge which enable the individual to get along effectively with other people. It includes the ability to cooperate in group activities, attitudes of intelligent tolerance of individual differences, social sensitivity and freedom from extreme dependence on other people. The socially mature individual enjoys social contacts, participates and contributes to group activities, and can manage his interpersonal relations with a minimum of conflict and difficulty. The socially mature person is a good friend, an interesting person, a successful husband or wife, an adequate parent, an enjoyable neighbor, and a good citizen.

Intellectual maturity is a complex of many aspects, some of the more important of which can be mentioned briefly. The mature person has acquired a considerable store of usable knowledge and is still learning. He has a strong desire to know and understand. He shows a healthy skepticism and does not accept things at their face value but looks for evidence and evaluates, weighs, and thinks for himself. He has a set of values and standards, which although not fixed and unchangeable, are an adequate guide to his behavior. He has developed a philosophy of life which lends meaning and significance to life.

Psychosexual maturity is built on adequate knowledge about sex and its place in human life. It includes healthy attitudes of acceptance of sex as important but not the center of living. The adult accepts the sensible taboos of his society and conforms with the essential social regulations of this basic appetite.

The mature person has not stopped learning and developing. He has merely reached a minimum level of this development for independent living. His maturity is far from static; it is a base for further progress. Even though he shows no further physical growth, he continues to widen his knowledge and deepen his wisdom, and there is continued character and personality growth. His accumulating experience makes him a more adequate person. So this minimum maturity is the goal of child training and education. Emancipation from parental control achieved in easy stages is an integral part of discipline and an important part of the attainment of the maturity of adulthood.

The greatest need of society today is for more and more genuine adults. The passage of time and the addition of birthdays is no guarantee that maturity will be achieved. There is nothing more dangerous than child minds, emotions, and attitudes in adult bodies. Most of the woes of mankind can be traced to immature adults. An effective plan of discipline built around the central idea of a progressive shift of control from without to within, from parental control to self-discipline is our only hope for a better world. The parent's reward is the deep satisfaction of seeing the helpless immature infant grow into a mature, independent effective adult, and life does not hold any greater or more lasting satisfaction.

part iii
A Developmental
View of
Discipline

In this final section, discipline is viewed
in a developmental context. Children can
be understood better when they are seen as
changing and developing. Perhaps the
most frequent comment made about any
child is, "My, how you have grown."

One can only understand a preschool child
if the months of infancy are known and
also what the child is becoming. In other
words, we know the child more completely
the more we take into account the road
he has already covered and what lies ahead.

What is true of understanding is also true
of a plan of discipline. Discipline derives
its meaning mainly from development.
The nature of the discipline depends on
the present stage of development of the
child and the kind of person we hope he
will become.

Some repetition is inevitable when the same set of ideas is used in formulating a general scheme of discipline, in a description of life situations, and now in various developmental stages. Perhaps the repetition may serve to emphasize some of the basic principles which we consider to be very important.

chapter 22

The Family Atmosphere, Feelings, and Values

I suppose we'll never stop wondering at the miracle of birth and development. Miracles are the unexplained in experience. Certainly, there is much that we can only marvel at and wonder about in human life: the miracle of conception, growth, learning, memory, feeling, and experience itself. Someday we may know some of the reasons for what happens. At present, we can only describe and marvel at what we describe. And even our descriptions are partial and incomplete. However, centuries of human experience and decades of careful research have given us some of the answers and we still seek many more. With this experience and the accumulated facts of our still very meager research, we can use that other miracle, our intelligence, and formulate our plans and select the guiding values, and thus do our best to give direction to the next generation. But, as we do so, we realize fully that what we do will only be a part, but a very important part, of all the influences that will determine the result.

The Family

Better ways may be discovered someday of managing the miracles of birth, childhood and growing up, but the best way we know at present is in the family. Of course, every family is unique, for a family is the merging of two personalities in the common purpose of wresting satisfactions from life and living and seeking realizations of vaguely perceived yearnings. From this merging of personalities, new life is formed, but the new lives are in part continuities of the old, for in this miracle something of the parent's make-up is continued in the children. But the children are themselves unique, never a mere copy of their parents and ancestors. So the family is a unity of diversities. It is a dynamic, ever-changing pattern of interrelated but different personalities. Each contributes and each receives from this interchange, and life for all can be serene and at the same time challenging: a struggle, but also fulfilling.

The family both reflects and incorporates the values, attitudes, and purposes of the individuals who are its members and the culture in which it functions. When two individuals found a family, they, of course, bring with them all the ideas and ideals, wishes and ambitions, worries and fears, attitudes and opinions, prejudices and biases, knowledge and wisdom they have accumulated up to that time. And these two individuals never think and feel exactly the same about anything. Part of their job in founding a family is to achieve some kind of agreement about the details of their life together. There are sure to be differences in both what they want and the methods of achieving their desires. These differences have to be resolved, or they remain to plague them and make family life both difficult and uncomfortable. How the differences are resolved will determine to a large extent the nature of the family structure.

The Head-of-the-household Family

Traditionally, marriage has been an unequal relationship. There has been a head of the household. In some cultures this head has been the husband, in others the wife. Even in those cultures where it has been traditional for the man to be the "boss," there have been many reversals where the wife has been the dominant figure. And sometimes, when there has been an outward acceptance of the husband as the head of the family, the influence of the wife has been persistent and effective so that she has been the power behind the throne. In the last few decades, the norm of family organization has been a partnership of equals. But such an equality partnership is not easy to administer and we have been having difficulty with it. True, we have abolished to a large extent the promise to obey which was a part of the older tradition, but we retain many of the features of the earlier dictatorship without being thoroughly aware of it.

A dictatorship arrangement in the family is the most efficient form when it is thoroughly accepted by the members. There is no room for disagreement, as it is the total responsibility of the head to make all the decisions and take all the responsibility. What he decides to do is "law" and all the other member of the pair has to do is accept and follow the decisions. However, this type of social relationship is now virtually impossible as the context of the family is such that individuals are not capable of being submissive, obedient followers of a dictator, no matter how benevolent he may be. Since women have largely won the battle for equality, they are not prepared to surrender their status and be submissive, obedient wives. They want, and should have, a partnership in the family scene.

Marriage as a Partnership

An equality partnership is not easy to manage. As differences are inevitable and must be resolved, there must be some method of doing so. As most people in our culture have been well trained in the importance of winning, the most common pattern at present is to try to resolve differences either by the old technique of one individual dominating the other and forcing obedience and acceptance or the newer family technique of a battle in which the more persistent or the louder wins, and the basic idea of equality is lost. The winning the argument picture has some unfortunate by-products. The winner may feel guilty, for after all the loser is a loved one. The loser cannot help but feel resentment.

There is a technique which we have difficulty in using but which is essential for an equality partnership, namely, the discussion method culminating in a compromise. The reason so many of us have difficulty with this method is that our training has been more in competition than in cooperation so that the discussion degenerates into an argument. A discussion is where the participants have common goals and purposes and strive to find the best solution. The best solution, all things considered, is rarely one person's ideas but rather the combined wisdom of all. In terms of the husband and wife situation, this best solution is usually a compromise in which each has given up something and accepted something of the other's. The ingredients, then, of an effective equality partnership are well-defined goals and purposes, free discussion in which no one is trying to win, and compromise solutions in which the desires, ideas, and wisdom of both are represented.

Perhaps we can digress for a moment here to comment on the training of the next generation of marriage partners. One part of this training can be sufficient experience with the "democratic" techniques of adopting common group goals, submerging individual desires in such group purposes, taking part in free discussion, and arriving at a consensus. A start can be made with this even in the preschool years when children can learn to share possessions, take turns, and respect the desires of others. Later in the school age period the discussion method can be developed. There can be a reduction of the amount of competition in routine activities. In fact, it would be well if we eliminated the deliberate use of comparisons, the pitting of one child against another, and the use of the competitive incentive except in games.

The Democratic Family

Now to return to the family organization. Let us suppose that in the months or years provided before the children start to arrive, the husband and wife have been successful in working out a partnership which works fairly smoothly. They can manage their differences in an adult manner. They are ready for parenthood. The family now becomes complex. It now includes another person, but this person cannot be immediately assimilated into the partnership, as this infant is completely helpless, ignorant, and dependent. All decisions have to be made for him, all responsibility for his care, protection, and well-being must be taken for him. But every day brings changes, for this new member of the family starts learning and moving on his long journey towards maturity. We want him to become fully self-disciplined, a mature adult who can manage his own life and fit in with a very complex society and contribute something to this society. The main problem is how to guide this journey so that the end result is what we hope. This does not mean that we will try to determine all the details of his life, what he will work at, whom he will marry, and the like, but rather that we will provide the kinds of experiences that will result in a person who is truly adult and healthy. This means mainly that he will gradually learn to accept the consequences of his own decisions and behavior.

Because this child is born into a family in which already there has been established mutual respect and effective partnership, his individuality will be respected. His affairs will be managed so as to provide him with the necessary ingredients of healthy growth and development. He will not be either indulged or dominated. He will feel the warmth and affection of parents who want him. He will begin to learn that life makes demands on him and that when he shapes his own behavior to fit these demands he gets more out of life. In other words, because there is a consistent core of treatment from his parents, he learns how to behave appropriately. But all this takes time—years in fact.

There are many reasons why the family is the ideal setting for the growing child. One of these is a feeling of dependence and trust in others which is the foundation from which the child develops his necessary feeling of self-confidence as well as his attitude toward others. In other words, it does seem necessary for the child to have a solid feeling of trust and confidence in his parents (or some parent substitute) before he can develop healthy social attitudes and adjustments. This means that the infant and young child must have a person who is dependable, which means two things, namely, consistency and affection.

The Good Home

One of our pressing problems is to know what constitutes a good home. Many details of current research have a bearing on this question, but no final answers are available. However, some things are becoming increasingly clear. One of these is that material possessions play only a small part in determining the goodness of a home for for children. Rather the relationships between the members of the home and the values translated into everyday behavior in it provide the core of a good home. Obviously, a child may have everything that money can buy and still be both an unhappy child and one who is acquiring distorted and twisted attitudes and emotional patterns. On the other hand, the child who lives in an atmosphere of affection, trust, and sensible adherence to reasonable standards and values has a very good chance of developing into the kind of person all of us like to have around.

"Like father, like son" is taken by many to mean that biological heredity is the main factor determining what the child will become. However, it is also possible to interpret this old saying to mean that the child absorbs from his parents the patterns of behavior, attitudes, and values which they exemplify. But this process of absorption depends on the nature of the relationship between parent and child. For instance, the father who depends on severe punishment to keep his son "in line" may find that the boy gradually moves out of his orbit of influence. Or the influence works in an opposite way; the boy tries to be as little like the father as possible.

The Changing Family

Many things have been happening to the family in the last few decades. Family life is never static; it shows the effect of the context in which it exists. The complexity of community life, with its insistent demands on the members of the family, has meant among other things that the family group is together less. The invasion of the outside world into the living room through radio, television, newspaper, phone, and magazine has brought other changes. The state, school, and church have taken over various functions which used to be taken care of by the family. On the other hand, the family roots in the community are more shallow; the family tends to move around more than it used to. But the fundamental functions of the family remain the same: the provision of settings for birth and rearing of children and a comfortable, sheltered haven in which the individual may feel at home and where he may be himself.

It is rather trite to say that the nature of the home in which the child grows up is the most important factor determining the kind of person he becomes. But trite or not, it needs to be said and even stressed. Many parents today are seeking simple answers to their problems of child rearing, are looking for simple formulas, and are asking about the surface features of their parental responsibilities. These simple answers and rules of child rearing are not nearly so important in the long run as the nature of the home atmosphere and the character of the relationships that exist among the members of the family. It is not so much what the parent does as *how* he does it that determines its results. We are sometimes tempted even to think that the "good" parent could spank the children without serious effects. However, more sober thought reminds us that the good parent would never resort to the level of the personal indignity involved in corporal punishment.

Democratic Values

The techniques used in the family to enforce the necessary rules of communal living and at the same time help the child to become a thoroughly socialized individual are always a reflection of the underlying values and goals of the parents. When, for example, individual human personality is considered more valuable than family pride and prestige, what is done and how is considerably different from what it would be if these values were reversed. All people have scales of value; the point is what priorities are assigned to the values. We are living in a culture in which we are striving toward a democratic ideal. This is very vague and relatively meaningless until we endow it with more concrete practical meaning.

In a democratic society nothing is more important than individual personality. This, of course, cannot mean that the individual can do as he likes. But it does mean that our values, which determine how we live and act, put persons ahead of institutions. The child, for instance, is more important than the home, the school, the church, or the state. Translated still further into practical terms, it means that the child is more important than housekeeping, furniture, or bank account. And it means that the individual is never used as an instrument to further other goals.

Feelings and Atmosphere

Sometimes we wonder if words are capable of conveying full meanings. So much of family life is compounded of feelings and meanings, and feelings often escape when we try to capture them and wrap them up in cold print. The so-called intangibles of experiences are at the core of effective family living. To say that much of what parents do is determined by how they feel about things, and that the effect of what they do is carried more in the feelings of the child, is easily understood, and accepted by most people. But to go on from there, to try to offer suggestions as to how to manage these feelings, is more difficult. Perhaps the best we can do is to remind parents that everything they do, say, and think is influenced by how they feel. And to point out at the same time that much of the behavior of children is directed by their feelings.

We often pride ourselves on being rational beings. By this, we seem to mean that our behavior is controlled and directed by reason. But this is only a part of the truth. We are also feeling beings. That is, what we do and say is at least partly determined by our feelings. We say we like certain kinds of food, music, books, people; this is the same as saying that we have a pleasant feeling toward these things, and our pleasant feeling leads us to take an attitude of approach toward them. We then tend to seek out, prolong, repeat our experiences with these liked objects. The same kind of thing is true in a reverse direction about the things we dislike. This means that we have an unpleasant feeling about these things and tend to withdraw from them.

It is our impression that these feelings are not taken into account by parents as extensively as they deserve. Take some simple and not too extreme examples. Here is a child who develops a dislike for a particular item of food because of a scene when it was first introduced, when his mother with all good intentions tried to force him to eat it. The unpleasant feeling generated at that time may take years for the child to get over. His food dislike (or attitude of withdrawal) may persist for the rest of his life but may also be changed with subsequent experience. Or take the child whose parents decided she should take music lessons and imposed the lessons and the accompanying practice on the girl, and helped her develop a dislike and withdrawal attitude toward music which may persist for years. Such examples could be multiplied many times over. The simple point is that it is not only possible but desirable to take into account the feeling factor in experience. Educators have been talking about education through interest for years. What they mean is simply that a child learns more, and more easily, if he is interested (has pleasant feelings and the attitude of approach) in the subject matter or activity.

Feelings are also central to social relations. Children can learn to dislike even their own parents and teachers, and they do so more frequently than we like to admit. When such feelings have been built up the parent or teacher is much less effective. This is another very good reason why the adult working with the child needs to be very careful that his methods are such that they appear to the child as being thoroughly reasonable. Although we do not want to train the child to do things just to please mother or teacher, we do realize that, when there is a pleasant relationship between the adult and the child, the leadership and guidance of that adult is much more successful.

So, when we talk about a good home we are dealing with a compound of attitudes, feelings, and values, the intangibles which add up to what we can call the atmosphere or climate of a home. It is this atmosphere which provides the setting for healthy growth and development or hinders it, depending on the nature of the atmosphere built by the parents. And it is this atmosphere which some people remember in their homes and look back on with feelings of thankfulness. This atmosphere is the creation of serious, hard-working parents, who incidentally enjoy the fruits of their own labors. It is this atmosphere that determines the effectiveness of the training techniques used. In other words, any technique used by parents with children depends for its success not so much on the technique itself as the atmosphere in which it is used.

It would be nice to be able to provide a simple formula for a good home and an effective child-rearing program. We are confident that the suggestions offered and implied in this book can be of help. But we are sure also that no mechanical application of rules will ever take the place of an atmosphere of trust and affection, or ever overcome the absence of such an atmosphere. However, we should not like to give the impression that all that is needed is that parents love their children and let "nature take its course." What we are trying to say is that the intelligent application of principles of child training requires attention to the feeling, attitude, and value aspects of the situation as well as the more purely rational features.

References

Baldwin, A. L.: "Socialization and the Parent-Child Relationship," *Child Development,* 1948, **19**, 127–136.

Bernhardt, K. S.: "Parental Dilemmas, Choices and Values," *Bulletin of the Institute of Child Study,* Toronto, 1958, No. 76.

Brim, O. S., Jr.: "The Parent-Child Relation as a Social System: I. Parent and Child Roles," *Child Development,* 1957, **28**, 344–360.

Burchinal, L. G.: "Parents' Attitudes and Adjustment of Children," *Journal of Genetic Psychology,* 1958, **92**, 67–79.

———, Hawkes, G. R., and Gardner, B.: "The Relationship between Parental Acceptance and Adjustment in Children," *Child Development,* 1957, **28**, 65–77.

Davis, W. A., and Havighurst, R. J.: *Father of the Man,* Houghton Mifflin, Boston, 1947.

Fromm, E.: *The Sane Society,* Rinehart, New York, 1955.

Glidewell, J. C. (ed.): *Parental Attitudes and Child Behavior,* Charles C. Thomas, Springfield, Ill., 1961.

Goodman, D.: *A Parent's Guide to the Emotional Needs of Children,* Hawthorn, Englewood Cliffs, N.J., 1959.

Symonds, P. M.: *The Dynamics of Parent-Child Relationships,* Teachers College, New York, 1949.

Wolf, A. W. M., and Dawson, M. C.: *What Makes a Good Home?* Child Study Association of America, New York.

chapter 23
From Birth to Maturity—
Discipline in the
Developmental Stages

Progressive change is the universal characteristic of childhood. Even though there is much that cannot be predicted about children, it is always safe to count on them growing, developing, and changing from month to month. No scheme of discipline could be adequate without taking into account this constant, progressive change. Obviously, what we do and how we do it will depend on where the child is in the developmental picture.

A Developmental Approach

A developmental approach enables us to avoid some mistakes we might otherwise make. We might, for instance, fail to realize that the child is ready for new experiences and learning opportunities and thus hinder his development by failing to allow him to try out new activities. On the other hand, we might expect faster progress than he is capable of and thus exert pressures and attempt to force development prematurely. The child's own developmental timetable is much more meaningful than any set of developmental behavior norms, to which very few individual children exactly conform. It is much better for the adult to be alert to the signs of readiness and plan in terms of the child's own developmental tempo.

Experience is cumulative. Every experience builds on what has gone before. What happens in infancy helps to determine what will take place in later years. And school age experiences and learnings will influence adolescent development. What is called transfer of training in learning experiments is a universal characteristic of all learning. For all learning, indeed all experience, builds on the past and all experience contributes to the continuous stream of change that is called learning.

Every experience leaves the child a slightly different person. This is why all training and discipline must have a future reference. It is never good enough merely to take care of the present situation and just see that things go well now; we must at the same time think in terms of the possible effect of the experience on the child's changing personality. It would be much easier, in some ways, if all we had to think about was getting the child to do something or keeping him from doing something at present. Then it would not matter how we got the child to eat, go to bed, dress, or do his homework. Any method that was successful in achieving the present purpose would be a good method. However, we are dealing with a child who remembers, who inevitably carries with him the effects of all his experiences. Discipline, then, has this double function of taking care of the present situation and at the same time preparing for the future.

This double aspect of discipline has another important feature. In administering requirements, and supervising children the adult must always take into account the simple fact that the methods used are going to affect the adult-child relationship. If the child is tricked into a way of behaving, if unreasonable or unjust demands have been made, if there has been inconsistent treatment, or if a promise has not been fulfilled, the child remembers and the adult-child relationship suffers.

Stages of Development

For purposes of description and classification we divide the developmental picture into stages or periods even though we realize that development is continuous. The boundaries between these stages are useful landmarks but are still artificial. These boundaries will be less artificial if we use developmental events, which by their very nature pose new problems of adjustment and call for new learning. This provides us with developmental periods which have their own char-

From Birth to Maturity 243

acteristic kinds of learning. A brief picture of such developmental periods will serve as an introduction to the following sections in which we shall try to offer practical suggestions for discipline in each of the successive periods.

The developmental events we will use to divide the picture into stages will not occur at the same time from child to child. It is the event, not the age of the child that is most important. For example, two children on their thirteenth birthdays may be very different developmentally, one an adolescent with all that this implies and the other still a preadolescent. The periods we will use are: (1) the prenatal period, (2) infancy, (3) the preschool period, (4) the school age period, (5) adolescence, and (6) young adulthood. Thus, in turn, we have the hidden prenatal period; the period of the helpless, ignorant, very immature infant; then the awkward toddler becoming an active preschooler; then the squirming, restless, noisy and often untidy school age child; the self-conscious, insecure youth growing into a full-grown promising adolescent; and finally, a mature young adult. Each period has its own characteristic problems and its own best techniques for discipline. The best guarantee of successful adjustment in any stage of development is that the child has been able to adjust satisfactorily in all previous stages of development.

Prenatal Period

The prenatal period is that important developmental time between conception and birth. In the short nine months that this requires, the individual grows from a single fertilized cell into a complex organism that is distinctly human in appearance. During this time he is protected almost completely from any external influence. He is provided with an environment which is highly constant and in which the intrinsic characteristics of the cell determine the growth and development. However, the isolation from external influences is only partial, for the organism is dependent on the external environment for the materials for growth. So there can be prenatal influences. These can include anything that is carried in the blood stream. If the nutrition of the mother is deficient in any essential elements needed for growth, then development is hindered. If there are foreign elements in the blood stream that can be transferred to the little organism, they too can have their effect on development. Glandular products associated with emotional disturbances can be carried in the blood and conceivably affect the unborn child. So, the condition of the mother, whether she is well, adequately nourished, and emotionally stable, will help to determine development in this hidden period. To some extent, then, the child's parents have started their part in shaping his development even before he is born.

Infancy

The period of infancy begins with the event of birth. Birth can be a serious shock to the immature organism or it can be a smooth developmental event, depending on the nature of the birth itself. Due to circumstances over which we have little or no control, in a small percentage of cases birth inflicts irreparable damage. Fortunately, such cases are rare and should become even more infrequent as our knowledge and skills increase. Whatever the nature of the birth, it is the signal for a whole series of radical changes in physiological functioning. The child changes from a parasite, dependent on its host for ready-made materials for growth and life, to an individual who must now extract from its environment what is needed. Breathing, taking in food, digestion, and elimination are now the infant's responsibility. Before birth it lived in a constant, protected environment; now it is in a changing environment and its sense organs which are beginning to function are being bombarded by a continuous flow of stimuli. The organism somehow stores up the effects of these stimuli and we have the beginning of awareness and memory. Gradually these effects become accumulated and related so that meanings emerge and learning, which will continue as long as the individual lives, has begun.

The most prominent characteristic of infancy is immaturity and helplessness. There are very few ready-made patterns of behavior, just a few simple reflexes such as sucking, swallowing, and the like. The infant must have care and protection that is constant, consistent, and adequate. As the process of maturation continues and is now complicated by the effect of external stimuli producing learning, development moves in a continuous sequence of activities. Slowly coordinated patterns of activity emerge, partly through the unfolding process called maturation and partly through exercise and learning. In this stream of development, it is possible to pick out specific features, as for example that series of events culminating in "learning to walk." Although not every child follows exactly the same sequence at the same rate, there is a fairly common pattern including such events as holding up the head, rolling over, sitting up, hitching, creeping, standing with support, standing alone, pulling up to a stand, taking a few steps with support, and finally walking. The child may achieve the ability to walk any time from his ninth to his eighteenth month (very infrequently even before or after these times). When the infant has acquired the ability to stand, balance himself, and move from place to place on his own two feet, we consider that he has moved into another stage of development. For our purposes we will think of him now as a preschool child, rather than an infant.

Preschool Period

This period of the preschool child is one in which the process of learning becomes more and more prominent. Maturation, that part of development which is largely determined by intrinsic organic factors, is still active but now appears to take second place to that other aspect of development we call learning which is directed mainly by influences coming from the external environment. The preschool period is a time of extensive learning. Many sensory-motor skills are developed. The child acquires eye-hand coordinations and many big-muscle skills such as running, jumping, and climbing. He is gradually gaining mastery of his environment by developing control of his bodily equipment. But even more important is the development of that uniquely human accomplishment, language. The preschool child normally acquires the foundations of his speech and thus sets the stage for many other activities which are usually classified as social. Because he is by nature disturbable, he will show frequent outbursts of emotional behavior. During the preschool period he will also show evidences of a beginning control of these disturbances. During the few short years of the preschool period the child will learn a great deal, possibly more than at any other comparable period in his life. He will, if his environment is right, lay the foundation for most of the activities and personality characteristics which he will possess during his whole lifetime.

This preschool period is a busy, exciting, and challenging time for the child's parents. So much is happening developmentally. Nearly every week brings some new development: new skills, new words, greater capabilities, and with these new problems. There is so much happening that the parent is sometimes hard pressed to keep up with events. Problems emerge almost daily that require thought and attention. Eating, sleeping, washing, dressing, and toilet habits seem to fill the day with active, exploring play activities filling in the minutes between these routine activities. The child seems to be into everything and demanding constant supervision to see that he avoids the danger pitfalls that his activity produces.

We have come to think of this preschool period as being extremely important in the total picture of development. This is partly because, it comes so early in the life of the child and because what happens now will condition later happenings. It is also the beginning of control and direction by the adult. Many directions of development get started during this period, and these directional tendencies will continue and cumulate and persist. Of course, nothing in human nature and conduct is ever completely fixed and unchangeable, but changes are sometimes difficult. It is better to make sure that development gets started in the right direction in these early years if at all possible.

The School Age Period

And then, in no time at all it seems, the child is old enough to start school and a new period of development is begun. This school age period is a different stage in development merely because there is such a radical change in the child's environment. He has moved out of the relatively protected environment of the home to that of a larger world where a whole new set of learnings and adjustments is required. From the highly personal and individual treatment of preschool days he is thrust into a situation where he is only one of many in a group. He meets many new demands, rules, and restrictions. He is expected to acquire many skills and accumulate knowledge. And there is no mother to run to for sympathy or protection when things get difficult.

For some children starting to school is a difficult time. The child who is not prepared for school may cling to his mother, resist being taken or sent to school, cry or throw a temper tantrum, and all in all present a picture of a very unhappy child. Such children, who have not been well prepared for the school experience, are too dependent on the presence, protection, and care of their mothers and find it difficult to manage the amount of self-reliance and independence that the school situation demands of them.

Most children, however, find school a thrilling, interesting, and challenging place and go to school eagerly and willingly. They are ready for school and can meet the demands of school; they also find the wider world an interesting place to explore, and the opportunities offered to acquire knowledge and skills are both stimulating and satisfying to them. Their preparation for the school experience has included learning to look after themselves: dressing, washing, and toilet needs, managing themselves in traffic, being able to accept and follow directions, rules, and restrictions.

In trying to understand the school age child, it helps if we remember that each one is unique, different from every other child, even though he is also like all other children in having the same basic needs and behavior equipment. And he does not stand still; he is growing, developing, learning, and changing. He carries within himself the effects of all that has happened to him so far. He may, for instance, have learned to trust adults, to be ready to accept their direction and depend on them for help when needed and protection from situations beyond his ability to handle. On the other hand, instead of trust and healthy dependency the child may be suspicious of adults and even hostile to them. He may have learned to classify teachers, policemen, and even neighbors as his enemies.

If so, his school adjustment will be neither easy nor very successful. Somehow or other he should be helped to find in some adults reasons why they can be trusted and their direction accepted.

It is during the school age period that the child moves outside the sphere of adult direction and supervision for some of his activities. He becomes a member of a child culture or gang with many customs and rituals which help him to feel that he belongs and is accepted by his contemporaries. He is beginning to find his place in a complex world of people. Although his home is still his base, his haven, and the center of his world, other settings are important to him as well. The school may be his second home; the haunts of the neighborhood gang, the club, the Sunday school, and the wider community all provide the locale of some of his activities.

During the school age period the child usually shows a decreasing suggestibility to his parents and teachers. While he is showing a decreasing readiness to be influenced by adults, he is more and more ready to allow himself to be swayed by members of his own age group. He is becoming more independent and likes to think of himself as an individual who can do things for himself. Being "grown up" is one of his most powerful ambitions.

Boys and girls in this period tend to seek different settings and groups. This sex separation is partly because of different interests and activities, but also because adults both expect it and arrange for it. It is well, however, to see that the separation is not too complete and that boys and girls have a chance to associate and get to understand and appreciate each other before the social and biological pressures of adolescence become too prominent. The boy or girl who has not had much experience with members of the opposite sex before adolescence may have a rather difficult time making the necessary adjustments in adolescence.

Adolescence

Another landmark in development is reached when the outward signs of beginning physiological maturity appear. The child is now entering adolescence. The bridge between childhood and adult is reached. This is normally the time for more rapid progress toward emancipation from parental control. It is a period when the effectiveness of early training becomes evident. If there have been a number of unsolved problems of adjustment in the early years, they tend to show up now. If, however, the early years have been well handled, then adolescence is usually a fairly happy period for both the adolescent and his parents. If the parent-child relationship has been good during childhood, the parent and the adolescent now enjoy and understand each other and the parent is able to provide the guidance and support which the adolescent needs.

Adolescence is the time when the most serious adjustment problems have to be faced. It is the time for vocational choice, heterosexual adjustment, emancipation from parental control, and the building of a satisfactory philosophy of life. These are difficult problems for most adolescents, so it is not surprising that they are insecure and often show this insecurity in restlessness, addiction to fads, temporary enthusiasms, resistance to authority, and similar symptoms.

The adolescent is neither a child nor yet an adult. He is leaving behind his childish characteristics, interests, and activities. But he is not yet adult in maturity, independence, and competency. He still needs the support, guidance, and sometimes even the protection of his adults. Yet he must not be treated like a child. One of the most frequent complaints made by adolescents is that their parents and teachers treat them like children.

We have assumed all through our discussion that adult direction, guidance, control, teaching, and other kinds of intervention are necessary for the healthy development of the infant, child, and adolescent. And we have also assumed that this intervention will vary as the child grows and acquires skills, knowledge, and experience. Now we shall look at each stage in turn and offer some practical suggestions about the application of principles of discipline.

References

Allport, G.: *Becoming,* Yale, New Haven, Conn., 1957.
Bowlby, J.: *Maternal Care and Mental Health,* World Health Organization Monograph, Series No. 2, New York, 1952.

Hymes, J. L., Jr.: *Understanding Your Child,* Prentice-Hall, Englewood Cliffs, N.J., 1952.

Levitt, E. E., and Ojemann, R. H.: "The Aims of Preventive Psychiatry and Causality as a Personality Pattern," *Journal of Psychology,* 1953, 36, 393–400.

Sears, R. R., Maccoby, E. E., and Levin, H.: *Patterns of Child Rearing,* Harper & Row, New York, 1957.

chapter 24

Discipline in Infancy

It may sound a little strange to talk about discipline in infancy, but the foundations of a reasonable scheme of discipline are laid in this early period. It is then that the child accumulates the impressions and experiences which will help to determine for him the meaning of many of the aspects of social relations and adult direction that he will experience later.

The main parental function in this early period is the provision of a protected, serene, comfortable, and satisfying environment. In this before-language period, the main communication between the parent and the child is through the medium of feelings. One gets the impression that feelings dominate infant experience. Parental care and attention are designed to make the infant's experience predominantly pleasant and satisfying. His comfort is the main parental concern. When the child's basic needs are met regularly and consistently the child's predominant feeling is one of pleasantness, and this provides the best foundation for the development of an even temperament and a pleasing personality.

Infant Development

There are two aspects of development to keep in mind. One is the slow unfolding of developmental possibilities dictated by the intrinsic nature of the organism. The infant is born in a very immature condition and the growth processes which began in the prenatal period are still continuing. This prepares the infant for various kinds of activity. When structures are ready to function they are exercised if there are no environmental hindrances. But the process cannot be hurried, and all infants do not show the same rate of unfolding. This is learning readiness. Until there has been sufficient growth the child is not ready for standing, walking, chewing, talking, bladder control, reading, and the hundred and one abilities that are the foundation of his varied activities.

The other feature of development that needs to be taken into account is the gradual acceleration of the process of learning. At first, there is very little evidence of learning, but as the days and weeks go by the effects of experience become more evident. This slow, early learning could be called *foundation learning*, as this gradual accumulation of experience provides the foundation on which later learning builds. In these early months there is very little in the infant's experience that could be called meaning. Meaning seems to be largely a matter of feeling. This is why it is so important that the infant's environment be such that pleasant feeling predominates.

There can be little doubt that the structure and functioning of the organism has a great deal to do with how the infant develops, his present comfort, and thus his outward appearance of pleasure or distress. Body chemistry does help to determine whether the food taken in will be handled easily or cause discomfort. The attending physician will do all he can to advise about the best kinds of foods and treatment to take into account the unique physiological organism that is your infant, but there still remain factors that affect body chemistry and yet are not dictated by it. These include features such as the way you handle the child, the degree of gentleness and warmth present, the degree of promptness with which you relieve distress, and the general character of the routine treatment you provide.

"Self-demand" or Schedule?

One of the most difficult problems facing the parent of the infant is whether the child should be fed and looked after on the basis of "self-demand" or a regular schedule. The self-demand idea seems to be based on the assumption that the infant must never feel frustration and that any delay in feeding the child when he signals his hunger is necessarily unpleasant. The regular schedule idea assumes that the infant will have to learn to fit in with many environmental demands and that he might as well make a start on it in infancy. It is possible to be too extreme with either, and it seems that the most desirable method is a mixture of both ideas. This is a flexible schedule which has been set up by taking into account the child's own rhythm of hunger and need for sleep and rest. To work on a split second, rigid schedule is neither sensible nor realistic. But equally unrealistic is to depend on the child's expression of need to determine when he should be fed and put to bed. Of course some infants show very clearly their needs and it is relatively easy to tell when they are hungry or sleepy. Other infants do not make their needs known so openly. There is the real danger in an extreme self-demand program that the infant will learn to demand all kinds of attention and thus get started on a direction of development that will be difficult to change later.

There is very little from the research literature to guide us with such questions as whether the child should be breast- or bottle-fed. There is no indication, for instance, that bottle-fed babies do more thumb sucking than breast-fed babies, as had been suggested formerly. Such decisions have to be made by the parents in the light of all the circumstances. However, if the infant is bottle-fed it is best that his mother hold him rather than use a bottle holder, because the warmth, support, and security that results from being held does appear to be very important. Feeding the baby serves other purposes than merely giving him food, as studies of institutionalized babies show. The individual, personal attention of the same person seems to provide the infant with a feeling of trust and security that is important for his well-being.

Sleep

Most infants go to sleep very easily and wake up very easily. An infant who has had his hunger satisfied, who has had food that his system can digest, who does not have discomfort from air taken in with the food, and who is otherwise comfortable usually drops off to sleep almost immediately. Wakefulness is almost always an indication of some kind of bodily distress. At first the infant sleeps nearly all the time, waking only to be fed, changed, or made comfortable. But soon the amount of sleep decreases as the baby stays awake to "play." His play at first is merely muscular activity with no particular pattern, and it seems to be exercise of developing structures. This will change in a few months as the baby's activity begins to take on more meaning and he now seems to be exploring and finding out about his world. The infant's sleep will soon show some degree of regularity, and take on a pattern which may not be the same as any other infant's but peculiarly his own. He may, for instance, sleep through the night and have two daytime sleep periods. Or he may have a period of wakefulness in the middle of the night. The infant's sleep pattern will depend on such factors as his hunger rhythm, digestion, and elimination. However, his sleep pattern can be modified and the child can be gently influenced into a regular and reasonable schedule.

Regularity

Regularity is a useful guiding principle in the care of the infant. It is not necessary for the mother to be a slave of the clock, and this regularity principle does not mean that a few minutes either way are so important. But regular times for feeding, the bath, being taken outdoors, and sleeping help to provide a feeling of security as things do not happen haphazardly but in a dependable way. However, it is important to build the regular daily routine on the basis of an observation of the baby's natural rhythm of rest and activity, hunger and satiation.

Sucking

Something over 50 per cent of all infants indulge in some kind of nonnutritive sucking. There seems to be little relationship between this and sucking to get food. Infants with plenty of food-getting sucking as well as those with little develop nonfood-getting sucking. The infant seems to derive considerable satisfaction from this sucking. Most children stop this behavior in the preschool period and the indications are that unless the thumb or finger sucking persists until the child is about seven years old there is little damage to mouth and teeth formation. Thumb sucking that persists or recurs in the older child may be an indication of some insecurity and calls for a review of the child's activity and treatment to discover possible causes. With the younger child it is safe to do nothing directly about the sucking but merely to see that he has other interesting things to do with his hands.

Toilet Training

It used to be a matter of some pride to parents to toilet-train their children as soon as possible. However, more recent studies indicate that it is better not to try to hurry the process. The child has to be ready for this learning. That is, there has to be sufficient growth of nerves and muscles, an ability to recognize pressure and to hold and release muscle groups voluntarily. Rarely is the child ready for this learning before his first birthday and frequently not until some time later. An observant mother can tell when the child is showing signs of readiness. The training itself should not be hurried or too much pressure put on the child. Punishment for failures or "accidents" is out of place. It is best to emphasize successes and ignore failures. It has been shown that if parents can be patient enough the child can practically toilet-train himself. However, usually some help is desirable. The child can be provided with a simple word he can use to indicate his need to go to the bathroom, and he can be taken to the toilet on a regular schedule. Of course, he will eventually have to learn the ordinary customs and modesty associated with elimination, but in the early stages there should not be too much fuss or emotion and nothing that will cause the child to be ashamed of this natural bodily function. There are indications that too strict toilet training and too much parental pressure for early training are associated with less desirable personality development.

Crying

Crying is the natural expression of any kind of distress by the infant. The amount of crying varies enormously from child to child.

Mothers soon learn to interpret the meaning of the baby's crying, whether it is from hunger, colic, pain, distress, or for attention. It is natural that the child should learn to associate crying with the attention it brings. For this reason some parents let the infant cry for long periods lest he learn to cry to get attention. However, most of the crying of the young infant is a signal that he does need attention and should have it. Of course, it does not hurt the infant to cry for a short time, but in the main it is best to answer the child's expressed need for some kind of attention when he cries.

Infant Discipline

Discipline in the period of infancy is mainly providing for the child's needs, making him comfortable, protecting him from danger, and arranging a suitable environment. As he can take very little if any responsibility for anything, the responsibility rests with the parents. They have to make all the decisions and accept the consequences. But the beginnings of control and guidance are there in the care, protection, and nurture of the helpless infant.

Some parents are tempted to introduce controls and punishments while the child is still an infant. They slap his hands, try to force him to do what he is not yet capable of, allow him to cry for long periods, and do similar things in their eagerness to hurry the child's development and learning. But all they succeed in doing is to make their job of parenthood more difficult. Strictness, forcing, and punishment have no place in dealing with infants, for this is the time for tenderness, warmth, and cuddling, expressed in constant care, protection, and providing for the needs of the baby. The nearest thing to control is the introduction of some degree of regularity in the daily care of the infant.

References

Aldrich, C., and Aldrich, M.: *Babies Are Human Beings*, Macmillan, New York, 1954.

Flint, B.: *Security of Infants*, University of Toronto Press, Toronto, 1959.

Landreth, C.: *Psychology of Early Childhood,* Knopf, New York, 1958.

Rand, W., Sweeney, M., and Vincent, E. L.: *Growth and Development of the Young Child,* Saunders, Philadelphia, 1953.

Smart, M., and Smart, R.: *Babe in the House,* Scribner, New York, 1950.

U.S. Children's Bureau: *Infant Care,* Publ. No. 8, U.S. Government Printing Office, Washington.

chapter 25

Discipline for

the Preschool Child

The preschool period should see a real beginning of the plan of training which we are calling discipline. Having now acquired the ability to get around for himself, the child has passed a very important landmark in development. He is no longer an infant but an active preschool child. He is of necessity introduced to a series of restrictions. His activity, ignorance, and impulsiveness can lead him into a lot of difficulty and danger, so that he must learn some necessary boundaries and prohibitions. And he will be launched on an extensive program of learning, designed to enable him to manage many things for himself that had been previously done for him.

In the preschool period we make a start on the process of handing over to the child the responsibility for the management of his own life. But it is only a beginning for it will take years of learning before he is truly self-disciplined. Remote as this is, what is done in the preschool period is fashioned with that end in mind. A responsible person is one who not only makes his own decisions but accepts the consequences of these decisions, whatever those consequences may be. This may sound general and theoretical and yet it is the key to a successful plan of discipline. The child has much to learn, but the ability to learn is his most prominent as well as his greatest asset. He will acquire the necessary skills almost without teaching but the more important attitudes, feelings, values, and social relationships will require planning and arranging by the parent.

The Beginning of Requirements

It is during the preschool period that the child can learn that there are two kinds of activities—those which he has to do whether he wants to or not and those which he can do or not as he likes. Later he will learn to classify these two kinds of activities as work and play. This does not mean that the child has to learn that life is hard and a burden, but it does mean that he cannot do everything he wants and must do some things whether he wants to or not. Nor does he need to learn that these required activities and restrictions are necessarily unpleasant and to be deplored. For the present, he learns that some things "are done" and some "are not done." Later he will learn why and gradually come to accept these social customs, taboos, laws, and requirements as sensible and necessary.

It does not help the young child to have the requirements disguised and his "work" made to look like play. Sometimes parents try to make a game out of eating, washing, going to bed, and other routine activities, thinking that the child will be able to accept them more easily and conform if they are thus disguised. However, one difficulty is that the child may choose not to play the game. It is better that he should learn that there are some activities which are truly play and which he can do or not as he likes, but that there are other activities that are required, a part of everyday living, and whether he enjoys them or not they are still necessary and must be done. Of course, where possible and as soon as possible the child should be helped to understand why they are necessary and thus required. What we have been saying does not mean that the routine activities cannot be made pleasant, interesting, and satisfying, but pleasant or not they are still necessary and required.

We believe this is the essential core of discipline: the demands of living and the restrictions of society either must be met or the individual suffers the consequences of his failure. Of course, not everyone agrees with this point of view. There are those who believe that we should work entirely through the child's wants; that is, they try to get the child to want what is required by society. This is the meaning of what is often called the technique of "reasoning" with the child. This is actually trying to talk the child into doing what we want him to do, a technique which is not always successful. This is the difference between a reasonable scheme of discipline and the reasoning technique. Everyone will agree that discipline should be reasonable to all concerned, but many do not agree that this means that the child should be reasoned into doing something.

Several generations ago parents were advised that it was necessary to "break the will of the child" and thus make him a submissive, obedient child. This does not appeal to us today, for we like to see children with spirit and not just obedient robots. On the other hand, it does seem to be sensible that the child should learn early that there are elements of necessary compulsion in his world and that he cannot do as he wishes.

Consistency

The preschool period is the time for the parent to establish the basic principles of the plan of discipline. The most important of these principles is consistency. This implies a number of things. One is that what the child is required to do is thought out and planned rather than spur-of-the-moment whims. This planning is in terms of the ability of the child to perform, the possibility of enforcing the requirement, and how necessary it is to make such a demand of the child. There is no use trying to require a child of three to sit still for any length of time because most three-year-olds are unable to do so. Nor should the preschool child be expected to participate in an adult conversation or eat like an adult. The test of a requirement—is it necessary?—can be rather tricky. It is easy for an adult to justify almost any requirement. But what we mean by "necessary" is necessary for the safety of the child, the convenience of the total group, and the ultimate good of the child himself.

There is no use making a requirement that cannot be enforced. For example, it is virtually impossible to enforce a requirement such as, "You must eat your dinner" or "You must go to sleep." It is possible, of course, if thought to be desirable, to say, "If you do not eat your first course you can not have your dessert." And it is always possible, though not necessarily desirable, to say, "If you don't get enough sleep you will not be able to go on the picnic tomorrow." A very real danger in this type of direction is that the consequence stated may not be carried out and becomes a mere threat that the parent had no intention of enforcing. It is not just the possibility of a consequence but its inevitability that controls behavior and produces learning by the child. Parents should be careful that they never threaten a consequence that they do not intend to administer. Nor should they use frequent warnings such as, "Don't climb, you'll fall and hurt yourself." There is no inevitability about falling and hurting himself and when stated consequences do not occur the parent's warnings are weakened. When the young child is subjected to frequent warnings, one of two things usually happens. The child either learns to pay no attention to what the parent says in such situations or he does take each warning seriously and becomes a timid, fearful child.

Another way of describing what is meant by this core principle of consistency is to say that requirements are situational rather than personal. This means that the requirements are dictated by the nature of the situation and are not just personal whims of the parent. Perhaps the easiest way to establish this is to make sure that the requirements are the same for the child in a situation no matter who is supervising him. When mother requires one thing, father another, and grandmother still a different one then the child can hardly help but learn that he is being controlled by the personal whims of the various adults. When, however, there is a standard set of requirements so that no matter which adult is in charge the same kind of behavior is required of him, he can learn that it is really the situation that is making demands of him, not mother or any one person.

We have found it convenient in thinking about the control of the preschool child to designate three kinds of situations: routine, play, and danger situations. Of course this is an artificial classification because nearly all situations have elements of all three. However, some situations are clearly routine in nature, happening regularly and with the requirements clearly central. Other situations are clearly play situations with any requirements or rules in the background and the child has considerable freedom to do as he likes within limits. Although most situations have an element of danger in them, there are some situations for the preschool child where the danger element is more prominent. We shall look at each of these in turn.

The Routines

The routine situations such as eating, rest time and bedtime, toilet, washing, dressing, and putting away play materials are all situations in which the child is required to behave in a certain way. In other words the external compulsion is a central feature. They are serious business or work for the young child. They are situations where he is being required to learn skills, to accept social customs, and to conform to specific requirements. But they are also situations where the child can have considerable enjoyment and satisfaction. They make up a large part of the "curriculum" of the preschool period.

In planning these routine situations for the preschool child there are a number of goals and results we have in mind. We want the child to experience satisfaction and pleasure in living up to the requirements; we want him to make progress in acquiring skills; we want him to become self-directing and independent in these situations; and we want him to learn how to manage in socially acceptable ways. Perhaps we should state a fairly obvious fact, that learning how to behave in these routine situations takes time and that the preschool child will only make a beginning. The important thing is that he make a good start on this long and gradual process of learning how to live with other people, accept willingly the necessary and sensible rules of society, and begin to understand the importance of taking into account the feelings and desires of other people.

Eating. The child has made a start as an infant in learning to eat. By the time he has learned to walk and is classified by us a preschool child, he has probably learned to take some of his food from a cup or a spoon. He has been, or is being, weaned, a process that is best managed gradually, each new food or utensil being introduced one at a time. If there is too much novelty all at once there will be difficulty and resistance. The natural response of the young child to new tastes, temperatures, and consistencies is rejection. If the child is forced or hurried, or if there is too much fuss and emotion, the resistance may become stronger and we have the beginning of a food dislike or some other eating difficulty. The key to success in these early years is a little at a time, no emotion, and no forcing, coaxing, or bribing.

If it is possible, the preschool child should eat at his own small table by himself. He does not have the skill nor is he able to give his attention to the serious (for him) business of eating when his high chair is pushed up to the family table. He can be introduced to this gradually as he becomes ready for it. Play should be discouraged and the child should be helped to give his whole attention to eating. Small helpings, repeated as often as necessary, help him to learn to eat what is put before him. Then, even if he does eat the most preferred foods first, the less desired food is not too formidable for him.

By the end of the preschool period he will have acquired considerable skill in the mechanics of eating and will be ready for the family meal. However, there will still be lapses, spills, and immature behavior. The only kind of discipline that is desirable is removal to eat by himself until he is ready and able to eat in an acceptable manner. Mealtime is a poor time for scenes, and the inevitable accidents should be accepted as a part of learning. Manners can be left until later when they will have more meaning for the child. Anyway, he will learn the manners shown by the group more easily and naturally than what he is taught directly.

Sleep. The daytime nap routine should present little difficulty if it is regular, comes at approximately the same time every day, and happens without exception. Of course, it is wise to prepare the child for it by making sure that there is nothing exciting happening. Any emotion destroys the ability to relax and go to sleep. The physical setting for the nap is arranged also to be conducive to relaxation and rest; comparative quiet and a darkened room with play materials and other distractions out of sight are desirable. The daytime nap should not be so long as to interfere with night sleep. There is no standard amount, as children vary greatly in their sleep requirements. If the child does not sleep he should be helped to lie quietly and rest anyway.

A regular bedtime should be planned and followed consistently. Again the child can be prepared for bedtime by making sure that exciting play and interesting events are not taking place. The child will naturally object to breaking off an exciting game or romp to go to bed. But he will go more willingly if nothing very interesting is happening. He can be warned that his bedtime is approaching and the clock can be the control rather than the person. It is difficult to argue with a clock; it does not answer back. Fears and insecurities tend to come to the surface at bedtime. If possible it is wise to try to help the child to balance his emotional books and not be left to try and go to sleep with worries and unresolved conflicts plaguing him. Many parents of young children find that bedtime can be an occasion for the warm, intimate expressions of affection that puts the child's mind at rest and makes him feel that he is loved and wanted and not being put to bed to be got rid of.

Some preschool children have difficulty going to sleep. Life has become so exciting and interesting for them that they find it difficult to let down and woo sleep. Some parents make the mistake of thinking that if bedtime is delayed the child will fall asleep from fatigue. But the overtired child often has even more difficulty in getting to sleep. A fairly common fear in preschool children is that their parents will disappear while they are asleep, so they try to stay awake or find excuses to call the parents so that they can be reassured of their presence. This fear is sometimes strengthened by the parents going out when the child has gone to sleep and the child waking up to find someone else there and his parents absent. If the parents are going out it is best that the child knows it and has been told where the parents are and when they will return. And if possible, the child should know and trust the baby-sitter.

Toilet. We discussed toilet training in a previous section and nothing much needs to be added here. As the child begins to recognize the sensations of pressure and to associate them with the emptying of the bladder and when he has learned a signal such as a simple word, he can be helped to take some responsibility for getting to the toilet in time. Usually daytime control is learned before night control, which may take some months or even years longer to establish. The child can be helped to take some pride in his progress. Punishment, scolding, and the like usually hinder rather than help progress.

As soon as the child shows any interest and has sufficient motor control he can be allowed to do some of the washing, dressing, and undressing for himself. Considerable patience is necessary to watch the child's fumbling efforts, but it is only by trying to do these things for himself that he can acquire the skill. During most of the preschool period he will need help with the more difficult parts of these activities. But the help should not be so much that the child does not have to put forth any effort for himself. On the other hand, it should not be so slight that he has an unpleasant and difficult time with many failures.

Play

The preschool period is a time for play. It is through play that the child develops large and small muscle control, learns much about his world, gains a feeling of mastery over himself and materials, begins to experience the satisfactions in companionship and to learn the necessity for rules and regulations. When the child is not sleeping, eating, dressing, or washing, he is playing. That is, when there is no routine to attend to, his life is play. The most prominent characteristic of play at any age is the feeling of freedom, for play is something we do because we want to and because we enjoy it. So play, in contrast to the routines, has very few requirements. Even though the requirements in the play situation are at a minimum they are still necessary.

Preschool children need constant supervision, that is, an adult within sight and hearing. Although constant, the supervision can be unobtrusive, so that the child can have both the security of a nearby adult and the feeling of being on his own, going about his own affairs. Play is free activity but the freedom is always within limits. These limits are dictated by such considerations as the safety of the child, the protection of property, the rights of other children, and what the child is learning.

In some ways the foundation of adequate control of the preschool

child in play situations is provision of a suitable place, suitable
materials, ideas, and companionship part of the time. Many difficulties are avoided if a suitable play place both indoors and out
can be provided. The outdoor play space should be enclosed if at
all possible, otherwise the parent must be on the alert to see that
the child does not wander off into traffic or other dangers. A part
of a room can be fitted up indoors as a play space with floor cover-
ing, small table and chair, low shelves or boxes or baskets to store
play materials. When a suitable place for play is provided then it
is both possible and sensible to require the child to keep his play
materials in the play space and avoid the common nuisance of
play materials scattered over the house.

One important essential about play materials for the preschool
child is variety. Play materials need not be expensive; in fact, some
of the best materials cost nothing. For outdoors a sandbox, a supply
of cans and large spoons or small shovels, large blocks or small packing cases, a wagon, and in the hot weather some large container for
water are some materials that have a variety of uses. Something to
climb on such as a jungle gym, boards that can be used for a variety
of things, and a swing are not indispensable but are useful. What
is provided depends on the size of the space and the nature of the
ground. For instance, if there is a suitable place, a kiddie car and
later a tricycle are useful. Indoor play materials can be of great
variety with materials for play on the floor and at the table. Blunt
scissors, plenty of paper and discarded picture magazines, crayons,
plasticine, paints with wrapping paper or newsprint, blocks, push-
around toys, nests of cans or blocks are but a few of the kinds of
materials that are conducive to interesting and creative activities.

One requirement which is sensible and which can be enforced
consistently is that the play materials must be put away after use.
This can be started very early with the young child helping to put
his toys away and gradually he takes over and does it all. It helps to
establish the idea that a material is put away when the child has
finished with it, so that at the end of the playtime the job of clearing up is not too formidable. Materials that are not put away may
be confiscated temporarily as a consequence for failure to live up
to the requirement. Toys that are misused or destroyed are not re-

placed immediately, so that the child can learn that if he fails to care for materials he has to get along without them.

Preschool children often need suggestions for play activities. This is especially true when the child has no older brothers or sisters to set patterns and provide ideas. It is wise to provide a number of suggestions so that the element of choice in activities is always present and the child is not merely doing what he is told. When new materials are provided the child will need to have demonstrations of their use. Simple rules can be established for the use of such things as scissors, paints, crayons, and plasticine. Although playtime is free time, the child's freedom always has limits. The bored child is usually the child with insufficient variety of materials or lack of ideas of how to use the materials he has.

Most young preschool children are ready for some companionship with children of their own age. This is one of the values of nursery school or play school. But the preschool child who does not go to such a school can usually have playmates some of the time if the parent arranges for them. Such a small group of preschool children needs to have an adult nearby to see that the necessary rules of taking turns, use of material, and the like are enforced. All children are required to live up to the rules and neighbor children are treated the same as one's own. It is wise to have times for solitary play as well as social play so that the child does not become so dependent on other children for play that he cannot entertain himself.

Danger Situations

There are a number of goals to keep in mind in situations which have an element of danger. Some of these are the protection of the child, the training of the child in self-management, the development of understanding rather than fear, and the building up of skills and knowledge that will enable the child to cope with the common life situations which are dangerous. While the child is learning it is wise to make the environment as safe as possible so that he is protected from traffic, open fires, boiling water on a stove, sharp knives, and poisons.

The core of training is not to make the child fear danger situations but assist him to understand them and learn how to cope with them. Thus every opportunity is taken to help the young child watch the traffic and to know when and where it is safe to cross the street. He can learn about fires and the dangers without becoming terrified. He can learn the sensible precautions about water. He will need to have many experiences under supervision and direction before he will be able to manage for himself. While he is learning, adults will have to see that the child is not exposed to dangers he does not yet understand or have the skills to manage.

Summary

Thus, in the routine situations the child will learn to accept the requirements and restrictions and learn how to behave in a socially acceptable manner. Before he starts to school he will have made considerable progress toward managing eating, dressing, sleeping, and toilet habits for himself. In the play situations he will have acquired some concentration, ability to entertain himself, ability to play cooperatively with other children, and have learned to accept the necessary boundaries and rules that make play productive and satisfying.

It is rather easy for the preschool child to learn to conform for the sake of winning approval or even tangible rewards. And it is always a temptation for the parent to exploit the child's desire for approval and rewards. Of course, the trouble with this is that the child learns to do things mainly for approval or reward and he fails to discover that there are some activities that are satisfying and worthwhile for themselves. And he may fail to learn that there are some activities that are necessary and must be done without expectation of reward or approval.

Most preschool children are good conformists. They feel more secure when they know what is expected of them and when they are living up to these expectations. They are still largely dependent on their parents for protection and the satisfaction of their basic needs. There is the danger of the child learning to conform for the sake of conforming or conforming in order to win approval. We would hope that the preschool child would begin to see the value of conforming to the rules that make the group function more adequately. In other words, it is not too soon for the child to begin to build an understanding of the simple societies of which he is a member such as the family and the play group.

The preschool period is the time to build foundations. His present experiences will be the foundations on which he will build later learning. If the requirements are planned and their enforcement gentle but consistent he will have made some important first steps towards self-discipline. It is not enough that he be protected and trained to meet the necessary requirements of his little world. He will need to make a start on self-management and self-reliance. To be ready for the wider and more complex world of the school he will need to have a good start in doing things for himself, taking directions from others, and fitting in with the rules and requirements of group activity.

We do not want to leave the impression that the preschool period is all work, supervision, enforcing requirements, and serious business for parents. There can be a lot of fun and much deep satisfaction too. The child is in one of his most interesting phases of development. So many dramatic events take place in this period as the child moves fairly quickly from being quite helpless and almost completely dependent to an individual in his own right, capable of doing much for himself. Communication between parent and child becomes more and more possible as his language skill increases. His ability to understand meanings shows very rapid development. His personality structure is taking form and his preschool experiences will help to determine its essential pattern.

References

Black, I. S.: *Off to a Good Start,* Harcourt, Brace, New York, 1953.
————: *The Preschool Years,* New York State Department of Health, Copp.
Faegre, M. L., Anderson, J., and Harris, D.: *Child Care and Training,* University of Minnesota Press, Minneapolis, 1958.
Fletcher, M.: *The Adult and the Nursery School Child,* University of Toronto Press, Toronto, Canada, 1958.

Hymes, J. L., Jr.: *The Child under Six,* Educational Services, Washington, 1961.

Landreth, C.: *Psychology of Early Childhood,* Knopf, New York, 1958.

Read, K. H.: *The Nursery School: A Human Relationship Laboratory,* Saunders, Philadelphia, 1960.

U.S. Children's Bureau: *Your Child from One to Six,* Publ. No. 30, U.S. Government Printing Office, Washington.

chapter 26
Discipline in the
School Age Period

When school days begin the child enters a new era in his life. Mother usually has mixed feelings as this day approaches. Her baby is growing up, but she will now have time to catch her breath and do some of the things that have been crowded out by the constant care and supervision that were necessary. For the child it is an exciting time; he has looked forward to this day for some time, for to him it is a sign that he is growing up. He is now one of those big children who go to school. He may go with eager anticipation or with some trepidation, depending on the nature of his preparation for it.

Different Standards

For the school age child there will be at least three kinds of discipline: the discipline of his home, the discipline of the school, and the discipline of the play group. As long as these three spheres do not overlap too much there will be little confusion. The child is usually flexible enough to adjust to these different kinds of control. However, he may need help from his parents to understand the differences between the demands of the classroom and those of the home. No matter how important the school may be to the child, home will still be his headquarters and his emotional haven. In the classroom he will be only one of forty and in the school one of hundreds but in his own home he can still feel that he is an accepted, important member of the little family group. While he is finding his place in this wider world, he can feel at home in the family.

The school age child will be influenced greatly by the standards, customs, and values of his wider environment. When there are differences between these standards and values and those of his own family

271

he will want to know why. "Why can't I stay up later like the boy up the street?" "Charlie gets twice the allowance I do." "Billie isn't any older than I am and he can have a bike." "Why can't I wear the kind of clothes the other girls do?" "Why do I have to report home after school, none of the other kids do." These and similar complaints indicate the child's awareness of the customs and values of the neighborhood. Now the parents have to decide what is important and thus to be adhered to in spite of what is done in other homes, and what is not so important and on which compromises can be made. The wise parent attempts to achieve a balance between insisting on what he feels must be done and allowing the customs of the community to dictate what can be done. But in doing this he will try to get the child to understand the reason why he believes it is important to differ from the rest of the community.

Helping to Make the Rules

In the school age period the child can be taken more and more into the planning and making decisions about the daily routine activities. Rules are made after discussion and agreement. At first, this is difficult because the child is incapable of taking a very objective view of things and his part will be mainly fighting for what he wants. Gradually he will begin to understand the reasonableness of the rules and that his parents do not insist on certain requirements and restrictions just because they are mean and want to make life unpleasant for him.

There cannot be a rule for everything, and even if we could cover every possibility by a rule so that we had a long, long list of them, it would not be wise to do so. After all, rules are but stopgaps while we clarify some guiding principles. We might, for instance, have a rule dealing with getting to meals on time, but we need this rule only until the child develops sufficient awareness of the inconvenience he causes other people when he fails to be punctual in such situations. Punctuality in itself is no virtue, but consideration for others is. We should strive, then, not for the multiplication of rules but rather for as few rules as we can get along with. And for each rule there should be an attempt to help the child understand the meaning of the rule and its importance. When he has acquired this kind of understanding the rule gives place to a kind of inner control that makes the rule as such unnecessary.

Positive Discipline

Discipline needs to be of such a nature that the child can have the feeling of being approved of, accepted, and enjoyed by his parents. This supplies the necessary foundation for the growth of confidence in himself that is the core of a healthy personality. A plan of discipline that is too detailed and predominantly negative and disapproving makes it very difficult for the child to have this feeling of security and self-reliance. Discipline is supposed to help, not hinder, growth toward maturity and self-discipline. The kind of discipline that hinders is largely negative. It stresses the must-nots, the boundaries, limits, and restrictions. It includes many expressions of disappointment, disapproval, and regret. It fails to make enough of approval, acceptance, and even pride in the child. It is difficult for little Betty to feel that she is accepted when her mother frequently expresses her regret that Betty does not have curly blonde hair. And when little Harry hears his parents tell of his shortcomings as well as being reminded of them at nearly every meal, he has great difficulty in developing a feeling of self-confidence or self-worth.

A positive form of discipline emphasizes the desirable and provides the guidelines within which the child can use initiative. The necessary restraints are in the background rather than being the prominent aspects of the plan. The child can feel that the discipline is not just repressive but he can have the security that comes from knowing the limits. He can also feel the encouragement of adults who are on his side, who are proud of him and wish him well. A positive form of discipline is based on a strong faith in the child. His adults believe in him and he feels that they do. If this faith in the child is present it may be possible to perform the mental gymnastic of disapproving of the child's misdeed but not of him. This enables the parent to say in effect, "You are a fine person and I like you, but what you have done is undesirable and I know that you will learn to behave differently."

Nothing that we have been saying should be taken to mean that children should be allowed to do as they please or that their failures to live up to reasonable requirements should be ignored. School age children need to have some rules to guide them. They need a few clear rules, not a large number which restrict their activities in all directions. These rules will be fashioned to fit the family circumstances and will include such things as times for meals, bedtime, coming home from school, coming in from play, the boundaries within which they may roam, and the home chores for which they are responsible. And these few rules are enforced with logical, consistent consequences when necessary.

The Management of Time

The management of time by the child can be an important and difficult area of learning. As mentioned before, it is usually necessary to have a number of rules for the child's guidance. These may include reporting home from school before going anywhere to play, being on time for meals, coming in from play at an agreed hour, a time for schoolwork if there is any to do at home, and a time for practicing his music. First, the child should understand clearly what is required of him and why. This is achieved by sufficient discussion. Then the child's failure to live up to the rule brings the inevitable, consistent consequence, which he can realize is to help him to remember and live up to the rule. In giving the child a chance to explain his neglect, it is important that we are not just providing him with chances to practice making excuses and distorting the facts to justify his behavior. The consequences may be such devices as temporary loss of some of his freedom or privileges. These are best enforced without criticism, name-calling, or disapproval. The child should realize that we are just as sorry as he is, that we like and accept him just as much as before, and that we believe he can learn quickly by this method.

Care of Possessions

Another area in which there is often a need for some rules and planned discipline is the care of possessions such as clothes, play materials, and sports equipment, as well as family furniture and belongings. The child's idea of order, tidiness, and use of furniture rarely conforms with that of his parents. For instance, mother may put a high premium on order and tidiness and may consider almost any disorder as a cardinal sin. If this is the case, there are sure to be frequent difficulties as her school age children may not be able to see why they cannot leave some of their possessions spread around handy for the next time they want to use them. What is necessary is a kind of compromise, in which mother accepts some of their lack of order while insisting on a certain amount of tidiness.

One way to help the school age child to be responsible for the care of his possessions is to see that there are suitable places for him to keep his belongings. When there are drawers, shelves, cupboards, boxes, and the like for him to keep his things, there is liable to be much less disorder and what adults may call an untidy mess. Sometimes it helps the child to learn his responsibility for his possessions if he loses some of them when they are left lying around.

Personal Care

During the school age period the boy or girl can assume more and more responsibility for personal care. With an occasional reminder he can learn to look after cleaning teeth, washing, taking baths, changing underwear, selecting suitable clothes to wear, and putting his dirty clothes in the laundry. However, as long as mother takes the responsibility for these things the child will let her. So a typical scene in the home of a twelve-year-old boy on a school day finds mother getting him up, seeing that he gets washed, teeth cleaned, and hair combed, coaxing or nagging him into eating his breakfast, finding his school books, seeing that he has the right clothes, and getting him started for school on time. But, if we realize how important it is for the child to learn to take responsibility for these details of daily life, we will arrange matters so that it does become his responsibility and he gets the valuable practice of managing for himself. After all, by age twelve the boy or girl is quite capable of looking after the details of personal care and cleanliness. Of course, the child's standards and those of his parents may not coincide and again some compromises may be necessary.

Home Chores

Child labor has been abolished by law in most countries. However, work is an important experience for the child to have. Farm children have an advantage in this respect over most city children, for there are still many chores to be done, and children are usually given responsibility for various jobs. In modern urban living home chores for children are not so obvious. But, by the time the child is twelve he should be able to put up his own lunch, prepare simple meals, take responsibility for grass cutting, wash the car, clean his own room, and perform similar tasks. Many people today find routine tasks disagreeable or even a burden. Work attitudes are catching. It may not seem important that mother seems to find all her household work a burden or that father attacks any chore with a groan, but it does not leave the children unaffected.

It may be easier for parents to do the work themselves, rather than letting the children have the experience of taking part in the work of the home. But taking part in the serious work can be a valuable experience for children, not just because of the skills they acquire but more because of the feeling of being a part of the busy life around them and a contributing member of their society.

It helps when the child has some choice of tasks to do and can be given some room for initiative in how he does them. Variety is also important, so chores should be changed from time to time. Working along with the child can also make the work more interesting as well as providing opportunities for companionship. And children should not be given a chance to think that it is only the unimportant tasks that are left for them. There is much more fun in preparing a meal than in washing up afterward, for instance.

Another kind of work for most school age children is schoolwork done at home or, as it has been called, homework. The child can be helped to accept this as his own responsibility. The parents can help by seeing that he has an uninterrupted block of time and conditions conducive for work. They should be ready to help provide materials and even some help when called on, when the child is engaged in a project requiring searching for information or materials.

Healthy attitudes toward work and good work habits are invaluable assets. The school age period is the time when foundations for these are built. Healthy attitudes include a willing and cheerful acceptance of work, a willingness to do one's share, an attitude of cooperation, and the absence of the idea that any kind of work is beneath his dignity to do. Good work habits include an ability to concentrate on the job at hand, a degree of intelligent persistence, a reasonable level of quality and accuracy, and the ability to carry through a task, without supervision or checkup. These attitudes and habits will not be acquired overnight; they will take time, but what we should expect is that the school age child will show progress in the right direction. The observant parent can be very helpful if he notices that the child is failing to obtain the feelings of achievement and joy in putting forth effort for worthwhile ends. A change in conditions, even a change in the pattern set by the parents themselves, a few positive suggestions and encouragement whenever there is evidence of progress, may all serve to get the child started in the right direction.

The Management of Money

Money becomes important to the child in this period and some direction is needed if he is to acquire desirable attitudes and useful habits. He can be helped to learn that money is for use, that intelligent management can bring much happiness, but that money is not the measure of all things. In order to learn how to manage money, the child has to have some money of his own. This is usually arranged by providing the child with a small regular allowance. The amount of the allowance is determined by circumstances, but it should be something less than the child can spend. This is to make sure that he can learn from experience that if he spends his money thoughtlessly he will have to do without something else. At first the allowance covers only a few rather simple and nonessential wants but as the learning goes on the allowance is increased and its scope widened until by middle adolescence the child is managing all the money the family can provide for his personal requirements. If the child is to learn to manage money he must be given freedom in how he uses his allowance. If the parents dictate how he is to spend his money then he learns very little. However, discussions about what the allowance is to cover, suggestions about values, help in planning and even bookkeeping can be useful as long as they do not become a form of direction in which the child's choices and experiences of doing without because he did not spend wisely are lost. Saving has meaning for the child, when it is saving for a specific object or purpose. The idea of saving for a remote future has little meaning for him yet. Giving is another important part of the money picture. For the child to learn to share means that he gives out of his own meager store of money and is not merely a messenger for his parent's giving. Earning can come into the picture as well, but any working for money in the home should be outside his regular chores which, of course, are done without pay. The allowance should not be dependent on good behavior, or be thought of as pay for doing what is reasonably required of the child.

The school age child will profit from being introduced gradually into the family finances. He hears and even takes part in discussions about the use of the family money. He is better prepared for that day in the not too distant future when he will be launching a new home and family if he knows something about taxes, mortgages, insurance, house repairs, budgets, and all the many details of making income and expenditures somehow balance.

Play

Although school, routine activities, home chores, extra lessons, and the like fill many hours of the child's time, play is precious to him. Play is his own activity; the others are dictated by someone else.

The meaning of play is freedom, and the school age boy or girl throws all of his available energy into it. Because it is self-chosen and what he most wants to do, there is enthusiasm, effort, and whole-heartedness in it. It stretches his imagination, it develops mind and body, it produces skills, it helps him to learn how to get along with others, to win gracefully and to accept defeat, and a hundred and one other lessons about life. He finds in play release from tensions, relief from serious work, and even solace for hurts and resentments.

The observant adult can learn much about the child from watching the child at play. In play, the child sometimes expresses some of his deepest feelings, attitudes, and values. Parents may sometimes see their own techniques in action as the child talks to dolls, pets, or playmates. It would be quite enlightening for some parents to hear their children scolding, name calling, or belittling a doll or a dog. Because play is so free, the child's behavior can reveal some of his fears, worries, and aspirations. We can learn much from children's free play activities.

The school age child is given to enthusiasms which, although intense, may not last very long. One week he may be collecting something with great zest, but next week the collection is collecting dust while the child has moved on to some other enthusiasm. This is one of the ways the school age child achieves variety in his play activities. And variety is important. So is balance. For instance, a balance between spectator activities and those in which the child participates is important. There is a tendency today for spectator activities to win out: watching games, television, listening to radio or records, being entertained. There is nothing wrong with any of these, but they should not crowd out the participation of the child. Another kind of balance is between social and solitary activities. Both are important, but what is more important is the balance between them.

Discipline and play do not seem to go together, yet discipline is needed even in play situations. It is a matter of limits and necessary rules, but arranged in such a way that the free and spontaneous nature of play is preserved. And the positive aspect of discipline is the key to success. This means the provision of time, place, materials, and ideas but not so directly as in the earlier years, for now the child should have the feeling that he himself is doing most of the arranging, managing, and providing. Perhaps the hardest part of this for some parents is being in the background. But their reward comes in seeing the child's happiness and progress.

Sex Education

The greatest worries of parents of school age children concern sex and character. Some parents remember the stories and distorted accounts they themselves listened to at the end of the schoolyard or behind the barn and they wonder if their children are hearing the same kind of thing. But this is where the parent needs to have a strong faith in his children; such a faith will not be misplaced if they have answered the children's questions earlier and made sure that they have a sound healthy knowledge of the "facts of life." They can also make sure that there is an atmosphere of confidence and trust so that the children will feel that they can discuss anything with their own parents and that they will get an honest answer to their questions.

Character

All parents want their children to grow up to be honest, law-abiding persons. They are concerned about their morals and character development. Their concern may be increased when they discover their child stealing, lying, or cheating. Of course, these are rather strong words to describe the child's excursions into what adults think of as crime. Most children in their immaturity distort facts, take what is not their own, and possibly cheat. What we sometimes fail to understand is that we almost force children into these patterns of behavior. For instance, why does Mary cheat at school? For any one of a number of reasons. Perhaps she wants desperately to please her parents and thinks that what will please them most is a good record at school and the only way she thinks she can achieve this is by cheating. Or perhaps she thinks her teacher is unfair in the way she treats her and so she is paying her back in the same manner. Or maybe she is afraid of failure and the disgrace that goes with it and so cheats to avoid disaster. Or, consider what are often called lies in children. Children may lie for many reasons such as fear, to attract attention, to bolster their self-confidence, to avoid being punished, or simply because they have not been helped to see that truth is always better than falsehood. Most school age children at some time or other take things that belong to someone else. They may be small articles from the dime store, small change from mother's purse, other children's belongings, or almost anything. Sometimes the child steals because the temptation is too strong for him and the chance so easy. Sometimes it is an indication of a lack of appreciation of ownership perhaps because the child has never had much feeling of having things that he can call his own. Sometimes he steals for revenge, striking back at adults who have been unjust to him. Sometimes the stealing is quite illogical from an adult point of view. For instance, the ten-year-old boy who had carried on a systematic program of stealing for some months and who was finally caught with a store of $18.40. When the tale finally came out it was both pathetic and illogical. He had stolen to make his mother happy. It seems that his mother had said that she could never be happy until the family had a summer cottage like all their friends. It was an innocent remark repeated several times by his mother and he had taken it very seriously and had gone to work systematically to get her what she needed. He had even taken money from the kitchen drawer, in fact wherever he could find it. He had dreams of the day when he would present his mother with her heart's desire.

But children need to be helped to learn to be honest. There are many character education techniques; some are helpful, some are harmless, and a few hinder the development of good character. For instance, severe punishment may result in resentment and hostility leading to even more undesirable behavior than that which brought on the punishment. And frequent preaching and lecturing the child about being good may not only be useless but may cause the child to think of goodness as unpleasant and forbidding. Sometimes our efforts produce such a load of guilt that the young child loses his feeling of self-worth.

The use of stories, drama, ritual, and similar devices may be of some help but the most powerful kind of character education is the example of those people the child admires, loves, and trusts.

Good character is built on understanding and accepted values, not fear. We do not want our children to learn to be good because they are afraid of being bad and being punished for it. Nor do we want them to learn to be good in order to win some reward. We want them to be good, because goodness is its own reward and because they believe that goodness is always better than badness. Living in an environment where goodness is taken for granted, where everyone is trusted and where we expect people to be honest and dependable, the child will gradually adopt this attitude as his own. Along the way he will need to have opportunities to deepen his understanding and learn not just how to behave adequately but the reason for so behaving. He will need also to experience the satisfactions of doing acceptable things and the consequences of unacceptable behavior.

The school age period is generally a happy, strenuous time. It is a time for far-reaching learning. Although the child's personality and character are never fixed and unchangeable, what happens in this period will shape, to a very large extent, the kind of person he is becoming. If the child receives treatment that is fair and just, if he lives in a home in which there are standards that are lived up to and not just talked about, and if he feels that his teachers and parents believe in him, are trying to understand him, and are helpful rather than punitive when he makes mistakes, then we can be fairly sure that he will build the kind of character of which we can be proud.

In the school age period, discipline that is not just correction and punishment but a positive planned program of training can guide the child through the crucial experiences that will tell the story of his development toward maturity. This plan will provide the experiences and settings that he needs to build his own attitudes and values. It is not merely an attempt to shape the child's life into a preconceived pattern but rather a program that will help him to meet and solve his own problems and adopt his own set of standards and guiding principles. It is a plan of training that is based on an abiding faith in the child himself as an individual and his great potential to learn to live in a way that will be acceptable to others as well as himself.

In what may seem like no time at all this child will show the unmistakable signs of approaching puberty and even though he may be still in school we now have to think of him or her as an adolescent, still part child but also part adult. And now we can only hope that we have helped prepare him for the exciting days of growing into manhood or womanhood.

References

Biber, B., Murphy, L. B., Woodcock, L. P., and Black, I. S.: *Life and Ways of the Seven-to-eight Year Old,* Basic Books, New York, 1952.

Colm, H.: "Help and Guidance as Discipline for Pre-adolescents," *Nervous Child,* 1951, **9,** 131–138.

U.S. Children's Bureau: *Your Child from Six to Twelve,* Publ. No. 324, U.S. Government Printing Office, Washington.

chapter 27

Discipline

in Adolescence

Every child passes three landmarks on his way to being grown up. The first is when he stands on his own two feet, takes his first steps, and demonstrates that he is no longer a helpless infant. The second is when he leaves the shelter of his home for the wider world of the school. And the third is when the developmental timetable brings the signs of puberty and the child steps over the boundary between childhood and adolescence. Another landmark is almost in sight, the time when he leaves home for a job or marriage. These years between puberty and stepping out on his own are the years of adolescence. Adolescence has accumulated the reputation for being a stormy time, filled with problems and difficulties, a worrisome period for parents. But it only partly deserves this reputation. It depends a great deal on what has gone before. When the problems of infancy, preschool, and school age have been solved as they occur, adolescence and its problems are not too serious or difficult.

Lengthened Adolescence

In primitive cultures adolescence is brief and the child steps from childhood to adulthood with hardly a pause. But as society becomes more and more complex, the transition lengthens. In our complex culture with the need for increased periods of preparation, training, and education, adolescence may occupy a whole decade. This lengthened adolescence poses problems as the adolescent may become impatient at the delay in his acceptance as a mature independent adult. With full physical and intellectual maturity, the adolescent may long for the time when he will be considered to be capable of economic independence and the management of his own life.

From Control to Guidance

One aspect of the transition from childhood to adulthood is a change in the nature of discipline from control to guidance. This cannot be an abrupt change but a gradual lessening of direction and a shift from control from without, to control by the adolescent himself. This seems to be difficult for some parents to manage. They tend to try to hang on to detailed control too long, or they give up rather abruptly and let the adolescent go his own way without direction or even advice. The key to success is to think of this period as one of transition in which nearly every month brings a small change in the plan of discipline.

Adolescence, then, is a bridge from childhood to adulthood, from immaturity to maturity, from dependency to independence, from needing control and direction to needing support and advice. But the bridge is a long one and the transitions will be gradual. The adolescent himself will show that he is part child and part adult, showing sometimes the need for direction and the outlining of limits, and at other times showing a strong desire for independence. Sometimes his behavior is a mixture of the childish and the mature. Charlie may show a high level of skill and knowledge as he repairs the car but may do so without changing from his good clothes, so that he succeeds in fixing the car but at the same time ruining his suit. In the same day Mary may show the emotional immaturity of childhood and the poise of an adult. Perhaps the most puzzling aspect of adolescence for parents is this mixture and the quick shifts from childish to mature patterns of behavior and back again.

The greatest need of the adolescent is to have the faith, trust, confidence, and support of someone, preferably his own parents. He needs to believe in himself, to accept his limitations and potentialities, and to have the kind of confidence in himself that will enable him to face and solve his problems. This self-confidence depends on a realization that someone else believes in him and is pulling for him. An effective plan of discipline in adolescence is only possible if there is this strong, unwavering trust in the adolescent.

The "Awkward" Age

Early adolescence has been called the awkward age and to a certain extent it deserves the label. The reason for the awkwardness is not so much the rapid growth that is taking place but a kind of self-awareness or self-consciousness that makes the boy or girl socially awkward. The boy or girl who runs into furniture, drops things, falls over his own feet, and cannot sit straight on a chair does not lack motor coordination but does lack ease and poise in a social situation. It does not help the adolescent to be told how awkward he is; he knows it, and being told makes him feel even more awkward. This social awkwardness provides a useful clue to the underlying feelings of early adolescence. He is insecure because so much is happening to him and so many problems are approaching. We can only begin to understand the adolescent when we remember that biological changes and the social pressures are demanding new adjustments.

Adolescent Adjustments

The adolescent faces four of the most serious, difficult, and far-reaching problems of his whole lifetime. These are adjustment to the opposite sex, finding his place in the world of work, emancipation from parental control, and formulating a satisfying philosophy of life. Each one of these calls for a series of decisions and hundreds of adjustments. It is not surprising that the adolescent is temporarily insecure. And it is not to be wondered at that the adolescent is socially awkward, sometimes loud and noisy, tends to show off, swings quickly from one mood to another, occasionally reverts to childish behavior, becomes a slave to fads, and has periods of rebellion to authority. All these and other similar patterns of behavior may be trying to the parent, difficult to understand and accept, but any criticism of the adolescent, nagging at him, or punishment will only make him worse. What the parent needs to do most is to be patient, supportive, and understanding. If the adolescent feels the encouragement of an adult's strong faith in him he will come through this phase of growing up fairly promptly.

Heterosexual Adjustment. Adolescence begins with puberty, that is, the maturing of the reproductive system. This is signaled by well-known outward signs. There are great individual differences in time of puberty. Girls on the average are earlier than boys. Early or late puberty can be a source of worry to the child who feels that he is different from other children. But he can be reassured by the parent who helps him to see that every individual has his own developmental timetable, and that being different from most does not mean that there is anything wrong with him.

Nowadays many parents have answered the child's questions as they have been asked about sex, and have also made sure that the child is prepared for the dramatic happenings of puberty. But even if the child has been thus prepared he may need further information and reassurance when the events themselves take place. It is well to resist the temptation to make comments about the boy's changing voice or the girl's figure as they are usually a bit self-conscious about these developments anyway. We can assume that both biology and social custom will bring an enhanced interest in members of the opposite sex. The young adolescent will now begin the important series of activities related to heterosexual adjustment.

Discipline related to boy-girl relations is often a difficult matter for some parents. This can be a highly emotionally charged area for both parents and adolescents. Parents are sometimes afraid that the child will make serious mistakes and are tempted to try to postpone as long as possible the child's participation in dating and mixed parties. This fear is sometimes based on a realization by the parent that the child is ignorant and immature. However, rather than attempting to treat the child like a preadolescent, it would be better to try to provide the necessary knowledge and understanding.

Remembering that the beginning adolescent still needs some direction, it is desirable to have clear agreements and rules. The young adolescent feels more secure when he knows what the limits are and what requirements he has to live up to. However, it is better that these rules and requirements be determined by discussion than that the parent impose them on the child in a dictatorial manner. Such rules usually deal with hours, places, and kinds of activity. How the boy or girl will behave will be more a matter of his standards of behavior than any rules that can be set. Of course the child will need help in developing these standards himself. The parent who has been frank in discussion and has not hesitated to make known what he considers to be good standards of behavior and above all shows that he trusts the boy or girl can feel fairly sure that the child will make no serious mistakes.

Dating is an exciting time for the young adolescent, but it presents many problems. He feels more secure in the early stages if he is a member of a group rather than being on his own. Mixed parties for young adolescents seem to present puzzling decisions for some parents. The place of the adult is not clear today. The old institution of the chaperon has almost disappeared, yet some kind of supervision does seem to be necessary. Some parents have bowed to what they think is the modern custom and go out when the young people have a party and leave the house to them. Others stay on hand and wonder if they are being "wet blankets." But it does seem clear that in the early stages of this phase of the child's development there is a very definite place for adult supervision. Of course, the supervision can be quite unobtrusive and need not be constant. When the parents have met and greeted the guests they can find a place in the house not in use and leave the young people to carry on. And the parents can be very helpful in the planning of activities and the preparation of refreshments. But this does not mean that they do all the planning or all the preparation. It is well to have the adolescents themselves take some of the responsibility and do some of the work. After all, it is their party. So, even though chaperons have gone out of fashion, there is a place for adults in the picture, and the adolescents themselves feel more secure when they know that there are understanding parents in the background.

Boy and girl will seek advice about making dates, what to do, how to behave, and even such touchy subjects as petting and the like, when they feel that the parents will be understanding, will not dictate or preach, and will never laugh at them or treat their questions lightly. Of course, there will be many details which the adolescent will have to work out for himself. But this will not be too difficult if he feels the security of understanding adults in the background. Serious difficulties usually arise when the adolescent thinks that his parents do not trust him or try to understand him. Many young adolescents have been driven into unfortunate behavior mainly because they have been blindly and unintelligently rebelling against what has seemed to them to be unfair dictates of parents who have not learned to listen and try to understand what is happening in the deep and stormy feelings of the adolescent.

Emancipation. Many parents feel insecure as parents today because of the confusion and uncertainties of child-rearing practices in our society. This has meant that they have less confidence in what they have been doing as parents, and this lack of confidence has sometimes been transferred to the products. This has meant in turn some reluctance to let adolescents become independent and emancipation of adolescents from parental control has been hindered. Of course, normally, emancipation starts back in infancy and everything the child learns that enables him to look after himself, make his own decisions, and manage his own affairs contributes to the process. Adolescence is the final stage in this process. Sometimes the child has to fight for chances to practice independence and responsibility, but occasionally the adolescent clings to the safety of childhood dependence and the parent has to push him gently out of the nest.

Emancipation should present no serious difficulties if the parent is willing to let the child grow up, has confidence in the individual to start managing his own affairs, and is ready to support the child in his attempts to run his own life. The transition should be gradual, and this seems to present difficulties. Some parents have difficulty in modifying their role from control to guidance, from direction to leadership, and from being an authority to a near equal. This, of course, is the meaning of emancipation—a changed relationship. When the adolescent is eventually treated as an equal then emancipation is complete. But this means that the parent has been able to change his ways of thinking, feeling, and acting toward this child of his who is no longer a child but a near-adult. The child who has been given protection, care, direction, and correction for years has now become the adult who is to be treated as an equal. This is not an easy change for a parent to make and some fail to do so. Such failures are the basis of what is often called mother-in-law trouble.

Vocational Choice. Another feature of the period of adolescence which demands attention and calls for decisions is vocational choice and preparation. How long is the adolescent to stay in school? What courses should be taken? Should a university course be planned? These and similar questions must be answered. Who should supply the answer? The state provides some partial answers when it decrees that the child should stay in school until a certain age, and when only a limited choice of possible courses is provided. The rest of the answers call for cooperative effort by a number of people. The adolescent himself should be the central figure in these discussions and decisions, for in the final analysis it is the young man or woman who has to decide what the career is to be. Parents, teachers, friends, and guidance officers can help mainly by providing the needed information about vocations, training possibilities, and the abilities and aptitudes the adolescent has demonstrated. Parental pressures, both direct and more subtle, play a large part in vocational choices and can be desirable if they are not too specific or unrealistic. But when such pressures mean that the decision is virtually taken away from the adolescent, they can be unhealthy and even disastrous.

Religion. Another aspect of the adolescent period that sometimes generates difficulties is religion. Usually in adolescence, doubts arise about the religious teaching that the child received earlier. He may question the doctrines that he had accepted as a child. And he may search for a set of beliefs that he can accept. In this process he may come into conflict with his parents, should they be shocked by his skepticism and desire to stop going to Sunday school or church. But his doubts are usually honest doubts and his search serious. The adolescent is fortunate if he is able to discuss these matters with his parents. If not, he will usually find other people, possibly other adolescents, who will be ready to talk about it.

The adolescent is characteristically an idealist and a reformer. He is looking for a philosophy of life that will provide answers to some of the puzzling questions about life. He may modify some of his childish beliefs and develop a philosophy of life that will be satisfying and that will grow and deepen with further experience. Or he may try to put it all out of his mind and keep his childish views intact by locking them up in a logic-tight compartment safe from critical examination. Or he may become an agnostic or even an atheist. What the adolescent needs is not adults to tell him what he must believe, but sympathetic, understanding adults who will provide the opportunities and materials for him to work out a satisfying religion for himself. Perhaps more than anything else the adolescent needs the example of admired adults either within or without the family who have a religion that they are living by.

So discipline in adolescence is concerned with the serious problems of social relations, heterosexual adjustment, vocational decisions, and religion. The adolescent does need guidance but the guidance that will be effective is not so much rigid control and direction as advice, the chance to discuss his problems, moral support, trust, and confidence. In the early years of adolescence there will be some need for rules, restrictions, and limits but even these will be negotiable as compromise and agreement will be a prominent technique.

There seems to be so much to say about discipline in adolescence that it may be helpful to list a number of suggestions by way of summary.

1. Adolescents need recognition to combat their natural feelings of insecurity. They want to feel grown-up and important and to possess a feeling of self-worth. As long as the praise, approval, and recognition are sincere and deserved there is very little danger of overdoing it.

2. Adolescents need to feel that they are trusted, that people, especially parents, believe in them. And they tend to live up to the expectations people have for them, if the expectations are realistic.

3. Adolescents need to know the limits, reasonable restrictions, and requirements. But they also like to feel that these rules and regulations are things about which they themselves have had some say.

4. Adolescents need help in solving their problems. But help does not mean providing ready-made solutions. They can be encouraged to look carefully at the pros and cons of any course of action and to arrive at a decision on important matters only after careful thought.

5. Adolescents need to feel that some of the things they are doing are important. In the stirring time of becoming an adult there should be challenging activities, not just dull routine. Otherwise the adolescent just has to break out somewhere and make things happen.

6. Parents cannot afford to lose touch with their adolescents. The lines of communication must be kept open and the parents ready to talk about virtually anything. The adolescent may be wrestling with really big questions about careers, social relations, morals, and religion. He will have to find his own solutions but he can be aided immeasurably in his search by adults who are ready both to listen and express their own views.

7. Friends, companions, and acceptance by the group are of central importance to the adolescent. Parents should not try to select the adolescent's companions. Forbidding certain associations almost certainly produces difficulties. The open-door policy works wonders. So the adolescent should feel free to bring his companions into the home. And, of course, parents should try never to criticize or belittle these friends.

8. When there are opportunities for wholesome, interesting activities, there is little time for the unwholesome ones. If homes and community do not provide the facilities and opportunities for suitable adolescent activities, then the poolrooms, the dives, the street corners fill the vacuum. Parents who complain that their adolescents never want to stay at home but always want to be going out would be wise to examine the home to see if there is anything worth staying home for.

9. The adolescent has to prove himself. This may lead him into dangerous and even foolish behavior. This is usually because he does not have enough worthwhile, important things to do in which he can show the world, but really himself, that he is capable.

10. So, adolescents need, above all, understanding. They are not just wild, irresponsible youths, but young people trying to grow up and meet the challenge of life. They need the steadying hand of adults who can help them harness and use some of the abundant drive and energy of youth for good purposes. Youth cannot wait to live. One of the greatest unused resources of our society is the idealism and enthusiasm of young people. Too often we say to these young people, wait until you are older and you will have your chance. But to the adolescent with his dreams of achievement, his enthusiasm for making the world over, the time is now, not tomorrow.

References

Bandura, A., and Walters, R. H.: *Adolescent Aggression,* Ronald, New York, 1959.
Baruch, D. W.: *How to Live with Your Teenager,* McGraw-Hill, New York, 1953.
Cole, L.: *The Psychology of Adolescence,* Rinehart, New York, 1959.
Davis, M.: *Sex and the Adolescent,* Permabooks, New York, 1960.
Frank, L. K., and Frank, M.: *Your Adolescent at Home and School,* New American Library, New York, 1959.
Jersild, A. T.: *Psychology of Adolescence,* Macmillan, New York, 1957.
U.S. Children's Bureau: *The Adolescent in Your Family,* Publ. No. 347, U.S. Government Printing Office, Washington.
Wittenberg, R. M.: *Adolescence and Discipline,* Association Press, New York, 1960.

chapter 28

Discipline

in Adulthood

There are at least two good reasons why we should look at discipline in adulthood. One is so that we can clarify our goals in administering discipline with children, and the other is so that we can evaluate the nature and quality of discipline as it applies to ourselves.

In thinking about a scheme of discipline for children, we have been assuming that the major goal has been to bring about a condition which we have called self-discipline. By this we have meant that external controls would gradually diminish and when the child had reached maturity this external control would have been replaced by internal controls. Of course this is a greatly simplified account of an extremely complex process. And it is an ideal which is not always realized. Many of the adults in our society still require external controls. Our policemen and courts are kept busy. But we do not think it is too utopian to suggest that it is possible with an adequate scheme of discipline to achieve this goal of thoroughly self-disciplined adults.

It has been said many times, "You can't change human nature." This statement is usually meant to imply the futility of working for human betterment. It is true that any radical change in personality and character of the adult is very difficult, but probably never impossible. When, however, we focus our efforts on children, it is a different story. Here it is possible to take a more hopeful position. Children are more flexible, more subject to being influenced, and more amenable to change. Our greatest hope for improvement in human nature is in child rearing and education. Such improvement is slow and disappointing, mainly because attitudes, prejudices, distortions, and undesirable patterns of behavior tend to be perpetuated from generation to generation. The child acquires his standards and values mostly through absorption from those with whom he lives.

Morally deficient families tend to produce individuals who reflect the level of values of the group. Of course there are examples to show that it is not impossible for children to have standards and patterns of behavior which are much better than their own parent's. But these are exceptions. The usual picture is one in which the child's personality and character formation reflect that of the family in which he was reared. However, as the community through its schools, churches, and community agencies provides what some families are failing to do, there is some hope that the endless chain of maladjustment and failure in human life will not be perpetuated.

To produce mature, self-disciplined individuals through child rearing and education requires mature, self-disciplined adults as parents and teachers. This is one of the most pressing problems in the current scene. Part of the answer is the provision of opportunities and facilities for parent education and preparental education in family life. Another part of the answer is in some way to make sure that only those people who are capable of discharging the responsibilities of parenthood become parents.

When mature, self-disciplined adults enter marriage and found a family, they build the kind of setting and provide the kind of atmosphere which is conducive to the healthy development of children. But anything short of maturity and self-discipline produces a setting and atmosphere that is less than effective. Although most of us are aware of what maturity and self-discipline mean, it may not be out of place to try to describe some of the central features of these essentials of adequate parents and at the same time to indicate the possibilities of improvement in areas in which immaturities persist.

Every individual is faced with a number of problems of adjustment and his degree of success in them is a measure of his maturity and self-discipline. Some of the more important are adjustment to people, to social requirements, to ideas, to his own feelings and emotions, and to his material environment. A brief examination of each of these in turn may provide some basis for an evaluation of what is involved in discipline in adulthood.

Adjustment to People

People are, of course, the most important part of the world of any individual. To be happy and efficient, he must learn how to live, work, and play with them. Very early in life he learns that people are important to him. He discovers that the satisfaction of his needs for food and comfort are provided by them. And every day brings added experiences of his social dependence. If he is fortunate in having parents who are dependable and consistent in their care and protection, he develops a basic dependent trust which is the foundation of his social adjustment. From this trust in a person or persons he develops self-trust, and later a realization of his social interdependence, and is thus able to participate in mature relationships of mutuality.

The child develops strong wants to be accepted, to be loved, to belong, and to be approved. He will seek satisfaction of these wants, and if he receives adequate guidance will find ways which are successful. He will derive deep and lasting satisfactions from his relationships with other people. He will form affectional attachments with his parents and other intimates. If he is fortunate enough to feel that he is loved, approved, and accepted, he will have a solid foundation for the development of social maturity and healthy social relationships.

The social development of the individual will be influenced by another factor. In our culture, getting ahead of other people is considered very important. Winning is applauded and losing is deplored. Social competition plays a large part in the life of the child just as it does in that of the adult. His self-picture is formed by comparison of himself with others. The jungle philosophy of the survival of the fittest dominates social values. These sweeping generalizations obviously do not apply to all individuals but do characterize the majority in our culture. This means that some people are inevitably doomed to failure and thus forced to find indirect and often distorted means of achieving satisfaction.

The socially mature adult is one who does find satisfaction in his relations with other people. He enjoys his social contacts, feels that he belongs in his social environment, and that his desire for self-importance and social approval is satisfied by his acceptance by others. He feels at home with other people. He seeks not only to derive pleasure and satisfaction in social situations, but to contribute something of himself to them. He has learned the joy and deep satisfaction of giving as well as receiving. He is not merely interested in people; he likes them, and because of this he looks for and discovers the best in them. He has moved out of the narrow circle of his earlier egocentricity, he is aware of the feelings as well as the rights of others, and he takes them into account. The self-disciplined adult has learned that his own desires and wants must be limited by consideration of the desires and wants of other people. His inner controls go beyond his personal satisfactions and encompass the satisfactions of his associates.

The self-disciplined adult has accepted the fact that personal freedom is limited by social responsibility. He knows that freedom and responsibility are inseparable. Freedom without responsibility is merely license. He knows, also, that membership in any group makes demands on him that should be met, things he should do and limits he should not violate.

So one important dimension of self-discipline and the mark of the mature adult is the discharging of his social responsibilities. He has his individual and personal satisfactions in satisfactory balance with his relations with others. He is more concerned with what he can contribute than with what he gets. He is a good friend, associate, parent, and citizen because of this concern for more than his own individual satisfactions.

Conformity and Nonconformity

Another general area of adjustment is to the demands and restrictions of organized groups and to society in general. The child is born into a highly organized, complex society. He will be a member of a number of groups such as his family, the school groups, play groups, and later clubs, teams, work groups, and the community in which he lives. Each group will make demands on him and limit his freedom. Part of his attainment of maturity will be his learning to meet these demands and accept the limitations of group membership. This means abiding by the rules and regulations, laws and taboos of the groups of which he becomes a member.

The mature, self-disciplined adult will have learned intelligent conformity and also nonconformity. This means that conformity for him will not be a virtue or an end in itself, but a simple necessity. That is, he will conform with the reasonable, sensible, and necessary rules, laws, and mores of his society and at the same time he will participate in activities to improve these laws when necessary. Outside this core of necessary conformity he will show an intelligent nonconformity. That is, he will not be a slave to fad or fashion but will develop his own tastes and preferences where these do not hinder or interfere with other people. This maturity of conformity and nonconformity is a fine balance of social responsibility and personal individuality. The mature adult will be both an individual with his own standards, values, and preferences and a socialized person who is a participating and contributing as well as conforming member of society.

Adjustment in the World of Opinion and Ideas

We live in a world that is made up of material things and people, but also of thoughts, ideas, opinions, and beliefs. To be a mature, self-disciplined adult, the individual must learn to be at home in this part of his world. This means acquiring the knowledge necessary for effective living, but it means also the development of the ability to use knowledge wisely, to choose, weigh, discriminate, and form judgments. Disciplined thought is the result of mature thinking that avoids the pitfalls of distortion, exaggeration, and self-justification.

In a very real sense we are what we think. And in a very important way, maturity and self-discipline are based in the individual's private world of ideas, opinions, thoughts, and beliefs. The self-disciplined person is master of this world, that is, his thinking is organized and controlled. He is open-minded, ready to consider any idea, but free to accept or reject what such consideration indicates.

He is an intelligent skeptic, demanding evidence and ready to weigh evidence when it is available. He is aware that there are areas where objective evidence does not exist and where faith must take its place.

The mature adult knows that human experience must depend on faith. There is much that we can only "know" by faith. We live much of our lives by faith—faith that there will be a tomorrow, that the sun will shine, that we can trust some people, that life is good, and that the universe has meaning and purpose. The more we know the more we realize how much we do not know or can only know by faith. This is true not just in terms of those areas of experience in which we do not have facts but also where there is an abundance of objective facts. Even with plenty of scientific results to use we must go beyond the facts to form insights or interpretations that endow them with the meaning and significance that make them live in human experience.

Adjusting to the Dynamo of Human Emotions

The mature adult has disciplined emotions. He does not deny nor repress his emotions but puts them to work as harnessed energy for daily living. Feelings and emotions are a part of human nature and as such can neither be denied nor completely hidden. And emotions can be respectable.

The mature adult has his experiences of joy, satisfaction, happiness, and affection. He is not ashamed of his enthusiasms or his enjoyment of simple satisfactions. Nor does he deny his fears or even his angers. On the other hand, he controls his emotions rather than allowing them to rule him.

Emotions are emergency equipment. They are responses to threats and hindrances. They prepare the individual for strenuous activity. They need not be disruptive, and are not when channeled into activity. The mature adult keeps control and uses this mobilized energy to solve problems or protect himself from danger. Everyone has experiences of fear and stirrings of anger. The sign of maturity and self-discipline is not absence of emotions but their management and use in healthy expressions and activity.

Adjusting to Failure, Disappointments, and Hurts

Perhaps the clearest indication of maturity and self-discipline is to be found in the individual's adjustment to his disappointments and failures and his ability to accept his own personal limitations.

During childhood he gradually built a picture of himself. If he was fortunate his parents and teachers helped him to see himself as capable and worthy. On the other hand, he may have lacked the acceptance, encouragement, and reassurance he needed to build a healthy self-portrait. The attaining of full maturity is only possible when the individual acquires the self-confidence that enables him to make his own decisions and accept the consequences of these decisions. Only then is he a truly independent individual and such independence is an ingredient of self-discipline.

Failures and disappointments come to all of us. What we do with them determines our maturity. Failures can be steppingstones to success. They can yield the insights needed for more adequate activity and they can provide the spur to further effort. They can be the basis of more realistic evaluation of strengths and weaknesses. In short, failure to the mature adult is a valuable experience and not food for self-pity.

Adult Mental Health

To plan and carry through a reasonable scheme of discipline for children, a parent or teacher must be mature, self-disciplined, and in good mental health. This is a tall order, and few of us qualify completely. However, our immaturities and failures in self-control, if infrequent and not too pronounced, may not be too serious or keep us from being adequate parents. But both for the sake of ourselves as well as our children, we should give some attention to our personal mental health. With this in mind, some simple but useful suggestions are given which, if followed, should strengthen an individual's mental health.

The mature adult lives in the present. The mentally healthy person makes the most of each experience at the time and lives one day at a time. He does not dissipate his energies in regret for the past or in dread of the future. He takes his lessons from past successes and failures but accepts the consequences of his activities without distortion or emotion.

It helps to minimize strains and stresses and develop the habit of living easily. Modern living seems to be a series of tensions and stresses for most people. Being "on edge," resorting to pills or alcohol, feeling constantly fatigued, and having frequent emotional outbursts are some of the signs of failure to live easily. The way a person meets life situations is pretty much a matter of habit. He can learn to take things easily and not allow the trivial and the unimportant to disturb him. Compare the following three individuals in the same situation and draw your own conclusions. One stamps his feet in rage, stalks out of the room, slamming the door, and takes a few days to cool off. Another says "What's the use?" and goes off to sulk and tell himself how hard and unfair life is. The third accepts the challenge of the situation with a cheerful attitude and goes to work to find a solution.

Most of the things that make us irritated are just not worth the strain. The thousand and one things that make up the day of the busy mother and housewife can all become sources of tensions if she lets them. Or they can be just incidents in the day's work. Habit makes the difference, and what an important difference it is!

It is a good idea to learn to make decisions promptly; indecision drains away energy. Life is a succession of choices and decisions, some serious and important, some trivial and routine. But whatever the decision, delay and postponement can be dangerous because it provides reason for worry and conflict.

Worry can be a bad habit. Most of the worries of parents, and some parents have many, are unnecessary. The antidote for worry is action. If possible the activity should be related to the source of the worry, but if this is not possible, be active anyway; chop wood, scrub the kitchen floor, or at least go for a walk.

The person with a variety of interests which he pursues actively is both an interesting person and a mentally healthy one. One can be an interested and appreciative spectator, but participating in satisfying activities is needed to provide release from life's tensions and strains. Leisure is an asset when some of the free time is taken up with doing things for no other reason than the satisfaction in freely chosen and self-fulfilling activities.

The mature adult has a set of goals, purposes, aims, and ideals. These give direction and meaning to life. Other similar suggestions might be offered but these may serve to illustrate the fact that mental health can be cultivated and strengthened. Of course, no simple set of rules will guarantee mental health. Life is too complex for that, but even though these suggestions are simple and not a complete prescription, when put to use they do help. As a final suggestion, it might be mentioned that a sense of humor can keep an individual from taking himself too seriously.

References

Bernhardt, K. S.: *Practical Psychology*, McGraw-Hill, New York, 1953.

McKinney, F.: *Psychology of Personal Adjustment*, Wiley, New York, 1941.

Overstreet, H. A.: *The Mature Mind*, Norton, New York, 1949.

————, and Overstreet, B. W.: *The Mind Alive*, Norton, New York, 1954.

chapter 29

A Final Word

In every age since the beginning of mankind people have said, "We are living in a challenging age." Every period in our long history has been an exciting time, for every period has had its problems to solve, its obstacles to overcome, and its new worlds to conquer. True, there are few physical frontiers left to discover on earth; perhaps this is why we are looking for them in space. But the frontiers of the mind and human experience offer much scope for exploration and discovery. Man has been seeking the answers about the meaning of life and the whys of human behavior for many generations; he has found some answers but there is much that we still do not know. Parents occupy one of the best situations there is to carry on this search. In the progress of the individual from infancy to maturity are to be found many of the answers about human nature and conduct, for it is in the story of becoming that we can see many of the reasons why people behave as they do.

Being a parent can mean many things. It can be a burden and an unpleasant task. It can be a series of worries. It can be a nuisance and a hindrance to doing other things. It can be a career. It can be a challenge. It can be a thoroughly enjoyable and satisfying experience. It can be a duty and a responsibility. It can be a mixture of joy and sorrow, of achievement and disappointment, of success and failure. It will probably be most of these things to most parents. What parenthood will bring to the individual will depend to a large extent on his attitude and expectations. It will depend also on his degree of maturity and readiness for the experience. But whatever parenthood means to the individual parent, the nature of the collective effort of parents will largely determine what the next generation will be like.

No one is satisfied with the world as it is today. Although we have conquered space, split the atom, discovered the secret of atomic energy, and mastered our physical world, we are still unable to live at peace with each other. And the real tragedy is that we know enough about human nature and human relationships to prevent most of the failures and disasters of human life if we would only put our knowledge to work.

Most of the maladjustments, neurotic behavior, inability to get along with others, delinquencies and crime, hates and antagonisms, and other similar ills that plague mankind have their beginnings in childhood. If we spent even a fraction of the money it is costing us to try to remedy these ills on seeing that every child was given the kind of training and experiences that produce a healthy personality and approach to life, we would see a social revolution which would look like utopia in comparison to our present sick society. If this is asking too much, then perhaps it is not too much to expect that we can increase the number of parents who learn how to provide the kind of childhood which will build healthy personalities and sound characters in their children.

Down through the ages man has had flashes of insight that have transformed the world and led mankind a step nearer to a fuller and better life. Not all these insights have been developed and applied in living. Progress in civilization has resulted from insights which have been put to work. It is true that these insights have directly affected only a fraction of the people of the world, but in some cases this fraction affected has changed the world. The tragedy that has plagued us so often is that the insights have not been complete enough to result in firm convictions that are then translated into action.

Many centuries ago man achieved the insight of one God instead of many. But he has not even yet assimilated the implications of this great insight. For if he had, there would be no hesitation in accepting the idea of the brotherhood of man and the essential dignity of human life. He would be through with war and hate and injustice.

Some of the early Greek philosophers achieved at least partial insight into the enormous potential of man as a rational being. Later philosophers, such as Kant, sharpened this insight and raised the hope of many that man could live by reason. But it was only a partial insight because the enormous power of human emotions was overlooked. Then Freud called our attention to the hidden motivations that directed man's behavior and man as a rational being was overshadowed by this partial insight. Man is both rational and emotional, and the possibility of man harnessing his emotions and putting reason in control should never be forgotten. Our only hope is that reason will triumph before we unleash the powers of destruction that man has discovered.

Another insight that has meant a great deal but which could mean much more is that man can only function adequately as a social being if there is social justice for all. This is true whatever the group may be: the family, the nation, or the whole world. No marriage, no family, no community, no state can last and succeed as a social group unless it is based on fairness and justice for all. True, some groups have carried on without justice and have been maintained by force and fear, but their members were denied some of their deepest satisfactions.

We see dimly another insight that has far-reaching implications. It is that human personality is of greater value than anything else in the world. It is more important than the organizations man has invented, the laws he has formulated, the possessions he has acquired, or the products of his creativity. But we carry on as though houses and housekeeping were more important than children; that industry, government, church, and other organizations were more important than the people they were designed to serve.

We sometimes catch a glimpse of an insight, which if it were more fully seen, might transform the world. This is the insight that would produce the conviction that goodness is always better than evil, that mercy is better than revenge, that love is better than hate, and that man does not have to be mean or unjust to his fellows. This is related to another idea which has never been given a real trial: that it is not necessary to win out against other people and that cooperation is better than competition. We are still suffering from the idea that the law of Nature and therefore of human nature is the survival of the fittest.

There are many other insights that have helped to shape the history of mankind, but we will mention only one more. This is the idea that the individual will become what he does mainly because of the kind of treatment he receives as an infant, child, and adolescent.

He can become a mature, rational, self-disciplined adult or he can become instead an immature, fearful, or hostility-ridden person who must win at all costs, dominate others if possible, gain his revenge, make others suffer, and be himself as unhappy as he makes other people.

Being a parent is an awful responsibility. So much depends on what is done, and how it is done. But the greatness of the responsibility should inspire and challenge us rather than make us fearful. What we need most for the job is a deep respect for the little lives in our care. This respect for our children as individuals coupled with abundant common sense, some knowledge of how children grow and develop, abiding patience, fairness, and clear goals will enable us to fulfill our responsibility.

This parental responsibility is made up of two functions. One is the affectional function and the other is the discipline function. They complement each other. Love is important but love is not enough; there must also be discipline. Discipline as a plan of training is important, but discipline is not enough either; there must be love. This started out to be a book on discipline, but we found that we could not write about discipline without bringing in the essential context in which effective discipline functions.

It does not seem possible to overemphasize the importance of this context. Children must have air to breathe and food to eat to stay alive. And they must have an atmosphere of affection, acceptance, and understanding for healthy development. Children can be just as malnourished emotionally as physically. And emotional deficiency can have far-reaching effects. Another whole book could be filled with descriptions of the variety of quirks, distortions, and neurotic tendencies that can result from living in a poor home environment.

The home environment can be deficient in a number of ways. It can lack physical facilities, with crowded living quarters, no materials for normal childhood activities, inadequate necessities for comfort, no protection from disease and accident. The home can also lack an atmosphere of warmth and affection, of acceptance and approval, and of understanding and sympathy. And the home can be deficient in discipline, with no adequate plan, with inconsistent treatment, frequent use of severe punishments, or allowing the children to run wild. It is difficult to say which of these deficiencies is most serious. There is some evidence that suggests that deficient physical facilities are not as damaging in their effects as the other two. Certainly we can say that some children have had every comfort and material advantage but have become maladjusted, unhappy individuals. The parent has only partly fulfilled his responsibility when he has provided for the child's physical needs. The child also has important psychological needs that must be met.

It may not be out of place here to suggest that the readers of this book who will be serious, thoughtful parents who are providing rich, healthy climates for their own children can lend support to community efforts to provide compensating facilities and activities for children from less adequate homes. If we could somehow manage to spend even a fraction of what we are pouring into weapons of destruction on community efforts to provide a good life for all our children we would reap rich dividends.

Years ago, wise men decided there should be universal elementary education, and slowly this is spreading into every corner of the globe. It may be just as wise to make sure that every person who is to become a parent receives some sound preparation for the job. And it may be that some time in the future we will find ways to deny parenthood to individuals who are incapable of discharging such an important responsibility as being an adequate parent.

We cherish freedom. But there is much confusion about the meaning of individual freedom. Sometimes our treasured freedom seems to be freedom to damage other lives, for instance, freedom of parents to administer corporal punishment. We have made some slight progress, for no longer may parents grossly mistreat their children without being subject to punishment. But there are still all kinds of serious neglect and inadequate training that are tolerated in our society. There are two major methods of providing the framework of control within which individual freedom is possible. These are legislation and education. The more effective education is in producing self-discipline, the less we need to depend on laws and their enforcement.

Freedom and discipline are not necessarily in opposition. They

308 A Developmental View of Discipline

can be complementary. True freedom is only possible when there is discipline, either inner or external. Reasonable discipline makes individual freedom possible. The individual can enjoy freedom only when his freedom does not encroach on the freedom of other people. The lives of individuals are inevitably interdependent. What one person does affects others and he in turn is affected by what others do.

Discipline is control, but more important is the principle that discipline is training for self-control. A scheme of discipline with children is only partially successful if all it does is to keep children in order. This is important, but not nearly so important as the provision of training for self-discipline. This has been the theme that has run through all sections of this book. In various ways we have made the point that every adult contact with the child has two purposes: to take care of the present situation whatever it might be, and to move the child another step nearer to a maturity of self-discipline.

Much of what has been said and written about parents being responsible for the maladjustments and delinquencies of their children is at least partly true. But equally true is the fact that parents have been responsible for the larger number of successful, well-adjusted, creative, and effective individuals. Being a parent is a grave responsibility. This is unavoidable. But being a parent can be deeply satisfying too. To watch day by day, month by month, and year by year a young life unfold, a personality form, and a character develop, and to realize that you have had some part in it, is one of the greatest experiences that living provides. And it is even greater when we realize that we have not so much molded this new life as provided the conditions for the fulfillment of its own potentials.

No one knows the details of living in the next half century. We can only be sure that there will be change, perhaps as much change as there has been in the last half century. Even though we cannot train our children in the details of living in their world of tomorrow, we can help them to acquire some of the characteristics that will enable them to live and participate with other people in a society which will provide the setting for self-fulfillment of all individuals. We can help them build values that will provide them with guides to behavior. We can help them learn to cherish justice and fair play, to value sincerity and integrity, and to view their freedom and individuality as functioning in a framework of consideration for other people. We can help them learn to make their decisions in terms of the consequences, and to move nearer and nearer toward that serenity which comes from a willingness as well as an ability to accept the consequences of their own decisions and behavior.

General References

I. General Textbooks on Child Development

Almy, M.: *Child Development,* Holt, New York, 1955.

Anderson, J. E.: *The Psychology of Development and Personality Adjustment,* Holt, New York, 1949.

Ausubel, D. P.: *Theory and Problems of Adolescent Development,* Grune & Stratton, New York, 1954.

————: *Theory and Problems of Child Development,* Grune & Stratton, New York, 1958.

Baldwin, A. L.: *Behavior and Development in Childhood,* Holt, New York, 1955.

Baller, W. R. (ed.): *Readings in the Psychology of Human Growth and Development,* Holt, New York, 1962.

———— and Charles, D. C.: *The Psychology of Human Growth and Development,* Holt, New York, 1961.

Barker, R. G., Kounin, J. S., and Wright, H. F. (eds): *Child Behavior and Development,* McGraw-Hill, New York, 1943.

Blatz, W. E.: *Understanding the Young Child,* Clarke, Irwin, Toronto, and Morrow, New York, 1944.

Breckenridge, M. E., and Vincent, E. L.: *Child Development,* Saunders, Philadelphia, 1960.

Cole, L. E.: *Psychology of Adolescence,* Rinehart, New York, 1959.

Crow, L. D., and Crow, A.: *Child Development and Adjustment,* Macmillan, New York, 1962.

Cruze, W. W.: *Adolescent Psychology and Development,* Ronald, New York, 1953.

Dennis, W.: *Readings in Child Psychology,* Prentice-Hall, Englewood Cliffs, N.J., 1951.

English, H. B.: *Dynamics of Child Development,* Holt, New York, 1961.

Forest, I: *Child Development,* McGraw-Hill, New York, 1954.

Gesell, A., Ilg, F. L., et al.: *Child Development,* Harper, New York, 1949.

Goodenough, F. L., and Tyler, L. E.: *Developmental Psychology,* Appleton-Century-Crofts, New York, 1959.

Gruenberg, S. M.: *The Encyclopedia of Child Care and Guidance,* Doubleday, Garden City, N.Y., 1954.

Haimowitz, M. L., and Haimowitz, N. R.: *Human Development, Selected Readings,* Crowell, New York, 1960.

Horrocks, J. E.: *The Psychology of Adolescence*, Houghton Mifflin, Boston, 1962.
Hurlock, E. B.: *Adolescent Development*, McGraw-Hill, New York, 1953.
———: *Child Development*, McGraw-Hill, New York, 1956.
Hutt, M. L., and Gibby, R. G.: *The Child, Development and Adjustment*, Allyn and Bacon, Englewood Cliffs, N.J., 1959.
Jersild, A. T.: *Child Psychology*, Prentice-Hall, Englewood Cliffs, N.J., 1960.
———: *Psychology of Adolescence*, Macmillan, New York, 1957.
Kuhlen, R. G.: *The Psychology of Adolescent Development*, Harper, New York, 1952.
Landis, P. H.: *Adolescence and Youth*, McGraw-Hill, New York, 1952.
Landreth, C.: *The Psychology of Early Childhood*, Knopf, New York, 1958.
Lane, H., and Beauchamp, M.: *Understanding Human Development*, Prentice-Hall, Englewood Cliffs, N.J., 1960.
Lee, J. M., and Lee, D. M.: *The Child and His Development*, Appleton-Century-Crofts, New York, 1958.
McCandless, B. R.: *Children and Adolescents*, Holt, New York, 1961.
Martin, W. E., and Stendler, C. B.: *Child Behavior and Development*, Harcourt, Brace, New York, 1958.
——— and ———: *Readings in Child Development*, Harcourt, Brace, New York, 1954.
Merry, F. K., and Merry, R. V.: *The First Two Decades of Life*, Harper, New York, 1958.
Mussen, P. H., and Conger, J. J.: *Child Development and Personality*, Harper, New York, 1956.
Olson, W. C.: *Child Development*, Heath, Boston, 1959.
Pressey, S. L., and Kuhlen, R. G.: *Psychological Development through the Life Span*, Harper, New York, 1957.
Rand, W., Sweeney, M., and Vincent, E. L.: *Growth and Development of the Young Child*, Saunders, Philadelphia, 1953.
Sears, R. R., Maccoby, E. E., and Levin, H.: *Patterns of Child Rearing*, Harper & Row, New York, 1957.
Seidman, J. (ed.): *The Child: A Book of Readings*, Rinehart, New York, 1958.
———: *The Adolescent: A Book of Readings*, Holt, New York, 1960.
Stone, L. J., and Church, J.: *Childhood and Adolescence*, Random House, New York, 1957.
Strang, R.: *An Introduction to Child Study*, Macmillan, New York, 1959.
Thompson, G. G.: *Child Psychology*, Houghton Mifflin, Boston, 1962.

Thorpe, L. P.: *Child Psychology and Development,* Ronald, New York, 1955.

Watson, R. I.: *Psychology of the Child,* Wiley, New York, 1959.

Wattenberg, W.: *The Adolescent Years,* Harcourt, Brace, New York, 1955.

Whiting, J. W. M., and Child, I. L.: *Child Training and Personality: A Cross-cultured Study,* Yale University Press, New Haven, Conn., 1953.

Zubek, J. P., and Solberg, P. A.: *Human Development,* McGraw-Hill, New York, 1954.

II. Paperback Books of Interest to Parents

The number of good inexpensive books for parents is increasing. A few of the popular ones are listed here.

Bowlby, J.: *Child Care and the Growth of Love,* Pelican, London, 1953.

Child Study Association of America: *What to Tell Your Child,* Permabooks, New York, 1954.

Duvall, E. M.: *Facts of Life and Love for Teen Agers,* Popular, New York, 1957.

Edwards, M.: *Your Child from Two to Five,* Permabooks, New York, 1955.

English, O. S., and Foster, C. J.: *Fathers Are Parents Too,* Belmont Books, New York, 1962.

Ilg, F. L., and Ames, L. B.: *The Gesell Institute's Child Behavior,* Dell, New York, 1960.

Larrick, N.: *Parent's Guide to Children's Reading,* Pocket, New York, 1958.

Spock, B.: *Baby and Child Care,* Pocket, New York, 1959.

Valentine, C. W.: *The Normal Child,* Pelican, London, 1956.

III. Sources of Materials for Parents

American Institute of Family Relations, 5287 Sunset Blvd., Los Angeles 27, Calif.

Association for Childhood Education, International, 1200 15th St. N.W., Washington 5, D.C. Publishes *Childhood Education* ten times a year and also a series of bulletins.

Association for Family Living, 28 East Jackson Blvd., Chicago, Ill.

Bank Street Publications, 69 Bank St., New York 14, N.Y.

Child Study Association of America, 9 East 89th St., New York 28, N.Y.

Publishes much useful material for parents. A sample of literature available:

Auerback, A. B.: *How to Give your Child a Good Start*
———: *The How and Why of Discipline*
Burgess, H. S.: *Discipline: What Is It?*
Wolf, A. W. M., and Dawson, M. C.: *What Makes a Good Home?*
Wolf, K. M.: *The Controversial Problem of Discipline*
——— and Auerback, A. B.: *As Your Child Grows*
——— and ———: *When Children Ask about Sex*

Institute of Child Study, University of Toronto, 45 Walmer Road, Toronto 4, Ont. Publishes *The Bulletin of the Institute of Child Study.*
National Association for Mental Health, 10 Columbus Circle, New York 19, N.Y. Publishes a quarterly journal, *Mental Hygiene.*
National Congress of Parents and Teachers, 600 South Michigan Blvd., Chicago 5, Ill. Publishes *National Parent-Teacher* ten times a year and other pamphlets.
Parent's Magazine, 52 Vanderbilt Ave., New York 17, N.Y. Publishes *Parent's Magazine* monthly.
Public Affairs Pamphlets, 22 East 38th St., New York 16, N.Y. Some pamphlets of interest to parents:

127. Duvall, E.: *Keeping Up with Teen-agers*
141. Hymes, J. L., Jr.: *Enjoy Your Child, 1, 2 and 3*
144. Lambert, C.: *Understanding Your Child, From 6–12*
148. Frank, J.: *Comics, T.V., Radio, Movies*
149. Hymes, J. L., Jr.: *How to Tell Your Child about Sex*
154. Baruch, D. W.: *How to Discipline Your Child*
157. Neisser, W., and Neisser, E.: *Making the Grade as Dad*
163. Hymes, J. L., Jr.: *Three to Six: Your Child Starts to School*
216. Osborne, E.: *How to Teach Your Child about Work*
219. Wishik, S. M.: *How to Help Your Handicapped Child*
232. Polier, J. W.: *Back to What Woodshed?*
234. Landis, P. H.: *Coming of Age, Problems of Teen-agers*
239. Ross, H.: *The Shy Child*
254. Neisser, E. G.: *Your Child's Sense of Responsibility*
264. Wolf, A. W. M.: *Your Child's Emotional Health*

Science Research Associates, 57 West Grand Ave., Chicago 10, Ill. Publishes Better Living booklets (for parents); Life Adjustment booklets (for teen-agers).
Teachers College, Columbia University, Bureau of Publications, 525 West

120th St., New York 27, N.Y. Publishes a Parent-Teacher Series. A sample of titles:

Baruch, D. W.: *Understanding Young Children*
Beasley, J.: *Slow to Talk*
Hymes, J. L., Jr.: *Being a Good Parent*
Hymes, J. L., Jr.: *Discipline*
Redl, F.: *Understanding Children's Behavior*

U.S. Government Printing Office, Superintendent of Documents, Washington 25, D.C. Publishes much valuable material for parents. Examples of material available:

Prenatal Care, Publ. No. 4, Children's Bureau
Infant Care, Publ. No. 8, Children's Bureau
Your Child from One to Six, Publ. No. 30
Your Child from Six to Twelve, Publ. No. 324
The Adolescent in Your Family, Publ. No. 347
Your Gifted Child, Publ. No. 371, Children's Bureau
A Healthy Personality for Your Child, Publ. No. 337, Children's Bureau